빅토리아 시대의 사회계급과 욕망
Social Class & Desire in Victorian England
디킨즈의 『위대한 유산』

빅토리아 시대의 사회계급과 욕망
Social Class & Desire in Victorian England
디킨즈의 『위대한 유산』

권정기 지음

도서출판 경진

머리말

 빅토리아 시대의 계급갈등과 사회적 억압 속에서 입신을 도모하는 한 청년의 도덕적 성장을 다룬 『위대한 유산』의 메시지는 오늘의 우리에게도 유효하다. 찰즈 디킨즈는 주인공 핍을 통해 "늪의 안개가 햇빛 아래 사라지고 말듯" 어렵게 얻은 신분과 재산을 창졸에 잃음으로써 마침내 위대한 정신적인 유산을 얻게 되는 고금과 동서를 막론하는 삶의 진리를 역설한다.
 이 책을 통해 여러 이유로 19세기의 영어로 쓰인 원전에 쉽게 접할 수 없는 독자들이 당시의 잉글랜드의 사회상을 이해하고, 사회 질서에 대한 신랄한 비평과 함께 개인의 가능성에 대한 애정 어린 신뢰를 보여주는 디킨즈적인 해학과 낙관주의를 감상할 수 있기 바란다.

애초에 집필을 권면하고 후원을 아끼지 않으신 도서출판 경진의 양정섭 사장님과 탁월한 식견으로 무흠한 편집을 위해 애써 주신 노경민 선생님과 김현열 선생님께 감사를 드린다.

2013년 12월 1일

저자

<　차
　례
　∨

머리말 ___ 5
차 례 ___ 7

Part 01 작품 분석 ___ 11
　제1장 서론 ·· 13

　제2장 디킨즈와 그의 시대 ··· 15
　　1. 변혁의 시대 ··· 15
　　2. 민중의 작가 ··· 22
　　3. 성장소설과 풍자 ··· 33

　제3장 인물과 사건 ··· 41
　　1. 등장인물 ··· 41
　　2. 혼돈과 갈등 ··· 47
　　3. 야망과 절망 ··· 52
　　4. 성숙과 회복 ··· 56

제4장 주제의 분석 ·· 63
  1. 가족의 해체 ·· 63
  2. 죄와 벌 ·· 69
  3. 계급과 욕망 ·· 73

제5장 결론 ·· 79

참고문헌 ·· 81

Part 02 본문 해설 ___ 83

  Chapter ONE In the Churchyard ··· 85
  Chapter TWO Christmas Day ··· 109
  Chapter THREE At Miss Havisham's ·· 121
  Chapter FOUR The Pale Young Gentleman ···································· 137
  Chapter FIVE "I Must Become a Gentleman!" ································· 147
  Chapter SIX Great Expectations ··· 157
  Chapter SEVEN Learning to Be a Gentleman ·································· 167
  Chapter EIGHT Young Men in Love ··· 185
  Chapter NINE I Come of Age ·· 193
  Chapter TEN Abel Magwitch ··· 207

Chapter ELEVEN Secrets from the Past ·················· 225
　　Chapter TWELVE Escape ·················· 239
　　Chapter THIRTEEN Friends Together ·················· 247

Part 03 이해 점검 ___ 257
　　Chapter 1. In the Church Yard ·················· 259
　　Chapter 2. Christmas Day ·················· 260
　　Chapter 3. At Miss Havisham's ·················· 261
　　Chapter 4. The Pale Young Gentleman ·················· 262
　　Chapter 5. "I Must Become a Gentleman!" ·················· 263
　　Chapter 6. Great Expectations ·················· 264
　　Chapter 7. Learning to Be a Gentleman ·················· 265
　　Chapter 8. Young Men in Love ·················· 267
　　Chapter 9. I Come of Age ·················· 268
　　Chapter 10. Abel Magwitch ·················· 269
　　Chapter 11. Secrets from the Past ·················· 270
　　Chapter 12. Escape ·················· 272
　　Chapter 13. Friends Together ·················· 273
　　Overall ·················· 274

Answer Key ··· 281
Chapter 1. In the Church Yard ··· 281
Chapter 2. Christmas Day ··· 283
Chapter 3. At Miss Havisham's ··· 284
Chapter 4. The Pale Young Gentleman ································· 285
Chapter 5. "I Must Become a Gentleman!" ·························· 286
Chapter 6. Great Expectations ·· 288
Chapter 7. Learning to Be a Gentleman ······························· 289
Chapter 8. Young Men in Love ·· 291
Chapter 9. I Come of Age ·· 292
Chapter 10. Abel Magwitch ·· 294
Chapter 11. Secrets from the Past ··· 296
Chapter 12. Escape ·· 298
Chapter 13. Friends Together ·· 299
Overall ··· 300

작가 연보 ___ 301

Part 01

Dickens' *Great Expectations*

작품 분석

찰즈 디킨즈
(Charles Dickens, 1812~1870)

제1장 서론

　영국이 낳은 가장 위대한 소설가들 중 한 명으로 손꼽히며 19세기의 '문학의 거인(literary colossus)'으로 평가 받는 찰즈 디킨즈(Charles Dickens, 1812~1870)는 사회 부조리에 대한 폭넓고 깊은 이해와 인간에 대한 연민에 기반한 치밀한 구성으로 그가 살았던 시대의 양심을 대변했다. 빈부귀천을 막론하고 누구에게나 큰 호소력 가진 그의 작품은 당시 과학기술의 괄목할 만한 진보 덕분에 빠른 속도로 전 세계로 소개되었다. 생전에도 전례 없는 명성을 누린 디킨즈는 20세기에 들어선 대부분의 학자들과 비평가들에 의해 문학적 천재를 인정받았으며 그의 작품들은 시간과 장소를 초월하는 고전의 자리에 올랐다.

오늘의 독자들은 그의 대표작 중 하나로 열세 번째이자 마지막에서 두 번째 소설인 『위대한 유산(Great Expectations)』을 읽으면서 주인공의 신분상승에 대한 욕망이 어떻게 전개되어 어떤 결과를 초래하는가를 지켜보면서 속물주의와 배금주의에 물든 당대의 인간 군상의 적나라한 모습을 일별함과 동시에, 이 소설에서 '신사'로 상징되는 시대와 문화를 초월하는 이상적인 인간형이란 무엇이며 진정한 행복의 열쇠는 무엇인가를 숙고하게 된다.

이 책에서는 우선 2장에서 디킨즈가 살았던 시대와 그의 삶, 그리고 그의 문학에 대해서 알아봄으로써 그의 대표작인 『위대한 유산』을 보다 쉽고 깊이 있게 이해할 수 있도록 하고, 3장에서는 이 작품의 구성요소 중 가장 중요하다고 여겨지는 등장인물에 대해 소개하고 사건의 전개를 요약해 본다. 이어 4장에서는 가족의 해체, 죄와 벌, 그리고 계급과 욕망이라는 세 가지 중심 주제를 분석해 보기로 한다.

제2장 디킨즈와 그의 시대

1. 변혁의 시대

 복잡다단한 변혁기였던 19세기를 거치면서 영국은 오늘날 알려진 바대로의 영국이 되었다. 디킨즈가 활약한 빅토리아 시대[1]에 이르러 산업혁명[2]을 계기로 기존의 중세 및 초기근대의 가치

---

[1] 빅토리아 시대(Victorian era)란 1837년부터 1901년까지 거의 64년간 영국을 통치했던 빅토리아 여왕(Queen Victoria, 1819~1901)의 치세를 이른다.
[2] 산업혁명(Industrial Revolution)은 1760년경부터 1840년경까지 영국에서 시작된 제조업 중심의 산업구조 이행과정에서 발생한 기술혁신과 이로 인한 사회경제적 변혁을 일컫는다. 이를 통해 사상 최초로 일반 민중의 생활수준이 지속적인 성장을 시작하게 되었다.

와 질서가 새로운 변화의 물결에 서서히 자리를 내주기 시작했다. 즉 산업구조가 1차 산업 중심에서 2차 산업을 중심으로 재편됨과 동시에 과학과 기술의 급격한 발전으로 인간 중심의 사회가 기계 중심의 사회로 급변하고 있었던 것이다. 영국은 이러한 경제구조 상의 변동을 겪으면서 점진적인 정치개혁을 통해 근대적 민주주의를 발전시켰고 대외적으로는 대영제국이란 이름으로 전 세계에 그 위세를 떨쳤다.

산업혁명을 통해 영국은 농업국가에서 산업·상업국가로 변모해 가고 있었다. 산업과 상업의 발흥은 새로운 돈을 필요로 했고 새로운 돈은 또 새로운 수요를 만들어 냈다. 19세기 전에는 소수를 제외하곤 금융 거래를 필요로 하지 않았기 때문에 은행업은 명성이나 평판에 따라 이루어지는 아주 비공식적이고 개인적인 사업이었다. 중앙은행(Bank of England)이 1694년에 설립되었으나 주로 정부의 사업만을 담당해 왔다. 그러다 19세기에 들어 산업화 과정에서 투자자금을 조달해야 할 필요가 급증하고 꾸준한 경제성장의 결과로 중산층이 확대됨에 따라 은행들이 우후죽순으로 생겨나게 되었다.

수백 년 동안 지속된 지주와 자작농, 그리고 소작인이나 일일 노동자들로 이루어진 19세기 영국의 농촌 체제에서 영원히 가난할 수밖에 없는 운명에 처한 땅이 없는 가난한 농부들은 자신의 재산을 소유하는 인생 역전의 꿈을 안고 신흥 산업이 넘쳐나는 도시로 몰려들었다. 그러나 도시의 산업에서는 증기기관과 방적기 같은 발명품들이 등장하여 기계가 인간의 노동을 대체하는 공장 체제가 도입됨에 따라 대규모의 실직이 발생했다. 이렇게 해서 일자리가 모자라게 되자 기업가들은 노동자들에게 돈을 조금만 주고서도 장시간의 중노동을 시킬 수 있게 되었고 이와 더불어 자본가들도 쉽게 돈을 벌 수 있었다.

이렇게 19세기 초 잉글랜드의 고용주들은 최소한의 임금만으로 어린이들과 부녀자들을 극심한 노동으로 내몰았는데 이들은 노동조합을 결성하지 않기 때문에 사업주에게는 더없이 이상적인 노동자들이었다. 이들은 때로 위협을 당하거나 매를 맞기도 했으며 이런 학대에 항의라도 하게 되면 곧바로 해고되었다.[3] 도시빈민들이 자녀들을 하루에 열두 시간 이상이나 일하는 공장으로 보내는 일이 다반사였다. 이런 어린이들은 불결한 환경에서, 심지어는 탄광의 갱도와 같이 위험한 작업조건 하에서 일하기도 했다. 학교는 자녀들을 일터로 보내 돈을 벌어오게 하지 않음은 물론 오히려 돈을 들여 자녀들을 위한 개인교사를 고용할 수도 있는 부모들을 둔 어린이들에게만 허락되는 사치였다. 최초의 공립학

---

[3] 19세기에 이르러 노동시간을 줄이고 작업환경을 개선하며 노동에 투입할 수 있는 아동의 최소연령을 올리는 일련의 법률이 생겨났다. 아동과 부녀자의 노동에 관한 최초의 입법은 아동의 일일 노동시간을 10시간 이하로 규제한 1833~1844년의 공장법(Factory Acts)이다.

교[4]는 숙련 노동에 대한 필요가 증대되던 1870년대에서야 설립되었고 고등학교의 필요성은 20세기 초까지도 제기되지 않았다.

당시 청운의 뜻을 품고 도시로 간 사람들은 비참한 처지를 감수할 수밖에 없었다. 세계의 수도라 할 런던엔 미처리 하수가 거리에 넘쳐났고 템즈(Thames) 강을 따라선 험악한 빈민가가 형성되었다. 대부분의 가정이나 산업에서 석탄이나 토탄을 사용했기 때문에 대기오염은 심각했고 폐질환도 흔했다. 실업자 수가 늘어나면서 돈이 도는 도시에는 밀수꾼, 소매치기, 도둑, 사기꾼들이 들끓었다. 빚을 지고 갚지 못하는 사람들도 많이 생겨나게 되어 큰 사회문제로 대두되었다. 이들을 수용하여 빚을 다 갚을 때까지 일을 하게 하는 구빈원[5]이 운영되었는데 일을 할 수 없는 채무자는 그나마 여기에도 들어가지 못하고 채무자 감옥으로 가야 했다.

---

[4] 영국에서는 학생으로부터 비교적 높은 수업료를 받으며 독립적으로 운영되는 초중등 교육기관인 사립학교를 돈만 있으면 누구나 종교, 직업, 지역과 관계없이 자녀들을 보낼 수 있다는 뜻에서 '공공학교(public school)'라 부르게 되었는데, 따라서 나중에 생겨난 전체 또는 부분적으로 국가의 지원을 받는 초중등 교육기관인 일반적인 의미의 공립학교는 전자와 구분하기 위해 '국가학교(state school)'라 한다.

[5] 구빈원(poorhouse; workhouse)은 빈곤층에게 제공하는 주거시설로서 빅토리아 시대 초기에는 거의 소년원(reformatory)과 흡사하게 운영되었다. 한 가족이 같이 들어가는 경우에도 서로 떨어져 살면서 소식도 모르는 채 지냈다. 수용자들은 할당된 노동의 대가로 초라한 보수를 받았으며 잘못이 있을 경우 체벌을 받기도 했다. 원칙적으로는 극빈 상태를 면할 정도로 돈을 모으면 이곳을 떠나도록 되어 있었으나 실제로는 거의 불가능했다. 이러한 상황은 19세기 후반으로 가면서 점차 개선되었다.

도시를 중심으로 삶의 모든 측면에서 급격한 변화가 몰아치는 가운데 멀리 시골에 사는 사람들만이 몇 백 년 동안 이어져온 전통적인 생활방식을 유지했고 돈 있는 사람들은 런던 도심의 지저분한 환경을 벗어난 외곽에 소도시(town)를 만들기 시작했다. 1860년대가 되어 기차가 도시와 시골, 그리고 과거와 현재를 연결해 줄 때까지 모든 사람들은 마차를 타거나 걸어서 여행했다.

산업혁명과 함께 과학과 신학 사이에서 또 하나의 혁명이 일어났다. 다윈과 헉슬리는 인간은 이전의 형태로부터 오랜 발달의 시기를 거쳐 진화했다는 새로운 주장을 함으로써 세상을 발칵 뒤집어 놓았다.[6] 인간은 하루 동안에 신의 형상을 따라 창조되었고 신으로부터 동물의 세계를 지배할 권리를 받았다고 믿는 사람들과 인간은 과학적으로 진화했다는 사람들 사이에 전쟁이 일어났다. 이 시대의 인간의 가치를 경시하는 보편적인 경향을 당시 지식인들은 산업사회의 과도한 발전에 따르는 부작용이라고 진단했다. 이러한 영국 사회 내부의 급격한 변화는 대외적 팽창정책인 제국주의와 맞물려 돌아갔다.

'대영제국(British Empire)'은 15세기 후반부터 18세기 중반까지 유럽의 배들이 세계를 돌아다니며 항로를 개척하며 탐험과 무역에

---

[6] 영국의 자연주의자이자 지질학자인 찰즈 다윈(Charles Darwin, 1809~1882)이 『종의 기원(On the Origin of Species)』이란 저서를 통해 진화론을 주장하였고, 후일 '다윈의 불독(Darwin's Bulldog)'이란 별명을 얻게 되는 영국의 생물학자 토머스 헉슬리(Thomas Huxley, 1825~1895)가 이를 강력하게 지지하고 널리 전파했다.

열중하던 '탐험의 시대'[7] 이후 1931년 영연방(British Commonwealth)이 성립할 때까지 영국에 복속되거나 영국이 건설한 식민지 등을 통틀어 일컫는 말이다. 한때 전 세계 인구의 약 4분의 1이 대영제국에 속해 '해가 지지 않는 나라'[8]라는 말이 생기기도 하였다.[9]

영국은 대외 팽창 및 국내 치안유지의 방법으로 죄수들을 해외 유형지로 추방해[10] 식민지 건설에 활용하기도 했다.[11] 영국은

---

[7] 세계사에서 문예부흥(Renaissance)과 함께 중세에서 근대로 넘어가는 가교 역할을 한 15세기 초반부터 17세기까지를 '발견의 시대(Age of Discovery)' 또는 '탐험의 시대(Age of Exploration)'라 한다. 유럽은 1453년 오스만(Ottoman) 제국에 의해 현재 터키의 이스탄불(İstanbul)인 콘스탄티노폴리스(Constantinople)가 함락되면서 육로로 아시아에 접근할 수 없게 되자, 해로를 통한 탐험을 가속화하여 아프리카, 아메리카, 아시아, 오세아니아를 발견했다. 이런 과정에서 유럽에는 근대 국민국가(nation state)가 나타나게 되고 이들의 해외 팽창의 결과로 식민제국(colonial empire)이 등장한다.

[8] '해가 지지 않는 제국(the empire on which the sun never sets)'이란 말은 원래 16~17세기의 스페인 제국을 지칭하던 말이었다.

[9] 영국의 역사에서 1815년부터 1914년까지는 '제국의 세기(imperial century)'라 부르는 시대다. 이때를 가리켜 라틴어로 '팍스 브리태니커(Pax Britannica)'라 하는데 이는 '영국의 평화(British Peace)'라는 뜻이다. 프랑스의 나폴레옹을 상대로 승리를 거둔 영국의 경쟁국은 중앙아시아 지역을 장악한 러시아 이외에는 존재하지 않았으며 전 세계의 주요한 해양 교역로는 완전히 영국이 장악했다. 영국은 전 세계적인 패권국(hegemon)으로서 세계경찰의 역할을 수행했는데, 19세기 후반에는 증기선의 발명과 전신 등의 신기술의 개발로 제국 지배력이 한층 더 강화되었다. 이 시기에만 2천 6백만 km^{2}의 영토와 4억의 인구가 증가했다.

[10] 강제로 귀양을 보내는 형벌은 로마시대 이전부터 죄수를 처형하지 않으면서 사회로부터 항구적으로 격리하기 위한 방식으로 사용되어 왔다.

[11] 유형지(流刑地, penal colony)는 죄인들을 사회로부터 추방하고 격리하기 위해 국내의 섬과 같은 오지나 해외 식민지에 설치한 거주지다. 1597년 영국 의회는 '불량배, 방랑자, 건장한 걸인의 징벌에 관한 법(An Act for the Punishment of Rogues, Vagabonds, and Sturdy Beggars)'을 통과시켜 일부러 일을 안 하고 구걸하는 걸인들은 출생지로 보내 일을 하겠다고 할 때까지 수감하도록 하고, 좀

1610년대로부터 미국으로 죄수들을 보냈었는데 1776년 식민지였던 미국이 독립하고 국내에 죄수가 폭증함에 따라 새로 오스트레일리아에 유형지를 건설하게 되었다.[12] 영국은 1770년에 오스트레일리아 동쪽 지역을 뉴 사우스 웨일즈(New South Wales) 식민지로 만들었다.[13] 그리고 1788년 1,500명을 태운 11척의 배가 시드니 항구에 도착하여 식민지 건설이 시작된 이래 1868년까지 약 16만 명에 달하는 영국의 죄수들이 이곳으로 유배되었다.

이와는 별개로 1790년대부터 세계 각지에서 자유 정착민들이 오스트레일리아로 이주해 오기 시작하였다. 특히 1850년대의 금광시대(Gold Rush)엔 중국을 포함한 다양한 국가의 사람들이 모여들어 1850년에 40만이었던 인구는 10년 후엔 백만 명 이상으로, 30년 후에는 2백만 명 이상으로 증가했다. 그 이후 인구가 차츰 늘면서 다섯 개의 자치 식민지를 추가적으로 건설하여

    더 심각하지만 사형은 너무 가혹하다고 여겨지는 중죄(felony)에 해당하는 범죄자들은 바다 건너 다른 지역으로 유배할 것을 결정했다. 이곳의 수감자들은 강제노역에 동원되는 등 노예와 같은 생활을 했다. 유럽과 라틴아메리카의 많은 국가들도 죄수를 여기저기 널리 흩어진 유형지에 추방하기는 했지만 이러한 유형지는 대부분이 영국과 프랑스가 개발하고 운영했다.

[12] 죄수의 노동력을 농부들이나 목장 운영자(pastoral squatter), 그리고 도로건설과 같은 국책사업에 할당해 주지 않았더라면 오스트레일리아 식민지 건설은 불가능 했을 것이다. 특히 19세기 후반에는 금광 개발에 가용한 일반 노동자들의 노동력이 대거 빠져나가 죄수의 노동력이 식민 건설에 절대적으로 중요한 위치를 점하게 되었다.

[13] 네덜란드는 1606년 4만 년 이상 원주민들만이 거주해왔던 오스트레일리아를 발견했다.

1901년에는 이 여섯 개의 식민지를 합하여 오스트레일리아 연방(Commonwealth of Australia)을 설립했다.

초기에는 오스트레일리아로 죄수들을 유배하는 수송선에 의료장비 등이 부족하여 수송 중에 질병이 발생하여 많은 인명을 잃기도 하였으나 이후 정부의 규제 및 관리 강화로 일반 이민선보다 더 안전하게 인명을 수송할 수 있게 되었다. 수형기간을 마친 죄수들은 자신이 알아서 본국으로 귀환해야 했기 때문에 많은 사람들이 자유민으로 오스트레일리아에 남게 되었다. 또한 수형기간의 일정 기간을 마친 사람에게 결혼을 할 수 있게 하는 등 부분적인 자유를 허락하여 이들이 식민지 건설에 참여할 수 있도록 하기도 하였다.

2. 민중의 작가

정식 교육은 별로 받지 못했지만 찰즈 디킨즈에게는 어린 시절의 가난과 고난의 경험이 무엇보다도 소중한 교육이었고 그는 결국 이를 바탕으로 작가이자 사회비평가로 성공했다. 디킨즈는 스무 해 동안 저명한 주간지를 편집했으며 완성하지 못한 것까지 포함해서 열다섯 편의 소설과 수백 편의 단편, 수필 등을 집필했으며 아동, 교육 등의 사회개혁 문제를 위한 사회운동가로서도 활동했다.

1812년 2월 7일 잉글랜드의 포츠머스(Portsmouth)[14]에서 팔 남매들 중 두 번째로 태어난 그는 어린 시절을 잉글랜드 남동부의 해안지역인 켄트(Kent)[15] 북부의 채텀(Chatham)이란 마을에서 보냈다. 병약하여 고생은 했지만 그는 부모와 보모가 들려주는 신나는 이야기들을 들으며 행복한 어린 시절을 보냈다. 그는 밖에서 놀기도 좋아했지만 아버지의 존(John)의 서재로부터 악한소설(picaresque novel)을 포함한 수많은 책들을 즐겨 탐독했다. 그러나 해군 경리국(Navy Pay Office)의 공무원인 아버지는 친절하고 사교적이긴 해도 금전 관념이 희박했다. 디킨즈가 열두 살이 되던 1824년에 그의 어머니와 막내 동생은 빚을 갚지 못해 수감된 아버지를 따라 런던 서덕(Southwark)[16]에 있는 마샬시(Marshalsea) 채무자 감옥에서 살게 되었다.[17] 이때 그의 어머니는 디킨즈는 밖에 따로 살면서 한 일 년쯤 런던 중심부에 있는 한 흑색도료[18] 공장에서 하루 열 시간 이상씩 병에 상표딱지를 붙이는 일을 하도록

---

[14] 런던에서 100km 정도 떨어진 잉글랜드 남부의 해안도시로 영국에서 인구밀도가 가장 높다. 해군기지와 상업 항구가 있는데 디킨즈의 시대에는 영국 해군의 중심기지로서 유럽에서 가장 강력하게 요새화한 도시였다.

[15] 잉글랜드 남동부 해안의 군(郡, county)으로 북서쪽으로는 대런던(Greater London)과 접해 있고, 남동쪽으로는 프랑스를 바라보고 있어 영국의 유럽대륙과의 교류에 있어 교두보 역할을 한다. 풍광이 아름다워 전통적으로 '잉글랜드의 정원(Garden of England)'이라 불린다.

[16] 런던 중심부 템즈 강 바로 남쪽에 있는 구역으로 런던교(London Bridge) 남단으로부터 시작된다.

[17] 감옥에 가족들이 들어와 함께 사는 것은 당시 일반적인 관행이었다.

[18] 흑색도료(blacking)란 19세기에 사용되던 검은 색소로 구두약이나 성냥, 비료 등을 만드는 데 사용되었다.

했다.¹⁹ 가족과 따로 살면서 굶주리고 버림받은 느낌으로 중노동을 한 이때의 경험은 평생토록 그에게 큰 상처로 남았다. 가세가 기울었음에도 누나는 장학금을 받고 왕립음악원(Royal Academy of Music)에서 공부를 계속하고 있었기 때문에 상대적으로 더 힘들었다.²⁰ 설상가상으로 그는 스스로 생각하기에도 공장 일을 아주 잘 해냈는데 그런 자신의 모습에 어머니가 만족스러워하는 걸 보면서 더욱 비참함을 느꼈다.

얼마 후 그의 증조모의 사망으로 유산을 물려받게 된 아버지가 채무자 감옥으로부터 석방되어 디킨즈는 다시 학교를 다닐 수 있게 되었다.²¹ 이후 디킨즈는 중학교를 2년 정도 다니다 1827년 열다섯 살에 변호사 사무실에서 사환으로 일하게 되었다. 다음해인 1828년엔 법원의 속기사를 거쳐 한 신문사의 속기 기자가 되었다.²² 그러던 중 스물한 살의 디킨즈는 자신이 어릴 적부

---

19 그는 삐걱거리는 바닥에 쥐들이 들끓는 이 공장에서의 경험을 토대로 자서전적인 소설인 1849~1850년 작 『데이비드 코퍼필드』에서 중산층에서 빈민층으로 내려앉은 집안 사정과 나이 어린 노동자로서 겪게 되는 고통과 좌절을 생생하게 그리고 있다. 이 경험은 또한 그로 하여금 아동노동 등의 사회문제에 관심을 갖고 사회개혁 운동에 나서게 하였다.
20 디킨즈는 일요일이면 따로 공부하는 누이와 함께 마샬시 감옥에 가서 가족과 함께 시간을 보냈다. 그는 나중에 이 감옥을 『리틀 도릿』의 배경으로 활용한다.
21 디킨즈는 가사와 교육을 전담한 어머니, 또한 부지런하며 현명한 어머니 일리저벳(Elizabeth)으로부터 문학적이고 예술적인 재능을 물려받았다. 그러나 디킨즈는 그녀를 냉혹한 어머니로 기억한다. 그녀는 가세가 기울자 디킨즈를 공장으로 보냈고 석방된 아버지가 다시 학교에 보내려 할 때에도 반대했다. 이것은 디킨즈의 일생에 큰 상처로 남았고 그의 여성관에도 적잖이 영향을 미쳤다. 그는 후일 그런 자신의 어머니를 『니콜러스 니클비』에서 딸을 비참한 결혼으로 이끄는 니클비 부인(Mrs Nickleby)으로 묘사한다.

터 꿈꿔왔던 위대한 배우나 기자가 되기는 힘들다고 판단한다.[23] 대신 기쁨과 슬픔의 경험을 생생하게 글로 표현하여 이를 읽는 이들로 하여금 현실로 느끼고 보게 만드는 재능이 있었던 그는 소설가로 입신하기로 결심하고 이후 여러 신문사에 열정적으로 기고했으며 1834년부터는 신문기자로서 런던의 삶에 대한 여러 편의 글을 발표했다.[24] 마침내 디킨즈는 스물다섯 살인 1837년에 해학과 풍자, 그리고 개인과 사회에 대한 날카로운 관찰이 돋보이는 『피퀵 페이퍼즈(Pickwick Papers)』[25]로 유명인사가 되고, 이어 1838년의 『올리버 트위스트(Oliver Twist)』,[26] 그리고 1838~1839

---

[22] 당시에는 신문이나 법원의 공식적인 기록을 주로 속기에 의존했는데 디킨즈는 탁월한 기억력으로 보통 3년은 걸려야 습득하는 속기술(Gurney's system of shorthand)을 3개월 만에 완성하고 정식 속기사가 되어 빠르고 정확한 업무 처리로 인정받았다.

[23] 디킨즈는 오랫동안 배우가 되는 꿈을 키워왔다. 어린 시절엔 혼자 방안이나 들판에서 하루에 네댓 시간씩 연기 연습을 했고 어른이 되어서도 아마추어 극단에서 배우로 연기했다. 실제로 전문 극단에 배우로 지원하기도 했으나 우연찮게 감기로 입단 심사에 참석하지 못한 것을 계기로 배우의 꿈을 접게 된다. 이런 재능은 그가 후일 영국 전역과 여러 나라들을 돌며 자기 소설의 낭독회를 할 때 발휘된다.

[24] 디킨즈는 『먼슬리 매거진(Monthly Magazine)』이라는 잡지에 글을 실었으며, 『모닝 크로니클(Morning Chronicle)』의 정치부 기자로 의회 토론을 보도하고 선거 보도를 위해 전국을 여행했다. 1936년엔 기자로서 쓴 글들을 모아 보즈(Boz)라는 가명으로 『보즈의 스케치(Sketches by Boz)』라는 책을 출판했다.

[25] 당대 고전의 영향을 많이 받은 디킨즈의 처녀작으로 생동감 넘치는 희극적 풍자나 재담을 담아 대중문학의 새로운 전통을 수립했다. 이 소설의 마지막 연재분이 실린 잡지는 4만 부 이상이나 팔리는 대성공이었다.

[26] 어린이를 주인공으로 한 빅토리아 시대 최초의 소설로 희극적 요소를 포함하면서도 빈민가와 지하세계를 적나라하게 묘사하여 크나큰 사회적 파장을 몰고 왔다. 사회적·도덕적 악에 천착하는 디킨즈의 예술적 야망이 드러나는 작품이

년의 『니콜러스 니클비(Nicholas Nickleby)』[27]로 폭발적인 인기를 얻어 작가로서 위치를 확고히 다지게 되었다.

디킨즈는 1833년 머리아 비드넬(Maria Beadnel)에 대한 첫사랑에 실패한 충격이 너무나도 큰 나머지 그녀에 대해 썼던 모든 것들을 불태워 버리고 그 후에도 아무에게도 그 이야기를 하지 못했다.[28] 그리곤 몇 십 년 지난 후에야 자신의 전기작가인 절친한 친구에게 힘들게 지난 일을 털어놓을 수 있었다. 유력한 은행가의 딸을 사랑하는 일개 무명작가였던 디킨즈는 머리아가 사회적 계급의 차이 때문에 그를 거절했다고 믿었다. 그리고는 1836년 그는 당시 유력한 신문이었던 『이브닝 크로니클(Evening Chronicle)』의 편집인과의 인연으로 그의 딸인 캐서린 호가스(Catherine Hogarth, 1816~1879)와 결혼하여 런던의 첼시(Chelsea)[29]에 정착했고 이후 아이 열을 낳았다.[30]

다. 당시 젊은 빅토리아 여왕도 매달 연재되는 『피퀵 페이퍼즈』와 『올리버 트위스트』를 밤늦게까지 읽고 토론했다 한다.
[27] 유기되고 학대당하는 어린이를 사회비판의 근거로 삼아 문학에서의 중요한 혁신을 이룬 작품이다.
[28] 머리아의 부모는 그녀를 파리에 있는 학교로 보냄으로 디킨즈의 구애를 끝냈다. 머리아는 후일 『데이비드 코퍼필드』의 도라(Dora)라는 인물로 재현된다.
[29] 런던 중심가 템즈 강 바로 위의 부촌으로 디킨즈의 생전에는 미술가나 문학가들이 많이 살았다.
[30] 결혼하자마자 열일곱 살 먹은 처제와 함께 하게 되는데 그녀가 1837년에 갑작스러운 병으로 죽자 엄청난 충격을 받은 디킨즈는 순수했던 그녀의 모습을 『오래된 골동품 가게』에서 어린 넬(Nell)로 재현했다.

디킨즈는 1840~1841년 작 『오래된 골동품 가게(The Old Curiosity Shop)』[31]에 이어 1841년에 『바나비 러지(Barnaby Rudge)』[32]를 출판하고, 1842년 아내와 함께 미국과 캐나다를 6개월간 여행했다. 여기서 그는 감옥과 정신병원 등을 돌아보았고 미국의 노예제도에 대해서도 신랄한 비판을 서슴지 않았다.[33] 영국 성공회 신도였던 그는 1840년대 초반엔 삼위일체, 원죄, 예정, 성서무오 등의 주요 교리를 부정하는 단신론(Unitarianism)에 경도되기도 했다. 1843엔 『크리스마스 캐럴(Christmas Carol)』,[34] 1846~1848년엔 『돔비와 아들(Dombey and Son)』[35] 등의 중·장편을 통해 자신이 몸소 체험한 사회 밑바닥의 생활상과 그 애환을 생생히 묘사하여 세상의 모순과 부정을 지적했는데 그런 가운데서도 해학을 잃지 않았다.

---

[31] 외할아버지와 함께 사는 고아 소녀의 처절하고 비극적인 이야기를 통한 사회비평으로 당대 사회에 대단한 충격을 가져 왔다.

[32] 새로운 장르인 역사소설을 시도하는 이 작품에서는 18세기 후반을 배경으로 민중폭동의 참상을 심도 있게 다루고 있다.

[33] 그는 또한 미국에 자신의 작품의 해적판이 나도는 것에 대해 강한 불만을 표했으나 미국 언론은 이에 대해 별로 개의치 않았다. 이때의 경험은 같은 해에 『일반 배포를 위한 아메리카 단상(American Notes for General Circulation)』이라는 여행기로 출판되었다.

[34] 빈한한 노동자들과 어린이들을 보고 겪은 경험을 토대로 가난한 사람들을 위한 소설로 작정하고 쓴 작품으로, 크리스마스에 나눔과 돌봄이라는 의미심장한 가치를 새롭게 부여하여 이것이 지역사회에 기반한 교회 중심의 기념일에서 가족 중심의 축일로 자리 잡는 계기를 마련하였다.

[35] 디킨즈는 이 작품부터 광대한 배경과 소재로 수많은 인물들이 등장하는 대하소설을 연재 형식으로 집필하면서도 전체적 목적과 구성을 유지하려 노력했다.

그의 대표작이라 할 수 있는 1850년에 완결된 자서전적인 소설 『데이비드 코퍼필드(David Copperfield)』[36]부터 작품의 경향이 조금씩 변해서 사회 전체를 암울한 시각으로 드러내는 후기의 특징을 보인다. 이 작품을 기점으로 그는 주제를 더 심도 있게 다루고 구성을 더욱 치밀하게 조직하기 시작했다. 다음 작품인 1853년의 『황량한 집(Bleak House)』[37]이 그 좋은 예인데 이전의 작품에서처럼 한 사람의 주인공의 성장과 체험을 다루는 것이 아니라 많은 인물들을 등장시켜 여러 사회계층을 폭넓게 조명하는 이른바 파노라마적인 사회소설로 접근한다. 여기선 개인의 힘으로는 어찌할 수 없는 사회의 벽에 직면한 무력감과 좌절감이 전편을 흐른다. 이후에도 그의 창작력은 조금도 쇠퇴되지 않아 직공들의 파업을 다룬 1854년의 『고된 시기(Hard Times)』,[38] 신랄한 풍자로 이루어진 1856년의 『리틀 도릿(Little Dorrit)』, 프랑스혁명[39]을 무대로 한 1859년 작 역사소설 『두 도시 이야기』,

---

[36] 디킨즈의 소설 중 가장 자서전에 가까운 작품으로 개성이 강한 인물에 대한 다채로운 묘사를 통해 고아인 주인공이 어려운 환경을 딛고 입신하는 과정을 그렸다. 그는 또 한편의 자전적 소설인 『위대한 유산』을 집필하기 전 의도하지 않은 중복을 피하기 위해 『데이비드 코퍼필드』를 다시 읽어 보았다고 한다.

[37] 당대의 법원과 사교계의 허세와 위선, 억압적인 여성 이데올로기에 대한 냉소적인 사회비평이다. 사법체계에 만연한 권모술수와 관료주의를 생생하게 묘사하여 가난한 사람들이 법에 의해서 보호 받기는커녕 더욱더 소외되는 현실을 꼬집었다.

[38] 산업혁명 이후 자본가와 노동자의 대립으로 나타나는 당시의 사회경제적인 난국을 묘사함으로써 과도하게 사실을 중시하여 상상력을 말살하는 급진적 공리주의(utilitarianism)에 대한 신랄한 사회비평이다.

[39] 1789~1799년 자유·평등·박애를 기치로 일어난 프랑스혁명(Révolution française)은

그리고 자서전적인 『위대한 유산』 등의 작품 이외에도 많은 단편과 수필을 썼다.[40]

디킨즈는 1855년 어린 시절의 연인이었던 머리아 비드넬을 다시 만나게 되지만 곧 실망하게 되는데 이러한 환멸을 1857년의 소설 『리틀 도릿』[41]에서 묘사했다. 곧이어 마흔 다섯의 디킨즈는 스물일곱 살이나 차이가 나는 열여덟 살의 신인 여배우 엘런 터난(Ellen Ternan, 1839~1914)을 사귀기 시작한다. 이는 당시의 사회 정서상 용납될 수 없는 것인데다가 존경 받는 작가이며 가족을 대상으로 하는 유수한 잡지의 편집인으로서의 자신의 명성을 염려하여 터난과의 관계를 은밀하게 유지했다. 이 사실은 디킨즈가 죽고 난 다음 그의 딸이 말할 때까지 아무도 몰랐다. 결국 1858년 디킨즈는 아내 머리아와 이혼한다. 비평가들은 디킨즈와 그의 아내 캐서린과 터난과의 삼각관계가 『두 도시 이야기(A Tale of Two Cities)』[42]에 반영되었다고 말한다.[43]

자본가 혁명으로 정치권력이 왕족과 귀족에서 자본가에게로 옮겨지는 세계사적으로 중요한 전환점으로 민주주의 발전에 크게 기여했다.

[40] 그의 사후 64년 만인 1934년에 출판된 책으로는 1846~1849년에 쓴 『우리 주님의 생애(The Life of Our Lord)』가 있다. 이 글은 디킨즈가 자신의 자녀들에게 신앙보다는 본받음의 대상으로 예수 그리스도에 대해 쉽게 설명하기 위해서 쓴 책이다.

[41] 당대 정부와 사회의 문제를 지적하는 풍자소설로서 채무자 감옥 등 열악한 사회적 안전망, 무능한 정부, 계급 간의 소통의 부재 등의 문제를 다룬다.

[42] 프랑스 혁명 기간 중 런던과 파리에서 벌어지는 이야기를 담은 소설로 이제까지 2억 부 이상이 팔렸다.

[43] 이 소설에서 루시 마네트(Lucie Manette)에 대한 묘사와 주요 등장인물인 시드니 카튼(Sydney Carton)과 샤를 다네(Charles Darnay)의 마네트에 대한 행동이

전 작품을 통해 보통 사람들에 대한 공감과 함께 상류사회에 대한 회의적인 시선을 보여준 디킨즈의 인생에서 가장 흥미로운 것은 대중과의 교감이었는데 이러한 대중성과 사회 현안에 대한 성찰이 바로 그의 탁월성의 요체였다. 그는 사람들의 마음을 움직이고 경탄을 자아낸 작가 정도가 아니라 그들의 사랑하는 진정한 친구였다. 그는 평생 대중에게 충심을 다했으며 그의 일거수일투족은 대중의 관심의 대상이었다.[44]

그러는 한편 디킨즈는 스스로 잡지사를 경영하기도 했고,[45] 윤락녀들을 위한 재활, 교육 시설도 운영했다.[46] 빈민층 아이들이 아플 때 치료받을 수 있는 아동병원[47]과 이들에게 무상 교육을

디킨즈 자신의 터난에 대한 자세를 반영한다는 것이다.

[44] 디킨즈는 두 번째 소설인 『올리버 트위스트』를 출간하고는 바로 전 세계적인 유명인사가 되었다. 유럽과 미국의 항구엔 열렬한 독자들이 그의 소설이 연재되는 잡지를 싣고 들어오는 배를 기다리고 있었다. 독자들이 그의 작품 속의 이야기가 마치 현실인 냥 기뻐하기도 하고 슬픔에 잠기기도 할 정도로 디킨즈는 민중의 감성을 완전히 사로잡고 있었다.

[45] 디킨즈는 1850~1859년에는 『하우스홀드 워즈(Household Words)』, 1858~1870년에는 『올 더 이어 라운드(All the Year Round)』라는 잡지의 발행인 겸 편집인으로 일했다.

[46] 1846년 디킨즈는 런던 서쪽 셰퍼즈부시(Shepherds Bush)에 윤락녀들의 징벌보다는 재활에 초점을 맞춘 유레이니어 코티지(Urania Cottage)라는 주거시설을 설립·후원했다. 여기서는 주로 일반적인 기초과정과 가사를 가르쳤는데 설립 후 10여 년 간 100여 명이 과정을 수료한 뒤 결혼하거나 이민을 가면서 이곳을 떠났다.

[47] 지금은 그레잇 오먼드 스트릿 병원(Great Ormond Street Hospital)으로 개명하였지만, 1852년 설립된 이 아동병원(Hospital for Sick Children)은 어린이만을 대상으로 입원 진료를 제공하는 영국 최초의 병원이다. 개원 당시에는 기부금에 의존하여 운영했다. 디킨즈는 이 병원을 위해 열정적으로 모금 운동을 벌였고 자신의 작품 낭독회로 벌어들인 돈을 이 병원에 기부하여 재정적으로 자립할 수 있게 하였다.

제공하는 빈민학교[48]를 후원하는 운동을 벌이기도 했다. 그는 생애 마지막 10년 동안 소설 낭독을 위해 영국 곳곳과 미국을 여행했다.[49] 가는 곳마다 대중들은 그를 눈물 어린 환대로 열렬히 영접했다. 그의 낭독회는 일개 개인의 행사가 아니라 처음부터 끝까지 공적이며 국제적인 행사였다. 그는 이렇게 오늘날 최고의 인기 연예인 이상의 대중적 인기를 누렸으며 당대의 어느 지식인보다도 더 사회 현안에 미치는 영향이 지대했다.[50]

쇠약해진 디킨즈는 1867~1868년에 넉 달 동안 두 번째로 미국을 방문하여 80회 정도의 낭독회를 성공적으로 마쳤으나 1868~1869년에는 영국 전역을 돌며 고별 낭독여행(reading tour)을 하던 중 몸의 이상을 느껴 모든 일정을 취소하게 된다. 그러나 1870년 마지막으로 10여 차례의 낭독회를 더 연 디킨즈는 결국 거듭된 과로로 인해 집필 중이던 『에드윈 드루드(Edwin Drood)』를 완성하지 못하고 뇌동맥류로 1870년 6월 9일 자택인 '개즈힐 플레이스(Gad's Hill Place)'에서 향년 58세로 사망했다. 당시 신문

---

[48] 19세기 영국의 빈민학교(ragged school)는 극빈 가족의 자녀들에게 무상 교육을 제공하는 자선 교육기관이었다. 디킨즈는 1843년부터 빈민학교 후원을 시작하였으며 이 경험에서 영감을 얻어 후일 『크리스마스 캐럴』을 썼다.

[49] 그가 운집한 청중 앞에서 마치 배우처럼 자신의 작품의 일부를 읽는 낭독회는 언제나 대성공이었다. 1858~1859년, 그리고 1866~1867년에 본격적으로 잉글랜드, 스코틀랜드, 아일랜드를 돌며 수백 회의 낭독회를 열어 엄청난 수입을 벌어들였다.

[50] 칼 막스(Karl Marx, 1818~1883)는 디킨즈는 세상을 향해 그 어느 정치인이나 사회운동가들보다도 더 많은 정치사회적인 진실을 외쳤다고 했다.

과 잡지들은 며칠 동안이나 그의 일대기로 지면을 도배하다시피 했다. "그의 소설은 정말 그날그날의 대화 주제였다. 그것은 문학이 아니라 마치 정치나 뉴스와 같은 사회적 사건과도 같았다"고 적은 한 신문의 부고는 디킨즈의 소설이 갖는 시대적 의미를 잘 보여준다.

그가 생전에 고향의 자택인 '개즈힐'에 묻히고 싶다고 말했었지만 사람들은 이를 무시했다. 지금 그는 런던 웨스트민스터 사원(Westminster Abbey)의 '시인들의 모퉁이(Poets' Corner)'[51]에 묻혀 있다. 장례식에서 배포된 추모사(epitaph)에는 "그는 가난하고 고통 받고 박해 받는 자들의 동정자였으며 그의 죽음으로 인해 세상은 영국의 가장 훌륭한 작가 중 하나를 잃었다"고 씌어 있었다.

디킨즈가 세상을 떠난 지 140년 이상이 지난 지금도 여러 곳에서 그의 흔적을 찾아볼 수 있다. 2002년 영국의 공영방송 BBC는 가장 위대한 영국인에 대한 여론조사의 결과를 발표했는데 디킨즈가 그 중 41위를 차지했다. 또한 같은 BBC가 선정한 역사상 가장 위대한 문학작품 100선에 디킨즈의 작품 5개가 선정되는[52] 등 아직도 그의 위대한 유산을 뚜렷하게 느낄 수 있다.[53] 단

---

[51] 런던의 웨스트민스터 사원 남쪽 부근으로 1556년 제프리 초서(Geoffrey Chaucer, 1343~1400) 이래 영국의 유명한 시인·소설·극작가들이 많이 묻혀 있다.
[52] 『위대한 유산』이 17위, 『데이비드 코퍼필드』가 34위, 『크리스마스 캐럴』이 47위, 『두 도시 이야기』가 63위, 『황량한 집』이 79위에 뽑혔다.
[53] 1992~2003년엔 영국의 10파운드 지폐에 등장하기도 했다. 이뿐만 아니라 디킨즈의 출생지인 포츠머스에는 디킨즈 박물관과 그의 이름을 딴 학교도 있으며 성장지인 켄트에는 디킨즈 월드(Dickens World)라는 놀이 공원도 있다. 미국 필라델

한 번도 절판된 적이 없는 그의 작품들은 200편 이상의 영화와 텔레비전 드라마로 제작되었는데, 이 중 『위대한 유산』은 20편 이상의 연극과 텔레비전 드라마, 영화로 제작되었다.[54]

3. 성장소설과 풍자

체스터턴은 디킨즈의 모든 소설은 빅토리아 시대 서민들의 비현실적이지만 강렬한 기대를 그리고 있으므로 모두 '위대한 유산'[55]이란 제목을 붙여도 무리가 없지만, 막상 그 중 아무런 유산도 기대도 현실화된 바 없는 이 작품에 그 이름을 붙인 것이 흥미롭다고 말한다. 그러나 그는 디킨즈가 자신의 '인생과 명성의 오후에' 집필한 이 『위대한 유산』이야말로 일관성이 있고 진실된 작품이라고 평한다. 사실 디킨즈 자신도 생전에 작가로서의 완숙미를 보여주는 이 소설을 자신의 작품들 중 가장 훌륭한 작품으로 꼽았다. 당시 일부 비평가들은 그의 다른 작품들과 마찬가지로 이 작품에서도 여실히 드러난 구성과 인물을 과장하는 경향에

피아(Philadelphia)에는 그의 동상이 있다.
[54] 『위대한 유산』은 1917년 무성영화로 제작된 이래 여러 편의 영화로 제작됐다. 이 중 1946년 제작된 데이비드 린(David Lean) 감독의 영화는 아카데미상을 수상했는데, 이 작품은 1999년 100대 영국 영화 중 5위로 뽑혔다. 2011년에는 브라이언 컥(Brian Kirk)이 이 소설을 BBC의 3부작으로 영화화하기도 했다.
[55] 빅토리아 시대의 영국인들에게 'expectations'란 말은 '유산(legacy)'이란 뜻과 '기대(anticipations)'란 뜻을 함께 가지고 있었다.

거부감을 보인 반면[56] 독자들은 1861년 판이 다섯 번이나 인쇄될 정도로 열광적으로 환영했다. 반면 오늘날의 비평가들은 현실성의 문제보다는 디킨즈가 두려움과 흥미, 소외와 행운, 계급차별과 사회정의, 굴욕과 명예와 같은 시대를 초월하는 주제를 다룬 것에 대해 대체적으로 긍정적인 평가를 내리고 있다.

사상 유래 없는 급격한 사회변동의 결과로 정치, 경제, 역사 심지어는 윤리의 분야에서도 순수하다고 여기는 기존의 가치관들이 왜곡되는 상황 속에서 당대의 문학은 개인의 특성과 인간에 대한 존엄성을 어떻게 보존하고 발전시킬 것인가 하는 문제에 천착하게 되었다. 디킨즈는 이러한 변화의 시대에 인간을 고통스럽게 하는 사회적 요인은 무엇이며 이에 따라 인간의 내면적 진실이 어떻게 변하는지를 보여주었다.[57] 이리하여 빅토리아 시대의 문학은 상류층의 삶을 미화한 낭만주의[58] 문학을 민중을

---

[56] 체스터턴(G. K. Chesterton, 1874~1936), 톨스토이(Leo Tolstoy, 1828~1910), 오웰(George Orwell, 1903~1950) 등은 사회비평과 사실주의, 희극적 요소, 등장인물의 설정 등에서 보여진 천재를 찬양하고 있지만, 와일드(Oscar Wilde, 1854~1900), 제임스(Henry James, 1843~1916), 울프(Virginia Woolf, 1882~1941) 등은 심리분석의 부족, 과도한 감상주의 등을 비판한다.

[57] 버나드 쇼(George Bernard Shaw, 1856~1950)는 『위대한 유산』이 칼 막스의 『자본론(Das Kapital)』보다도 더 선동적이라 말한다.

[58] 낭만주의(romanticism)는 서구에서 18세기 말부터 19세기 중엽까지 문학적, 예술적, 지적 운동으로 이성과 합리성을 중시한 고전주의와 유물론에 대한 반발로 비합리성, 상상력, 감성 등을 강조했다. 부분적으로는 산업혁명에 대한 반응이기도 하지만 실제로는 계몽주의(Enlightenment)의 귀족적 사회정치적 규범과 자연의 과학적 합리화에 대한 반란이었다. 이러한 흐름은 주로 시각예술, 음악과 문학에서 두드러지게 나타났지만 역사서술과 교육, 자연과학에서도 큰 변화를 가져왔다. 정치에서는 자유주의(liberalism)와 급진주의(radicalism) 사상을

위한 문학으로 대체함으로써 문학 안에서의 혁명을 일으키고 있었다. 이 문학의 혁명에서는 잡지가 아주 유효한 매체로 등장하여 각계각층의 독자들을 끌어 모으게 되었는데 이에 따라 보다 많은 작가들에게 작품활동의 기회가 제공됐다. 잡지라는 특성 때문에 작가들이 매주 또는 매달 조금씩 글을 발표해 나가다 보니 대중의 반응과 요구가 글의 전개에 많은 영향을 미치기도 했다. 디킨즈의 『위대한 유산』은 1860~1861년 주간지 『올 더 이어 라운드』에 연재되었던 것을 단행본으로 출판한 것이다.[59]

디킨즈는 종종 어릴 때의 꿈과 지금의 모습을 돌아보았다. 아홉 살이던 어느 날 대저택 '개즈힐 플레이스' 앞을 지나갈 때 아버지로부터 열심히 일하면 이런 집에서 살 수 있다는 말을 들은 디킨즈는 이후 성장기 내내 이 집에 사는 걸 꿈꿔오다 마침내 40대 중반이 되던 1856년 이 집을 사게 된다.[60] 또한 그는 어린 시절의 처절한 고난의 경험뿐만 아니라 애정 관계에서의 격동과 환희의 경험을 소설 속에서 참담함과 기쁨으로 아주 사실적으로

잉태했고, 장기적으로 보아서는 근대 민족주의(nationalism)의 태동에도 지대한 영향을 미치게 된다.

[59] 디킨즈 자신의 잡지인 『올 더 이어 라운드』는 소설 연재로 많은 독자들을 확보하고 있었는데 갑작스레 판매고의 부진을 겪게 되자 이의 반전을 노리고 『위대한 유산』을 기획했다. 이 소설은 바로 대중의 관심을 사로잡아 매주 10만 부 이상의 잡지가 팔렸다. 연재가 끝나고 1861년 10월에 쳅먼 앤드 홀(Chapman and Hall) 출판사에서 3권으로 출판했다.

[60] 켄트의 하이엄(Higham)에 있는 이 집은 셰익스피어(William Shakespeare, 1564~1616)의 『헨리 4세(Henry IV)』 제1부의 무대가 된 곳이다.

현실감 있게 표현한다. 『위대한 유산』은 디킨즈가 자신의 성장 과정의 경험을 살려 한 나약한 소년이 엄격한 사회질서 안에서 성숙한 성인으로 자라나는 과정을 그린 '성장소설(Bildungsroman; coming-of-age novel)'[61]이다.

문학비평에서 성장소설이란 심리적이고 도덕적인 면에서 청소년에서 성인으로 성장하는 '야망(ambition)'과 '성숙(maturation)'의 과정에 중점을 둔 소설을 이른다. 즉 민감한 청소년이 여러 가지 풍파 속에서도 회의와 야망을 품게 되고 이를 위해 인생의 해답을 찾아 가며 성장하는, 즉 진정한 성인 되어가는 과정을 그리는 소설이다. 이러한 장르의 작품은 대개 정서적 상실감을 겪는 청소년이 자신의 운명을 개척하기 위해 세상으로의 여행을 떠나는 것으로 시작한다. 그리고 이 주인공은 어렵게 그리고 서서히 목표한 바의 인간적인 성숙에 이른다. 그 과정에서 주인공과 사회와의 갈등이 전개되는데 결국은 주인공이 사회의 가치를 점진적으로 받아들이면서 이전의 실수와 절망을 끝내게 된다. 어떤 경우에는 이제는 성숙한 주인공이 다른 사람들을 돕기도 한다.

이 시대의 영국 소설은 역사상 가장 급격한 변화를 경험하는 동시대인들의 이상과 현실, 그리고 좌절과 희망을 표현함으로

---

[61] 성장소설의 장르는 괴테(Johann Wolfgang von Goethe, 1749~1832)의 1794~1796년 작 장편소설인 『빌헬름 마이스터(Wilhelm Meister)』로부터 대중화되어 이후 영국에서 크게 유행했다. 대표적인 작품으로는 대니얼 디포(Daniel Defoe)의 『로빈슨 크루소(Robinson Crusoe)』, 샬롯 브론테(Charlotte Brontë)의 『제인 에어(Jane Eyre)』와 디킨즈 자신의 『데이비드 코퍼필드(David Copperfield)』 등이 있다.

사회적 인식의 저변 확대에 주력했다. 삶의 모든 문제를 누구의 도움도 없이 스스로 해결해야만 하는 『위대한 유산』의 주인공도 필연적으로 이어지는 시행착오를 거치며 자신의 의지와 욕망을 부딪치는 현실에 맞추어 나가게 된다. 당시 빅토리아 시대의 서민들의 이상과 희망은 '신사'[62]가 되고자 하는 욕망으로 집약할 수 있다. 19세기에 들어 계급관계의 구조적 변화를 거치면서 이 개념이 상당한 재력을 가진 중산층까지도 포괄하게 되면서 돈만 있으면 계층의 경계를 넘나들 수 있는 지경에 이르게 되었다.[63] 이러한 당대의 사회발전 과정을 직접 경험한 디킨즈는 신사의 개념에 내포된 사회적 역설(social irony)을 포착하여 빅토리아 시대의 문명과 그 가치관에 대한 심오한 분석을 제공한다.[64] 스스로도 신사가 되기를 열망하기는 했지만 디킨즈는 외부자로서 이를 관찰하고 분석함으로써 신사에의 열망과 노력이 아무리 평등주의적이며 도덕적이라 하더라도, 신사의 개념 자체가 신사와 비신사를 구분하는 배제(exclusion)에 기반하고 있다는 역설을 통찰

---

[62] 지금은 통상적으로 예의 바르며 교양 있는 남자를 신사라고 하지만 이 용어는 원래 잉글랜드에서 향사(esquire) 아래, 자유민(yeoman) 위에 있는 가장 낮은 귀족 계급(gentry)을 의미했는데 대개 혈통에 의해 결정되었다.

[63] 그러나 아직도 상류계급의 예절은 엄격하고 보수적이어서 돈만 있으면 쉽게 흉내 낼 수 있는 것은 아니었다. 신사와 숙녀는 고전 교육을 받고 수많은 사회적인 상황에서 적절하게 행동할 수 있어야 했다.

[64] 디킨즈는 의회의원 선거제도를 정비한 1832년의 개혁법(Reform Act) 이후에 성인이 되었고 당시 다른 사람들의 신사에 대한 갈망을 공유하는 등 그 시대에 속한 그러나 외부적인 관찰자로서의 심오한 이해에 기반하여 『위대한 유산』을 집필했다.

하게 되는데 이러한 깊은 이해의 산물이 바로 『위대한 유산』인 것이다.[65]

이렇게 역설적인 진실을 문학적으로 구명하는 『위대한 유산』은 성장소설이면서 해학이나 야유를 통해 인간의 죄악이나 어리석음을 조롱하는 날카로운 '풍자(satire)'[66]이기도 하다. 현란하고 시적인 문체로 인물과 장소와 사건을 묘사하는 그의 작품을 읽어가다 보면 당시 잉글랜드 사회의 사람들과 제도에 대한 그의 생각과 느낌을 접하게 되는데 귀족의 속물근성에 대한 그의 풍자는 사악할 정도로 익살맞다. 우스운 이름을 가진 인물이 등장하거나 단어를 가지고 말장난(pun)을 하는 경우도 있다. 이렇게 디킨즈는 해학과 감성에 희극적이거나 극적인 효과를 위해 인물의 신체적이거나 성격적인 특징을 과장하는 기괴한(grotesque) 요소를 가미하기도 하는데 그의 이러한 문학적 특성은 후일 '디킨즈적(Dickensian)'이라고 불리게 된다. 실제로 그의 소설에는 괴이한 인물뿐 아니라 유령이 등장하기도 하고 유령의 이야기가 나오기도 한다.[67] 한편 이러한 괴기한 인물이 등장하는 그의 작

---

[65] 체스터턴은 출신성분상 디킨즈는 당대에 신사로 여겨지지 않았음을 지적한다. 디킨즈의 딸도 자신의 아버지는 신사가 되기에는 너무도 복잡했다고 말하는데 이러한 평가는 그의 민중지향성을 반증해 준다. 디킨즈는 흔히 동시대의 작가인 윌리엄 새커리(William Thackeray, 1811~1863)와 비교되는데 새커리가 신사계급과 귀족계급 사이의 어느 곳에 있었다면 디킨즈는 신사계급과 민중계급 사이 어느 곳에 있었던 것으로 보인다.

[66] 풍자란 문학의 한 장르로서 개인이나 사회의 악덕, 우둔, 비행, 결점 따위를 조롱함으로써 이를 고발하고 개선을 촉구하기 위한 예술 형식으로 해학적인 요소를 가미한 건설적 사회비평이다.

품들 중 몇은 디킨즈의 동시대 작가 몇 명의 경우와 같이 반유대주의로 비판되기도 하지만 이는 오늘날의 관점에서 과거를 바라보는 측면이 없지 않다.[68] 디킨즈 자신은 『위대한 유산』이 희극과 비극의 혼합이라고 말했는데 많은 비평가들이 여기 동의한다. 이 소설의 서술자인 주인공은 재미있고 우스꽝스럽기도 한 많은 희극적 인물들을 묘사하는데 이들이 불행하면서 동시에 비도덕적이라는 점에서 비극적이다. 조용히 도덕적인 삶을 살아가는 인물들의 경우도 세상의 인정을 받지 못한다는 점에서는 비극적이다.

---

[67] 『크리스마스 캐럴』, 『피퀵 페이퍼즈』, 『니콜라스 니클비』를 포함한 많은 작품에 유령이 등장한다. 디킨즈 자신은 1855년 케임브리지 대학의 교수들의 유령과 심령현상을 토론하는 모임으로 시작하여 1862년 공식적으로 발족한 유령협회(Ghost Club)에도 참여했다.

[68] 반유대주의(anti-Semitism)란 유서 깊은 유대인에 대한 편견, 증오 등의 인종차별을 이른다. 예를 들어 『올리버 트위스트』에서 아이키 솔로몬(Ikey Solomon)이란 유명한 범죄자를 모델로 한 페이긴(Fagin)이라는 인물은 매부리코와 탐욕스러운 눈을 가진 장물아비로 전형적인 유대인으로 묘사되는데 이를 반유대주의로 보기는 어려울 것 같다. 디킨즈는 유대인 대학살(Holocaust)이 일어나기 훨씬 이전의 사회에 살았으므로 작품에서 단지 극적인 효과를 위해 그런 인물을 설정했다고 보아야 할 것이다.

제3장 인물과 사건

1. 등장인물

변혁기의 엄청난 물결에 휩쓸린 인간과 인간관계에 대한 새로운 성찰과 함께 등장인물[69]의 성격 묘사가 이 시대 문학의 아주 중요한 특질로 자리 잡았다. 디킨즈가 『위대한 유산』에서 당대의 그릇된 사회제도를 고발하며 새 시대의 새로운 윤리를 촉구

---

[69] 등장인물(character)은 문학 작품이나 연극, 영화 따위에 나오는 인물로 반드시 사람이어야 하는 것은 아니며 의인화한 동물이나 신화적 존재 등도 모두 포함한다. 소설 구성의 3요소인 인물, 사건, 배경 중에서 등장인물은 작품의 성패를 가늠하는 가장 중요한 기준인데 작가는 직접 '말하기(telling)'를 통하거나 간접적으로 '보여주기(showing)'를 통해 등장인물을 묘사한다.

하는 힘은 무엇보다도 빅토리아 시대 특유의 억압구조 속에서 복합적인 개성을 보여주는 등장인물들을 통해서 발휘된다. 단행본 출판에 앞서 잡지에 연재되었던 디킨즈의 소설들에는 다양한 등장인물이 중요한 역할을 하는데, 그는 평생 동안 5백만 단어 이상을 써서 2천명 이상의 작중인물을 만들어 내 그들의 언행을 세밀하면서도 생동감 넘치게 묘사하여 독자들을 매료했다.

『위대한 유산』의 주인공은 '필립 피립(Philip Pirrip)'인데, 그는 이 성장소설이 다루고 있는 그가 여섯 살일 때부터 서른 네 살 쯤까지의 기간 내내 이 정식 이름 대신 어린 시절의 이름인 '핍(Pip)'으로 불린다. 이 소설에서 핍은 동시에 두 인물로, 즉 욕망의 성취를 위해 인생의 역경을 헤쳐 나가는 주인공과 후일 지난 날을 되돌아보는 성장한 일인칭 서술자로 나온다. 서술자인 핍은 기억에 의존하여 자신이 겪었던 세상의 무게와 이에 대한 어린 시절 자신의 반응을 담담하게 회고하면서도 그 미숙하고 이기적인 모습을 신랄하게 비난한다.

핍은 열정적이고 낭만적이며 감상적인, 즉 다소 비현실적인 인물인 동시에 강건한 양심의 소유자이며 도덕적이고 사회적으로 자기 자신을 개선하기를 갈망하는 인물이다. 그는 돈과 명예에 눈이 멀어 진정한 친구들을 배신하는 자기중심적 인간이었지만 일련의 고통스런 사건들을 겪어가면서 서서히 우정의 진가를 깨닫게 된다.

'조 가저리(Joe Gargery)'는 인정 많은 대장장이로 핍의 매형이다.[70] 그는 배우지 못했고 세련되지도 못하지만 이 소설에서 유일하게 사랑하는 사람들을 위해 말없이 자기 자리를 지키는 사람이다. 그는 고아인 핍을 사랑하는 마음으로 드세고 오지랖 넓은 핍의 누이와의 결혼 생활을 유지한다. 늘 핍을 염려하며 거친 누이로부터 보호해 주며 핍이 부유해진 다음 자신을 모르는 척 할 때도 신뢰를 지켜 결국엔 핍이 스스로 용서를 빌게 되고 둘은 진정한 화해를 이루게 된다.

'가저리 부인(Mrs Joe Gargery)'[71]은 핍보다 스무 살이나 나이가 많은 누이로 타계한 부모를 대신해 핍을 양육한다. 그녀는 고압적이고 강인한 성품의 소유자로 집안을 언제나 흠 없이 정돈된 상태로 유지하며 동생 핍은 물론 남편까지도 일일이 간섭하며 위협한다. 어린 핍의 공포의 대상이던 가저리 부인은 결국 대장간에서 일하던 악한의 습격을 받아 죽는다.

범죄자로 등장하여 고결한 인품의 소유자로 사라지는 '매그위치(Magwitch)'는 자신이 탈옥했을 때 어린 핍으로부터 받은 작은 도움에 감동하여 후일 오스트레일리아의 유배지에서 번 돈을 익명으로 핍에게 유산으로 전해주어 그가 신사가 되도록 돕는다. 다시 영국에 온 그는 핍의 도움을 받아 국외로 탈출하려다 체포되어 감옥에서 죽는다.[72]

---

[70] 그는 이 소설에서 그냥 'Joe'로 불린다.
[71] 소설 속에서 그녀는 'Mrs Gargery'가 아니라 'Mrs Joe'라고 불린다.

핍이 사랑하는 여인인 '에스텔라(Estella)'[73]는 아기일 때 부모로부터 버림받아 해비샴의 양녀가 된다. 해비샴은 모든 남자들에게 복수하기 위하여 그녀가 어느 누구도 진심으로 사랑하지 못하도록 양육한다. 그녀는 자라면서 핍에게 계속 자신은 누구도 사랑 할 수 없는 사람이라고 경고한다.

'해비샴(Miss Havisham)'은 핍의 집 근처의 대저택에 사는 부유한 독신녀다. 약혼자에게 버림받은 이래 은둔 생활을 하며 자신의 양녀인 에스텔라를 세뇌교육하여 그녀를 좋아하는 남자들을 농락하고 파멸시키려는 욕망에 평생을 바친 괴이한 여자다. 핍은 한 때 자신에게 유산을 준 사람이 이 해비샴이라고 오해한다. 그녀는 에스텔라를 조정하여 핍을 농락하지만 죽기 전에 핍에게 용서를 구한다.

소설 전체를 통해 에스텔라와 모든 면에서 정반대의 인물로 표현되는 착한 시골 소녀 '비디(Biddy)'는 핍과는 아주 절친한 사이다. 핍과 사랑하는 사이가 될 뻔 했으며 핍이 매형인 가저리를 저버리는 행동을 나무라기도 하는 신중하고 사려 깊은 사람이다. 가저리 부인이 습격을 받아 거의 식물인간이 되자 가저리의

---

[72] 매그위치는 성이고 그의 이름은 '에이블(Abel)'인데 이는 곧 기독교 성경에 나오는 인류 최초의 인간인 아담(Adam)과 하와(Eve)의 둘째 아들 아벨이다. 형 가인(Cain)은 시기심에서 목동이었던 동생 아벨을 살해하고 도망자가 된다. 소설이 진행되면서 디킨즈가 왜 범죄자인 매그위치에게 무고하게 형에게 살해된 아벨의 이름을 붙였는지가 드러난다.

[73] 'Estella'는 '별'이란 뜻이다.

집으로 들어와 살며 그녀를 간호한다. 그녀는 나중에 가저리 부인이 죽고 나서 가저리와 결혼한다.

허장성세가 심하고 돈만 아는 장사꾼인 '펌블축 삼촌(Uncle Pumblechook)'은 가저리의 삼촌인지라 가저리 부인이나 핍도 그냥 삼촌이라 부른다. 핍이 처음 해비샴의 집에 드나들도록 주선한 바 있는 그는 매그위치로부터 유산을 물려받고 신사가 된 핍으로부터 뭔가 얻어 보려고 아무 한 일도 없으면서 행세를 하려 하나 핍은 여기 속아 넘어가지 않는다.

냉혹하지만 성공한 변호사인 '재거즈(Mr Jaggers)'는 핍의 유산과 해비샴의 저택을 관리한다. 그는 고아인 에스텔라를 해비샴의 양녀로 들이는데 역할을 했고 때때로 핍의 일들을 돌봐주기도 한다. 에스텔라의 어머니의 살인 혐의를 벗겨주는 등 유능한 변호사로 명성을 날리기도 하지만 인간적인 면모를 모두 상실한 거만하고 가부장적 인물로서 범죄활동에 은밀하게 관여하기도 하며 흉악한 범죄자들과도 어울리는데 이들마저 그를 두려워한다. 그는 마치 자신에게 남아 있는 범죄의 흔적을 씻어내려는 듯 강박적으로 손을 씻는 버릇이 있다.

재거즈의 사무장인 '웨믹(Wemmick)'은 핍의 친구인데 업무에 있어서는 아주 사무적인 인물이지만 사적으로는 아주 정이 많은 사람이다. 자기만의 은밀한 공간에서 늙은 자신의 아버지를 극진히 모시고 살고 있고 핍이 위험에 처했을 때 도와주기도 한다.

몰리(Molly)는 집시로 험한 삶을 살아오다 살인죄로 체포되었을 때 재거즈가 도와준 인연으로 그의 가정부로 일하며 안정을 찾은 여인이다. 재거즈의 비위를 맞추려 눈치를 보며 산다. 핍은 소설의 후반부에서 그녀가 에스텔라의 어머니임을 알게 된다.

핍이 늪에서 매그위치를 처음 만났을 때 나타나는 또 한 명의 죄수인 '콤피슨(Compeyson)'은 모든 면에서 매그위치와 대비되는 고학력의 신사이지만 실상은 악랄한 범죄자다. 그는 약혼녀 해비샴을 배신했고 순진한 매그위치를 범죄의 세계로 이끌었다. 소설의 말미에서는 매그위치가 체포되도록 경찰에 제보하고 강에서 매그위치와 다투다 익사한다.

'올릭(Orlick)'은 가저리의 대장간 조수인데 일이 서툴고 미련한데다 거칠고 폭력적인지라 핍이 내심 경멸하는 사람이다. 그는 사람들을 괴롭히는 것 자체를 즐기는 사람으로 핍을 몹시도 시샘한 나머지 핍의 누이에게 폭력을 행사하여 죽게 만들고 비디를 협박하기도 하며 핍을 죽이려고도 한다.

무례하고 우둔한 '벤틀리 드러믈(Bentley Drummle)'은 핍과 함께 신사 수업을 받는다. 그는 상류층 출신이라는 우월감에서 주위 사람들에게 오만방자한 행동을 일삼는다. 핍이 사랑하는 에스텔라와 결혼함으로써 핍을 괴롭게 한다. 그는 결혼 생활 내내 아내 에스텔라를 학대하다 먼저 죽는다.

어린 핍이 해비샴의 집을 방문했을 때 정원에서 처음 만난 '허버트 포킷(Herbert Pocket)'은 핍과 같은 또래로 해비샴의 친척이다. 오랜 시간 후 핍이 런던으로 갔을 때 다시 만나게 되는 그는 이후 핍의 가장 가까운 친구가 된다. 의리가 있고 명예를 중시하며 사교적인 인물이다. 핍은 자기가 유산으로 받은 돈의 일부로 허버트의 사업 자금을 대어 준다.

2. 혼돈과 갈등

한편의 시대극으로 독자의 눈앞에 펼쳐지는 『위대한 유산』의 주인공 핍의 성장 이야기는 빅토리아 시대의 런던과 켄트라는 시간과 공간에서 관찰되는 폭력을 반복적으로 드러냄으로써 새로운 이상세계와 새로운 정의에 대한 갈망을 표출한다. 이 소설이 그리는 핍의 삶은 고향인 켄트의 늪지대에서의 어린 시절의 이야기와, 런던에서의 야망과 갈등을 다룬 사건들, 그리고 새로운 깨달음과 함께 다시 고향으로 돌아오게 되는 과정 등 크게 세 단계로 나누어 볼 수 있다.

첫 번째 혼돈과 갈등의 단계에서는 고아인 핍이 그의 유일한 혈육인 거칠고 불친절한 누나 가저리 부인과 친절하게 사랑으로 대해주는 매부 조 가저리에 의해 양육되는 모습이 그려진다. 아무런 애정도 없이 단지 의무감만으로 동생 핍을 양육하는 가저리 부인은 이 일을 대단히 짜증스럽게 여기는 반면 매형인 가저리는 인정이 많고 순수하여 어린 핍을 언제나 따뜻한 사랑으로 감싸준다.

어느 크리스마스이브에 핍은 공동묘지에 가서 부모와 남매들의 무덤을 바라보면서 처음으로 인간의 삶 속에는 무언가 형용할 수 없는 두려운 세계가 존재함을 느낀다. 그런데 갑자기 죄수선[74]에서 탈옥하여 추위와 굶주림에 떨고 있던 험악하게 생긴 한 죄수가 안개 속으로부터 나타나서 핍을 협박하여 쇠사슬을 끊을 줄칼과 배고픔을 달랠 음식을 가져오도록 한다. 핍은 그 죄수와의 약속을 지키기 위해 매형의 대장간에서 줄칼을 훔치고 누이의 부엌에선 음식을 훔쳐 가져다준다. 그러나 결국 그 죄수와 그를 잡으러 죄수선에서 연이어 탈출한 또 다른 죄수 한 명이 병사들에게 체포되어 죄수선으로 되돌아가게 된다. 이 첫 번째 죄수와의 조우는 핍에게는 타인과의 첫 만남인 동시에 그의 앞날이 순탄치 않을 것임을 암시하는 만남이다. 이로써 핍은 도덕적으로 동정심과 죄의식이 복합적으로 얽혀 있는 심리적 혼란을 겪으며 성장하게 된다. 지금까지 누이에게 핍박을 받으며 아무 생각 없이 살아 왔던 단순한 단계에서 주변 환경과 자신의 존재를 견주어 보는 단계로 진화하기 시작하는 것이다.

---

[74] '죄수선(prison ship)'은 18~19세기 영국에서 노후하여 운행이 불가능한 배를 감옥으로 개조한 것으로서 주로 유배지로 추방할 죄수들을 수감했다. 보통은 폐선의 선체라는 뜻으로 'hulk'라고 불렸다.

이후 핍은 펌블축 삼촌의 주선으로 해비샴의 부름을 받아 그녀의 저택 새티스 하우스(Satis House)에 드나들게 된다. 해비샴을 만나 접하게 된 세상은 평범하고 지루한 늪지대에서의 삶과는 전혀 다른 별천지였다. 이곳에서 핍은 그녀의 양녀 에스텔라를 만난다. 소설의 뒷부분에서 드러나지만 늪지대에서 만났던 첫 번째 죄수인 매그위치의 딸로 태어난 그녀는 세 살에 해비샴에게 입양 와서 모든 남자를 증오하도록 세뇌된다. 아름답지만 오만한 그녀는 처음부터 핍의 신분을 조롱하며 내내 모욕적인 행동을 한다. 핍은 그녀에게 멸시를 받으면서도 그녀가 속해 있는 상류사회에 대한 동경을 품게 되고 방약무인한 그녀의 성품을 알면서도 그녀의 아름다움에 사로잡힌다.

해비샴은 외적으로만 보자면 그저 핍의 마을 가까이의 대저택에 사는 돈 많고 괴팍한 여인일 뿐이나 그 실상은 거의 미치광이 수준의 폐인이다. 해비샴은 오래 전 어느 날 약혼자 콤피슨에 버림받았던 그 상황 그대로를 간직하고 있다. 식탁 위의 상차림도 그대로 두어 이제는 모두 부패했고 시계는 9시 20분 전에 멈춰있다. 해비샴은 낡아서 누더기가 된 그날의 웨딩드레스를 입고 살며 복수를 꿈꾸고 있다. 그 복수의 도구는 그녀가 아름답고 교양 있는 괴물로 키워낸 양녀 에스텔라다. 그녀는 에스텔라를 잔인하고 무정한 사람으로 만들어 콤피슨이 자신에게 그랬던 것처럼 에스텔라를 만나는 모든 남자들이 불행해지도록 온전히 파괴만을 목적으로 한 왜곡된 복수를 실천하고 있다. 오로지 자신의 고통에만 집중하는 해비샴에게 그녀의 집착이 핍과 에스텔라에게 주는 아픔은 안중에 없다. 핍은 그 후 한동안 일주일에 세 번씩 새티스 하우스를 방문하여 해비샴이 다 부패한 음식들이 놓여 있는 방을 걷거나 바퀴의자를 타고 돌도록 돕는 일을 하게 된다. 이렇게 이삼 년이 지난 어느 날 해비샴은 그 동안 일한 대가로 핍이 자기 매형 가저리의 대장장이 견습생으로 훈련하도록 그 비용을 대준다.[75]

핍은 이제 새티스 하우스를 더 이상 방문하지 않고 매형 가저리의 견습생으로 일을 배우게 되지만 대장장이 따위엔 관심이 없다. 1년이 지난 어느 날 에스텔라에 대한 그리움을 못 이겨 새티스 하우스를 방문한 핍은 그녀가 프랑스에 유학 중이라는 말을 듣는다. 슬픈 심사를 안고 대장간으로 돌아온 그는 누이인 가저리 부인이 남편 가저리 밑에서 일하는 올릭과 말다툼을 한 뒤 누구로부터인가 잔인하게 폭행을 당해 거의 식물인간이 되어 말도 못하고 누워있는 모습을 본다. 핍은 모든 정황으로 보아 바로 올릭이 범인임을 안다. 몇 주가 지나도 가저리 부인이 거동조차

---

[75] 핍이 가저리의 견습생(apprentice)이 된다는 것은 가저리의 감독 하에 일정한 기간 동안 가저리의 직업적인 기술을 습득한다는 것이다. 이를 위하여 핍은 가저리에게 수업료(premium)를 내고 고용계약서(indenture)에 서명하여야 한다. 이 시대에는 핍처럼 열네 살 정도 되는 아이들이 견습을 시작하는 경우가 흔했다. 사실 많은 가난한 집안에서는 가족 부양의 수단으로 자녀들을 일찌감치 견습생으로 보냈다.

힘들게 되자 착하고 명석한 마을 소녀 비디가 들어와 같이 살면서 그녀를 간호한다.

이전까지는 주어진 삶이 불만족스럽기는 했지만 항상 자신을 아껴주던 매형 가저리를 믿고 단순하게 살았지만 일단 새티스 하우스에서 상류사회를 접한 핍은 가난과 사회적 신분에 기인하는 한계와 무력감을 느낀다. 그러면서도 핍은 자신이 해비샴의 무모한 복수의 대상이라는 것도 모르고 에스텔라의 사랑을 쟁취하기 위해서 기필코 신사가 되겠다고 다짐하며 막연하게나마 결혼을 통한 신분상승도 기대해 본다. 어처구니없이 눈높이가 달라진 그는 급기야 자신을 아껴주던 가저리와 가난한 생활을 더 이상 계속하기는 어렵다고 판단한다. 핍은 이런 자신의 마음을 외모는 에스텔라만큼 아름답지 못하지만 마음 착하고 상냥한 친구 비디에게 고백한다. 이에 대해 그녀는 조심스럽지만 진심 어린 충고를 하지만 핍은 이를 개의치 않는다.

핍이 가저리의 견습생 생활을 시작한 지 4년이 지난 어느 날 저녁 런던의 변호사 재거즈가 핍에게 와서 정체를 밝힐 수 없는 누군가가 그에게 큰 유산을 물려주었는데 자신이 그 유산의 상속을 관리함을 알린다. 이로 인해 오매불망 그리던 신사가 될 수 있게 된 핍은 그 유산을 준 사람이 해비샴일 거라고 추측하면서 대장장이의 길을 완전히 접고 런던으로 가서 상류계급의 신사가 되려 한다.

3. 야망과 절망

핍의 인생의 두 번째 장인 야망과 절망의 단계는 그가 신사가 되기 위한 준비를 하는 런던에서 벌어진다. 핍은 런던에서 허버트 포킷과 재거즈의 사무장인 웨믹을 사귄다. 그러면서 허버트 등의 또래들과 함께 신사수업을 받는다. 핍은 바탕은 선량하였지만 런던에서 함께 신사수업을 받고 있는 허버트 포킷, 벤틀리 드러믈 등 중산층 이상의 청년들과 어울리게 되면서 저속한 행동거지에 물들어 간다. 그는 드러믈이 런던의 친구들 중 누구보다도 지체 높고 부유하지만 도덕적으로는 가장 저급하다는 것을 익히 알지만 고향에 있는 가저리나 비디와 같은 사랑하고 존경하는 사람들의 말보다는 그의 냉소를 더 두려워하여 런던에 오기 전 대장장이 견습생이었다는 것은 물론 매형이 대장장이라는 사실도 숨긴다. 이렇게 핍은 진정한 신사가 되기는커녕 내심 경멸하는 친구들과 어울리면서 인격적으로 타락한다.

몰락귀족(fallen aristocrat)보다는 돈 많은 은행가나 제조업자가 상류계급의 필수조건인 부동산을 많이 보유하게 되면 귀족계급으로 인정받는 시대를 맞아 운 좋게 신사가 된 핍은 런던에서의 사치와 방탕으로 결국 빈털터리가 되고 만다. 자신의 생계유지를 위한 돈벌이를 하지 않는 조건으로 익명의 후원자로부터 유산을 증여 받았으므로 직장도 구할 수 없는 핍은 빚까지 지게 된다. 핍은 이제서야 가저리와 비디를 저버렸던 자신을 반성해 보기도 하지만 아직 진정으로 자신의 잘못을 깨닫지는 못한다.

　에스텔라를 짝사랑하며 괴로워하는 핍은 그녀로부터 사랑을 느끼지 못하는 것이 자신의 본성이라는 말을 듣는다. 그녀로서는 해비샴에게 '심장이 없는 괴물'로 양육된 자신의 불행을 핍마저도 겪지 않도록 하려는 작은 배려였던 것이다. 얼마 안 있어서 병상에 누워있던 누이 가저리 부인이 죽었다는 기별을 받은 핍은 그녀의 장례식에 참석하려고 고향으로 간다. 핍은 장례식을 마치고 잠시 대장간에 들러서 가저리와 비디에게 나름 진심으로 앞으로 자주 오겠다고 하나 비디는 그럴 수 있겠냐고 반문하고 가저리도 너무 자주 오지는 않아도 된다고 하자 상한 마음으로 런던으로 돌아온다.

　스물한 살로 성인이 된 핍은 자신의 유산에서 매년 거금을 받게 되어 빚을 가릴 수 있게 되고 금전적으로 어려운 친구 허버트가 사업을 시작하도록 은밀하게 돕기도 한다. 그런데 스물 세 살이 되던 해의 어느 비 오는 날 오래 전 어린 시절 늪지대에서 만났던 탈옥수 매그위치가 런던에 있는 핍의 거처로 찾아온다. 그리고 대화를 통해 핍은 자신에게 유산을 물려준 사람은 상류계급의 해비샴이 아니라 자신보다도 더 비천한 죄수 매그위치였다는 사실을 알게 된다. 그가 그토록 열망했던 신사라는 신분을 매그위치라는 범죄자의 도움을 받아 얻은 것임을 알게 된 그는 삶의 기반 자체가 무너짐을 느낀다. 자신이 추구했던 목표가 남을 괴롭히고 고통을 주었던 사람의 도움으로 이루어진 것이 분명해진 지금 핍은 스스로의 노력 없이 신분의 상승을 도모했던 자신의 어리석음과 태생적 한계를 절감할 수밖에 없다. 동시에 고향 늪지대의 매형 가저리로부터 세상 누구에게서도 얻을 수 없는 사랑과 위로를 받았건만 이를 애써 부정하고 부끄럽게까지 생각했던 과오를 떠올리며 괴로워한다. 이제 성인인 핍은 이 소설의 서술자로서 주인공인 어린 시절의 자신이 신사가 된 뒤 그를 사랑했던 많은 사람들에게 고통을 주었음을 뉘우치며 그들에게 사죄와 존경을 표한다. 이렇게 디킨즈는 모든 것을 해결해 줄 것 같았던 막대한 부를 얻은 핍이 타락할 수밖에 없었고 그 부를 모두 탕진하고 나서야 더 높은 가치에 대한 깨달음을 얻게 되는 역설적 진리를 통해 배금주의가 만연한 세태를 비판한다.

  핍은 엄청난 회의를 느끼면서도 그가 신사가 되기 위해 지금까지 노력한 것이 매그위치를 위함이 아닌 것은 분명하기 때문에 자신 앞에 불쑥 나타난 그에게 거부감을 나타낸다. 매그위치는 자신의 예기치 않은 방문을 받은 핍의 심리상태는 전혀 눈치 채지 못하고 자신은 사회의 지탄과 멸시를 받는 무식한 밑바닥 인생이지만 시골에서 대장장이로 살아갈 수밖에 없었던 한 사람을 신사로 만들었다는 사실에 감격한다. 여기서 매그위치의 훌륭한 점은 세상이 자신을 부당하게 대접했다고 믿고 이를 앙갚음 하려 하지 않고 악을 선으로 갚고자 했다는 것일 게다. 하지만 그가 상대방의 상태나 의사를 알아보지도 않고 돈은 누구나

원하는 것이고 돈만 있으면 누구든 신사가 될 수 있다고 믿었다는 것, 그리고 과도한 요구일지는 몰라도 그가 핍에게서 보고자 했던 신사의 모습은 도덕과는 무관한 외형적이고 물질적인 것이었다는 것 또한 만연한 황금지상주의를 그대로 보여준다.

 이제 핍은 인간성이 결여된 명예는 아무 의미도 없음을 깨닫는다. 매그위치는 그가 막연하게나마 후원자로서 기대했던 세련된 신사가 결코 아니지만 핍이 어린 시절 베푼 친절을 잊지 않고 그 은혜를 보답하려 했던 사람이다. 그는 오래 전 죄수선에서 탈출하여 우연히 핍을 만난 이후 이전과는 다른 인생을 살았다. 곧바로 다시 붙잡혀서 오스트레일리아에 유배되어 살면서 따뜻한 소년의 마음에 보답하기 위해 목장에서 열심히 일해 돈을 모았다. 매그위치는 그 돈을 자신을 위해 쓸 수도 있었지만 핍을 신사로 만들어 신분 때문에 자신이 겪어야 했던 여러 가지 고초를 덜어줌으로써 자신의 죄값을 치르려 한 것이다. 그리고 죄과 때문에 영국으로 돌아오면 교수형을 당하게 되어 있었지만 자신의 유산을 상속받은 핍이 성장해서 신사가 된 모습을 보기 위해 지구의 반대쪽 머나먼 오스트레일리아로부터 생명의 위험을 무릅쓰고 런던까지 온 것이다.

4. 성숙과 회복

핍의 인생의 세 번째 성숙과 회복의 단계에서는 이 소설의 나머지 모든 수수께끼들이 풀린다. 허황된 가치관에 매몰되어 타락의 길을 걷던 핍에게 매그위치의 출현은 양면적인 의미를 지닌다. 그 하나는 상류계급에 속하고자 했던 기대가 무너지면서 커다란 시련을 앞두게 되었다는 것이고, 다른 하나는 이러한 모든 과정을 통해 자신의 타락한 삶을 성찰하는 계기를 얻었다는 것이다.

핍은 자신은 누이라도 있었지만 사고무친으로 홀로 자란 매그위치는 온통 적대적인 환경에서 온갖 역경을 헤쳐 나가다 범죄자가 될 수밖에 없었음을 이해하고 그와 인간적으로 동질감을 느낀다. 매그위치가 세상에서는 이제껏 가해자로 알려졌지만 어쩌면 그 누구보다도 큰 피해자 일수도 있다고 생각하고 그에게 연민을 갖게 된 것이다. 이렇게 이들의 두 번째의 만남은 매그위치에게는 자신을 추방했던 사회에 대한 편견을 버리고 참된 인간성을 회복할 수 있는 기회를, 핍에게는 돈만을 최고의 가치로 삼았던 천박한 정신세계와 행동을 개선할 기회를 준다.

그런데 여기서 콤피슨이 등장한다. 콤피슨은 바로 오래 전 늪지대에서 매그위치를 따라 죄수선에서 탈출했던 두 번째 죄수로 겉은 번지레한 신사지만 실상은 간교한 범죄자다. 그는 약혼녀 해비샴을 자신의 이익을 위해 이용한 뒤 배신했을 뿐만 아니라 신분적 우위를 이용하여 매그위치에게 모든 죄를 뒤집어씌운 바 있고 그 밖에도 여러 사람들에게 불행을 안겨주었다. 이에 핍은 종신형을 받고 오스트레일리아로 추방된 매그위치가 런던에 돌아온 것이 발각되면 사형 당할 것이 확실하기 때문에 허버트 등의 친구들의 도움을 받아 그를 해외로 도피시키려 한다. 그러나 매그위치의 탈출은 불구대천의 원수 콤피슨의 방해로 실패로 돌아가고 그 과정에서 이 둘은 강에서 결투를 벌이게 되는데 여기서 콤피슨은 죽고 매그위치는 중상을 입은 채로 체포된다.

　디킨즈는 작품 초반에 야만적인 괴물로 그렸던 매그위치를 후반부에서는 전혀 다른 위엄 있고 고결한 인물로 그려 낸다. 매그위치가 오스트레일리아로 추방될 당시 영국으로 돌아오면 사형에 처한다는 조건이 있었으므로 이제 그의 체포는 곧 죽음을 의미한다. 여기서 핍은 매그위치도 아무리 힘들게 살아도 자신처럼 누군가 진심으로 돌봐주는 사람이 곁에 있었더라면 지금과 같은 처지는 안 되었을 거라고 동정하면서 결연히 그의 마지막 가는 길을 지킨다. 매그위치는 신사인 핍이 자신과 같은 죄수와 연관이 있는 것으로 알려지면 좋지 않은 일이 생길 수도 있으니 그저 떠나도록 간청하지만 핍은 어떤 위험이 따를지라도 은인인 매그위치와 함께 있을 것을 약속한다. 매그위치가 체포됨으로써 그의 모든 재산은 국가에 몰수되고 말지만 자신의 '거대한' 유산을 잃고 나서야 비로소 사랑이라는 보다 높은 차원의 '진정한' 유산을 얻은 핍은 개의치 않는다.

이즈음 에스텔라는 불량배인 드러믈과 결혼한다. 에스텔라를 드러믈에게 빼앗겼지만 매그위치를 얻은 핍은 이제 자아상실에서 성숙과 회복으로 나아가게 된다. 어느 날 핍이 새티스 하우스를 방문했을 때 해비샴은 마침내 자신이 받은 것과 똑 같은 상처를 핍에게 주었음을 인정하며 용서를 빌자 핍은 진심으로 용서한다. 그날 저녁 해비샴은 어쩌다 화롯불이 드레스에 옮겨 붙어 화염에 휩싸이게 되는데 핍의 도움으로 겨우 목숨은 부지하지만 병상에 누워 있는 신세가 되고 얼마 있어 한 많은 세상을 떠난다.

타락하기는 쉬워도 어떤 식으로든 상실된 인간성을 회복하기는 쉽지 않은바 핍은 타락의 대가를 철저히 치르고서야 매그위치와의 두 번째 만남을 통해 자아를 발견하고 진실한 인간으로 발전한다. 이로써 디킨즈는 악행은 회개와 연민으로써만 만회할 수 있음을 말하고 있다. 많은 부분에서 매그위치는 부패한 사회 환경에 의해 범죄자의 길을 걷게 되었고 결국은 그 사회에 의해 단죄되는 희생자다. 핍은 죽음을 앞둔 매그위치에게 죽은 줄로만 알고 있던 딸 에스텔라가 살아 있음을 알려 준다. 그리고 매그위치는 조용히 눈을 감는다.

핍은 매그위치의 죽음으로 인한 충격과 자신의 지난날의 과오에 대한 고민으로 한 달간 중병을 앓는다. 이때 핍이 무시하고 수치스러워했던 가저리가 찾아와 정신을 잃고 누워있는 그를 극진하게 간호하고 경제적인 어려움도 해결해 준다. 이를 계기로 핍이 가저리에 대한 어린 시절의 신뢰와 사랑을 되찾는 듯했으나 그의 건강이 회복되면서 그를 돌봤던 가저리는 왠지 그에게서 멀어져 간다. 그런 가저리의 태도를 보고 핍은 그 동안 자신의 그릇됨을 다시 한 번 각성하고 이제는 순수하고 인간미 넘쳤던 고향 늪지대로 돌아가 가저리와 함께 열심히 일하며 비디와 결혼해 소박하게 살 결심을 한다.

  핍의 진정한 고귀함은 그가 고향으로 내려오는 데서 발견할 수 있다. 그것은 마치 성경에서 탕자가 집으로 돌아오는 장면과도 흡사하다. 그러나 핍의 기대와 달리 그가 고향으로 돌아간 날 가저리와 비디가 결혼을 한다. 핍은 가저리와 비디에게 지난 세월 동안 자신이 너무도 교만한 나머지 그들의 굳건한 사랑을 알아 보지 못했음을 고백하고 때때로 그의 늪지대에서의 어린 시절의 삶과 그 시절의 친구들을 부끄러워했음을 인정하며 용서를 구한다. 이 소설은 핍을 꾸준히 지켜보며 묵묵히 사랑을 실천함으로써 새 삶을 살 수 있도록 이끈 가저리를 통해 진정한 유산은 돈이나 신분이 아니라 참다운 인간성의 회복을 통해서만 얻을 수 있음을 천명한다.

  드디어 자기 미래를 결정할 자리에 서게 된 핍은 자신이 몰래 도와준바 있는 허버트 포킷의 회사에 취직한다. 처음에는 거지와 다름 없었고 후에는 유한계급의 일원이었던 핍은 지난한 체험을 통해 진정한 만족과 자기가치를 알게 되고 마침내 중산층 근로자로서 세상에서의 자신의 자리를 찾게 된 것이다. 핍은 그

후 가지고 있는 모든 것을 청산하고 카이로로 가서 친구 허버트와 동업을 함으로 새롭게 출발한다. 결국 성실함으로 꾸준히 사업을 번창시켜 먹고 살 수 있을 정도로 성공한다. 이를 통해 디킨즈는 '위대한 유산'이란 정당한 노동의 대가로 얻은 재산과 인격의 완성을 동시에 갖춘 신사가 되는 것임을 말하고 있다.

핍은 십일 년이 지난 다음 카이로로부터 늪지대로 돌아와 새티스 하우스에 가보게 되는데 여기서 우연히 자신을 학대하던 남편이 죽음으로써 결혼의 질곡에서 이제 막 해방된 에스텔라를 만나게 된다. 소설의 끝부분에서 에스텔라는 자신이 저질러 놓은 잘못을 조금이나마 바로잡으려 하는 진화과정을 겪게 된다. 여기서 이 둘이 이제 앞으로도 함께 할 것이라는 암시와 함께 이 소설은 막을 내린다.

이 소설은 애초에 주인공이 인생의 역경을 이겨내고 현실적인 깨달음을 얻는 것으로 끝났는데 후에 에스텔라와의 재회와 행복한 미래를 향한 출발을 암시하는 이야기로 바뀐다.[76] 비평가들은 주인공이 양모로부터 모든 남자를 증오하도록 양육된 에스텔라에 대한 집착을 포기함으로 참된 깨우침을 얻는 원래의 결말이

---

[76] 『위대한 유산』의 다소 논쟁적인 새롭게 수정된 결말은 핍이 정원에서 에스텔라를 우연히 만나 "다시는 헤어지지 않을 것이며…결코 보내지 않을 것"이라며 끝나는 것이다. 수정되기 전 원래의 내용은 드러믈이 죽고 나서 에스텔라가 쉬롭셔(Shropshire)의 시골 의사와 재혼했다는 소식을 들은 핍은 어느 날 가저리와 비디의 어린 아들과 런던 거리를 걷다 우연히 에스텔라와 마주쳐 악수를 하고 몇 마디를 나눈 뒤 헤어지는 것이다.

더 현실적이라고 주장한다. 그러나 주인공의 사랑과 인내가 마침내 결실을 맺을 것이라는 믿음을 갖고 하나하나의 사건 전개에 몰입하며 연재되는 이야기를 열정적으로 따라왔던 당시의 독자들은 이 소설의 통속적인 무대와 더불어 이 수정된 결말을 더 좋아했다.[77]

---

[77] 이런 수정의 배경에는 소설이 연재되었던 잡지의 판매고를 늘려 보려는 고려도 있었던 것으로 추정된다. 디킨즈의 작품을 읽을 때에는 그의 모든 작품들은 먼저 잡지에 주간 또는 월간으로 연재된 것을 나중에 모아서 출판한 것이라는 걸 염두에 두어야 한다. 디킨즈 이전에도 소설 연재는 있었지만 19세기 영국 문단에서 소설 연재의 표준을 수립한 이는 바로 디킨즈다. 디킨즈는 독자들이 다음 회의 연재를 기다리게끔 손에 땀을 쥐게 하는 상황(cliff-hanger)으로 한 회를 끝냈다. 연재라는 방식을 취함으로써 독자들에게 친숙해지기 쉬운 보다 많은 인물이 등장했으며 독자들의 작품의 전개에 관하여 작가나 잡지사에 편지를 써서 자신의 의견을 밝히기도 하였다.

제4장 주제의 분석

1. 가족의 해체

　디킨즈의 작품에서 주목할 만한 점은 빅토리아 시대의 사회에 대한 통렬한 비판인데 그 중 하나가 가족해체에 대한 고발이다. 당시의 부패한 사회의 제도와 도덕이 필연적으로 전통적인 가족 관계를 파괴하는 모습이『위대한 유산』에서는 극단적인 성향의 인물들을 통해 가족관계에서의 부부 간의 성역할의 전도, 부모와 자식 간의 억압적인 관계 등으로 형상화된다. 이 작품의 등장인물들은 가해자가 아니면 피해자이며 핍이 역할모범으로 삼을 만한 사람들은 매그위치와 가저리, 어느 면에서는 재거즈까지다 부정적이다. 인격적이고 사회적인 측면에서 볼 때 이들 모두는 세상을 자기 식대로 살아가지 못할 만큼 연약하거나 정상적인 행복한 삶을 영위하지 못할 정도로 손상되어 있는데 이것은 일차적으로 그들의 가족관계에서 여실히 드러난다.

가족해체를 보여주는 대표적인 반사회적 인물은 바로 핍의 누이 가저리 부인이다. 늪지대의 거친 노동자들 사이에서 사는 그녀는 남편 가저리와 펌블축 삼촌 외에는 친구라 할 사람이 없고 더구나 여자 중에서는 알고 지내는 사람도 없다. 그녀는 이웃이 될 수도 있었던 많은 사람들에게 적대적이고 거칠게 대하여 고립을 자초함으로써 스스로 문제를 만들어 낸다. 일반적인 가정에서의 아내와 남편의 역할이 전도된 가저리 부부의 기형적인 가부장제는 어른과 아이들의 관계도 왜곡한다. 핍보다 스무 살이나 많은 가저리 부인은 핍에게는 누이라기보다 어머니 같은 존재이지만 "대장장이 마누라 노릇도 힘든데 네 엄마 노릇까지 하려니 힘들다"며 자신의 고단한 삶에 대해 불평만 할 뿐 어머니의 역할은 물론 누이의 역할조차도 제대로 수행하지 못한다.

결혼에 안착하지 못한 사회적으로 실패한 괴이한 여자인 해비샴은 자신이 콤피슨에게 실연 당한 것에 대해 직접 콤피슨에게 복수하지 못하고 양녀 에스텔라를 통해 그녀 주위의 남자에게 고통을 줌으로써 대리만족하려 한다. 그녀는 스스로를 보호하기 위해 다른 사람들의 감정으로부터 자신을 격리시키는 사랑 없는 삶을 선택하고 에스텔라에게 왜곡된 가치관을 심어 비극적으로 자기 목적을 추구한다. 결국 심각하게 손상된 가정에서 자라난 에스텔라도 후일 병약해진 해비샴을 학대한다.

정상적인 가정에서 남편과 아버지의 역할을 할 기회를 놓쳐버린 매그위치는 핍에게 막후의 아버지와 같은 인물이다. 그는 처음에 반사회적인 범죄자로 나오지만 후반에선 자식을 위해 자신을 희생하는 아버지의 역할을 한다. 그는 핍에게 자기 이름 외에는 자신에 대해 아는 것이 없으며, 살기 위해 먹을 것을 훔치다 감옥을 들락거리게 되었고, 그 후 어딜 가던 처벌을 받게 되었으며, 조금 읽고 쓸 줄 아는 걸 빼고는 불학무식함을 고백한다. 그는 일방적이긴 하지만 한때 작은 사랑을 베풀어준 핍을 아들처럼 여겨 막대한 유산을 물려주어 자신은 못 이룬 신사의 꿈을 이룰 수 있도록 하는데, 이렇게 그는 자신이 상상으로 만들어낸 가족을 실제로 부양함으로 대리만족을 추구하는 것이다.

디킨즈는 많은 작품들에 고아들을 등장시켜 산업혁명이라는 화려한 역사의 부끄러운 이면을 드러낸다. 그가 살았던 빅토리아 시대에는 가난한 집안의 많은 어린이들이 노동을 했으며 부모들이 양육을 기피하거나 형편이 아주 어려운 어린이들은 고아원으로 보내졌다. 그의 많은 소설들에서 어린이들은 질병과 가난에 허덕이고 있거나 주위의 어른들에게 학대를 당한다. 『위대한 유산』에서 디킨즈는 고아 소년을 주인공으로 하여 가족해체의 문제를 다룬다. 여기서 부모 또는 보호자와 자식 간의 관계는 어른들의 무책임한 현실 인식으로 심각하게 왜곡되어 있다. 이 소설은 이러한 가정에서 핍과 에스텔라와 같은 고아가 학대를 받는 경우 그들이 성인이 되어가며, 또 성인이 되었을 때 어떤 일이 벌어지는지를 보여준다. 두 경우 다 세심하고 긍정적인 역할모범이 없다는 사실이 이들로 하여금 옳고 그름을 구분하지 못하도록 하였고 스스로뿐 아니라 남들에게까지도 씻을 수 없는 상처를 입히게 된다.

핍의 이야기는 어린 그가 음울한 교회 공동묘지의 부모의 묘지 앞에 서있는 것으로 시작한다. 어린 핍은 그의 어머니에 대해 묘비석에 아버지 이름 아래 적혀 있는 대로 '위 사람의 아내'라는 것 밖에는 모른다. 누이로부터 종종 위협을 받아온 핍은 우연찮게 만난 죄수 매그위치에게도 협박을 받는다. 부랑자 올릭마저도 성인인 핍을 죽이려 한다. 도시 생활을 시작한 후에도 핍의 주위에는 냉담하며 위험하기까지 한 많은 사람들이 들끓었고 친구들은 거의 없다. 다만 매형인 조 가저리가 처음부터 끝까지 유일한 친구이자 가족이었다.

해비샴의 저택 새티스 하우스에서 핍과 에스텔라가 노는 모습은 같은 또래의 평등한 친구들이 아니라 마치 고양이와 쥐 같은데 이게 바로 에스텔라가 모든 남자들을 농락하고 상처를 주도록 하는 해비샴의 복수의 일환이었다. 결국 성인이 된 에스텔라는 생기도 없고 사랑하는 마음도 없는 채로 늘 상심 가운데 산다. 마음 깊은 곳에 핍을 사랑하는 감정이 없는 것은 아니지만 마음이 비뚤어진 해비샴의 손에서 자라난 기이한 어린 시절의 경험으로 해서 어떤 사랑이나 우정도 주지도 받아들이지도 못한다.

이와는 달리 세상적으로 성공한 변호사인 재거즈는 가족 없이 외롭게 그러면서도 활기차게 살아간다. 그는 자칫 방심하여 실수하거나 감정을 드러내기라도 하면 바로 치명적인 약점이 될 것처럼 경계를 늦추지 않는다. 핍이 아무리 열린 마음으로 선의를 보여도 재거즈는 늘 거리를 둔다. 오히려 그는 자신이 원하는 것을 알아내고 얻으면 그만이라 생각하는지라 돈 많고 사악한 드러믈같은 인물들을 가까이 한다. 가족의 사랑보다는 세상의 힘을 택한 재거즈는 결국 그 어느 곳에서도 위로 받지 못하며 부패하고 비인간적인 세상의 일부로 살아간다.

이렇게 주위엔 온통 소외된 사람들 투성이이건만 핍은 이상하게도 런던을 떠나 고향 늪지대로 돌아와 가저리와 비디와 다시 함께 살거나 허버트 포킷이 자기 회사에서 함께 일하자고 하는 제안을 받아들이기를 꺼린다. 그러다 결국 유산을 다 탕진하고 갈 데가 없게 되고 나서야 사회적 신분과 관계 없이 한 인간으로서 자신을 아끼는 두 친구가 고향 늪지대에 있다는 것이 얼마나 큰 행운인가를 깨닫는다. 디킨즈는 이러한 깨달음이야말로 거저 주어지는 것이 아니라 건전한 가족관계를 통해서만 얻게 되는 정신적인 유산임을 말한다.

『위대한 유산』에서 아름다운 가족의 모습은 재거즈의 사무장인 웨믹과 그의 연로한 아버지의 관계에서 볼 수 있다. 핍은 때

때로 런던 교외의 웨믹의 집 안에 작은 해자와 대포까지도 완전히 갖추어 놓은 작은 모형 성으로 놀러 가곤 했다. 웨믹의 집은 숨가쁜 도시 생활과 밀접해 있으면서도 동떨어진 마법의 세계였다. 세상의 악에 대항하는 이 비밀의 요새에 있으면 모든 좋은 일들이 다시 가능해질 것만 같았다. 그곳이 좋은 이유 중 또 하나는 웨믹의 연로한 아버지다. 성격 좋고 귀먹은 이 노인은 나이 들어 연약해져 누구에게 위협이 되기는커녕 힘 있는 사람들이 보호해 줘야 할 존재다. 웨믹이 늙은 아버지에게 지극한 것을 보면서 늘 감탄하는 핍은 자기를 찾는 눈들을 피해 이 집에 숨어 있을 때 웨믹과 함께 그의 아버지를 돌보며 정상적인 가족, 회복된 가족의 모습을 배운다.

웨믹의 가정뿐 아니라 핍이 이집트에서 십일 년을 보내고 고향으로 돌아와 보게 된 가저리와 비디, 그리고 그들의 아들 또한 모두가 꿈꾸는 아름다운 가정의 모습을 보여준다. 이 아들을 보고 핍은 제 아들처럼 돌보겠다고 말하며 자신은 결혼하여 가정을 꾸릴 수 없을 것 같다고 말한다. 건강한 가정에서 자라나지 못하고 애정 관계에서 큰 상처를 받은 핍은 자신이 경험했던 것과 같은 불행한 가정을 재현하고 싶지 않았을 것이다.

2. 죄와 벌

　디킨즈는 『위대한 유산』에서 범죄에 연루된 사람들과 그 피해자가 된 사람들의 유무죄를 폭로함으로써 당대의 범죄의 본질을 탐구한다. 당대 사회의 관찰자이며 개혁가로서의 작가의 특성은 작품 전반에 걸쳐 자주 등장하는 죄수와 형벌 및 감옥의 묘사를 통해 엿볼 수 있다. 범죄와 관련되는 물건들, 즉 가저리가 수리하는 수갑, 자주 등장하는 막대기들, 런던 감옥의 교수대, 심지어는 에스텔라가 사실상 갇혀 있는 일종의 감옥으로서의 새티스 하우스 등이 범죄에 대한 배경의 역할을 한다.

　가저리 부인은 핍을 자기 '손으로(by hand)' 키웠다고 자랑하는데, 이는 누구의 도움도 받지 않았다는 말도 되지만 "매를 아끼면 아이를 망친다(Spare the rod and spoil the child)"는 자기 생각을 드러낸 것이다.[78] 어린 핍은 그녀의 회초리로 수도 없이 매를 맞아야만 했다. 디킨즈는 가저리 부인이 결국은 올릭의 잔인한 손에 죽도록 함으로써 인과응보의 교훈을 주고 있다.

　또한 디킨즈는 어린 핍의 성장에 결정적 역할을 하는 인물을 반사회의 전형인 탈옥수로 설정하여 당대의 징벌제도의 문제를 제기한다. 자신의 죄과를 뉘우칠 기회를 갖기도 전에 피해자가 되어 버린 매그위치는 범죄 활동이 아니라 유배지 오스트레일리

---

[78] 원래 이 표현은 사람의 몸으로부터 직접 모유를 먹이지(breast-feed) 않고 숟가락으로 먹이거나(spoon-feed) 병으로 먹여(bottle-feed) 키운다는 뜻이다.

아에서 피땀 흘려 번 돈으로 핍을 돕는다. 그러다 핍의 성공을 눈으로 확인하고픈 열망만으로 모든 위험을 무릅쓰고 잉글랜드로 돌아와 악랄한 콤피슨에게 쫓기는 신세가 되어 결국 체포되고 사형 선고를 받는다. 법은 매그위치에게 혹독하지만 그는 이를 담담하게 받아들인다.

한편 몰리는 재거즈에게 길들여진다. 집시로 태어나서 살기 위해서 범죄의 길로 들어섰다 질투심 때문에 살인을 저질렀던 그녀는 이제 재거즈의 집에서 하녀로 살고 있다. 따라서 더 이상 방황하거나 법을 어기지 않지만 그녀는 자신의 딸 에스텔라의 운명에 대해 전혀 알지 못하는 무력한 피해자다. 그녀가 아는 것이라곤 자기 딸이 음식과 보금자리를 제공할 수 있는 부유한 가정에 입양되었다는 것과 재거즈의 집을 떠나면 또다시 험난한 인생이 시작될 것이라는 사실뿐이다.

증오와 복수에 불타 인생을 허비한 인색하고 매정한 노파인 해비샴은 후반부에 다소의 심경의 변화를 보인다. 허버트 포킷의 사업 자금을 대주기도 하고 죽기 전에는 마침내 핍의 용서를 구한다. 핍은 인생의 마지막에 이르러 지난 날을 후회하며 괴로워하지만 변화된 양심의 열매를 맛보기에는 때가 너무 늦은 해비샴을 보면서 죄와 벌에 대한 귀한 교훈을 얻는다.

에스텔라는 냉혹한 양모 해비샴에게 학대 받는 피해자였지만 나중에는 스스로가 핍과 해비샴을 학대하는 가해자가 된다. 그리고는 저열한 드러믈에게 학대 받으며 사랑 없는 결혼생활을 견딘다. 에스텔라는 해비샴의 갑작스런 죽음으로 그녀와 화해할 기회는 놓쳐버렸지만 핍과는 대등한 입장으로 화해함으로써 죄의 고리를 끊는다.

이 소설에서 자기 자신만 아는 구제불능의 드러믈과 콤피슨 같은 인물들은 죄과를 인정하지 않은 채로 죽을 수밖에 없지만 매그위치와 몰리, 그리고 에스텔라는 정당화할 수 있거나 불가피했던 악행에 대해 용서를 받는다. 여기서 디킨즈는 서술자 핍의 목소리를 통해서 용서의 힘이 위대함을 보여준다. 그것은 남을 궁휼히 여김으로써 자신이 용서받기 때문이다. 핍은 한때 두려워했던 이 세상의 법은 진정한 정의와는 거리가 멀며 남에게 손가락질하기보다는 자신의 죄과를 인정함으로써만 용서받고 행복을 찾을 수 있음을 배운다.

법과 그 결과에 대해 잘 아는지라 당연히 정직한 시민일 것이라고 추정되는 변호사 재거즈는 사실 냉혹한 범죄자다. 그는 인생은 끊임없는 권력투쟁이며 인정사정 보지 않는 사람이 언제나 승자라고 믿는다. 그는 직업상 가해자들과 피해자들을 매일 접하면서도 세상 권력이 자기 확신의 힘과 결코 같을 수 없음을 깨닫지 못하고 평생을 보낸다. 자기편이 아닌 모든 사람들이 자신을 두려워하는 일시적일 수밖에 없는 권력을 즐기는 것이 그의 삶의 전부일 뿐 그에게는 어떤 양심의 갈등도 없다. 이를 통해 디킨즈는 사회계급이 개인의 가치에 대한 의미 없고 피상적인 척도인 것과 마찬가지로 영국의 사법제도, 즉 경찰, 법원, 감옥 및 죄와 벌에 대한 사회적 태도까지도 도덕성에 대한 피상적인 척도일 뿐임을 지적한다.

반면 핍은 자신의 양심과 대외적으로 표방하는 도덕성에 미치지 못하는 당대의 사법제도 사이에서 갈등한다. 어린 시절 죄수가 도망가도록 도운 일에 대해 핍은 늘 큰 죄의식 가운데서 살면서 언젠가는 어떤 큰 힘이 그를 잡아내 처벌할 거라고 생각한다. 그러나 핍은 성장과정에서 영국의 사법체제가 아니라 자기 자신의 양심과 부딪히게 되면서 모든 행동에서 법을 준거로 생각했던 죄의 문제가 처음 생각보다 훨씬 더 복잡함을 알게 된다. 한편 그는 주위의 선량한 사람들을 무시하여 그들에게 상처를 준다. 그는 처음 야망에 사로잡혀 대장간을 떠난 뒤 그들을 모르는 척 하며 지냈고, 모든 것을 잃고 해외 생활을 하던 십일 년 동안에도 연락 한 번 하지 않았을 뿐 아니라, 비디에게는 말로도 많은 상처를 주었다. 그러면서도 핍은 필요에 따라 그들의 우정을 남용했다. 그러던 핍은 오랜 고통을 겪고 모든 재산을 다 날려 버리고 거의 죽을 지경에 이르면서 순진했던 어린 시절의 단순한 진리를 기억하는 돌아온 탕자로서 용서를 구한다. 디킨즈는 핍이 과거의 행동과 현재의 결과를 함께 고려하게 되면서 얼마나 강한 사람이 되는가를 보여준다. 핍은 소설의 말미에서 매그위치에게서 단순한 고결함을 보게 된다. 이제 인간의 법을 넘어 더 큰 세상을 볼 수 있게 된 그는 자신이 주위 옳지 않은 일을 할 때마다 끊임없이 그를 괴롭히는 양심만을 신뢰하기로 한다.

3. 계급과 욕망

 디킨즈는 『위대한 유산』에서 빅토리아 시대의 영국의 계급구조를 전체적으로 보여준다. 이 소설에는 극악무도한 죄수로부터 늪지대에 사는 가난한 농부들, 중산층뿐만 아니라 아주 부유한 사람까지 다 등장한다. 디킨즈는 이러한 다양한 신분의 사람들 사이에서 주인공 핍의 야망이 전개되는 과정을 보여줌으로써 사랑과 양심이 신분이나 부보다도 더 중요함을 역설한다.
 핍은 사랑하는 에스텔라를 얻기 위해 그녀가 속한 상류사회로의 진입을 꿈꿨지만 그녀가 자신보다도 더 못한 사회의 맨 밑바닥에 있는 매그위치와 몰리의 딸이라는 걸 알게 된다. 또한 상류사회에 속한 그녀의 양모 해비샴이나 콤피슨, 드러믈 같은 인물들의 사악하고 참담한 실상과 서민층인 조와 비디, 그리고 사회로부터 버림받은 매그위치의 순전하고 숭고한 인격을 보면서 사회가 자연스러운 것으로 받아들이는 계급구조의 전제가 잘못된 것임을 알게 된다. 핍의 각성을 통해 디킨즈는 상류층에 있는 사람들은 그럴만한 자격이 있다는 생각이야말로 허구라는 것, 즉 사회계급과 성품 사이에는 아무런 관계가 없음을 보여주는데 이는 사회적 신분이 사람의 일생을 좌우하는 빅토리아 시대의 영국에서 상당히 논쟁적인 주장이었다.
 『위대한 유산』의 주인공인 핍에게서 볼 수 있는 가장 뚜렷한 특징인 '자기개선'의 욕망이 이 소설의 중심 주제다. 핍은 주어진 신분을 넘어 엘리트 계급에 진입하고자 하는 빅토리아 시대의 야망의 표상이다. 핍은 처음에는 개선에의 욕망을 삶의 모든 측면에 적용되는 일반적인 개념으로 여기고 모든 개선은 좋은 것이라 생각하지만 여러 경험을 통해 그것이 그리 단순하지만은 않음을 알게 된다. 그는 언제나 모든 일에서 최선을 추구하지만 불행히도 자신의 욕망에 일치하는 최선의 상태가 도덕적으로도 최선은 아니며, 때로는 한 사람의 개선이 다른 사람에게 부정적이며 심지어는 파괴적인 영향을 미칠 수도 있음을 거듭 경험한다.

나이에 비해 몸집도 작았고 신체적으로나 기질상 연약했던 어린 핍은 누이인 가저리 부인, 펌블축 삼촌, 에스텔라 그리고 해비샴으로부터 모욕을 당하며 산다. 누이에게 얹혀서 살아가는 고아인 핍은 야단맞지 않으려 누이의 눈치를 보는 것이 매일의 일과다. 해비샴이 처음 자기가 지켜보는 가운데 에스텔라와 카드 게임을 하라고 명령했을 때 핍은 너무도 두려웠고 어린 그였지만 그렇게 누가 시키는 대로 뭐든 해야 하는 자신의 처지가 참담함을 느낀다. 핍은 사랑하는 에스텔라를 얻기 위해 사회적 신분상승을 갈망하던 중 익명의 후원자의 등장으로 그 꿈을 이룰 수 있게 되어 런던에서 신사로서 정중한 대접을 받는 것을 즐긴다. 그러면서 지난 시절의 우정과 사랑을 자연스레 배신하는 자신을 발견한다. 그는 매형 가저리가 런던으로 자신을 찾아왔을 때 그의 남루한 옷차림과 촌티 나는 말투를 부끄러워한다. 매그위치 때문에 큰 돈을 갖게 되고 신분상승을 이뤘건만 그가 막상 목숨을 걸고 자신을 만나기 위해 잉글랜드로 왔을 땐 될 수 있는 한 빨리 그를 보내 버리려는 마음뿐이다. 종종 해비샴과 에스텔라를 방문하려고 고향을 찾았건만 자기가 살던 대장간에는 한 번도 들르지 않았고 그에게 소식을 전하지도 않는다.

  디킨즈는 핍이 신사의 세계를 탐험해 나가는 이야기를 통해서 당대의 계급구조를 풍자하여 상류층과 그들의 욕망이 얼마나 허망한 것인가를 보여준다. 인간의 개성과 인격이 무시되는 타락한 사회적 분위기에서 진정한 삶의 가치는 도외시한 채 오로지 상류사회로의 진입만을 도모하며 경험하게 되는 정신적 위기는 핍만의 문제라기보다는 당대의 공통된 문제다. 핍이 실제로 신사가 되고 보니 그 삶은 그의 이전의 삶보다 더 만족스럽지도 않으며 도덕적이지도 못하다. 신사라는 신분을 가능케 한 것이 자신이 땀 흘려 벌지 않은 거저 들어온 돈 때문인지라 결국 그 돈마저 다 탕진한다. 내면적인 자기개선보다는 겉으로 드러나는 모습에만 치중하여 낭비를 일삼고 타락의 길로 들어선 핍은 부지불식간 부패한 사회구조를 지탱하는 역할을 하고 만다.

  이상주의자인 핍은 모든 면에서 최선을 추구한다. 그의 자기개선에 대한 믿음은 사회적 신분상승에만 국한되지 않는다.『위대한 유산』전체를 흐르고 있는 하나의 주제는 핍의 신사뿐 아니라 도덕적이고 사려 깊은 인간이 되고자 하는 야망이다. 그는 자신의 의지와는 무관한 알 수 없는 어떤 외적인 힘에 의해 허황된 욕망을 좇아 살다가 자신이 소중하게 여기는 가치관과 물질적 기반을 전부 상실하고 정신적인 고통과 양심의 가책을 철저히 겪고 난 다음에서야 도덕성과 신뢰를 회복하게 된다.

소설의 처음부터 핍은 자신이 비도덕적으로 행동했을 때 아주 힘들어 했다. 핍은 자신이 가저리와 비디를 대했던 방식에 대해 죄의식을 갖게 되며 해비샴과 에스텔라를 통해서 다른 사람들의 감정을 무시하는 것이 얼마나 잔인한 것인가를 배운다. 마침내 지난날을 회상하는 서술자로서의 핍은 주인공 핍이 주위의 사람들을 편협한 마음으로 대했다고 비난하며 어린 핍이 자기개선의 욕구가 너무 큰 나머지 가저리와 비디와 같은 주위의 선량한 사람들의 존엄성을 침해했음을 고백한다. 이제 이런 행동을 부끄럽게 생각하게 된 핍은 가저리와 매그위치에게 사과할 뿐 아니라 자신을 학대했던 해비샴이 임종을 맞았을 때 그녀를 용서한다. 핍의 자기개선에의 열망은 단지 사회적으로 신사만 되고 말겠다는 저급한 욕망이 아니다. 그것은 남의 눈과 관계없이 스스로 더 나은 사람이 되고자 하는 열망이며 주위에 있는 다른 신사들과 같지 않은 도덕적이고 사려 깊은 인간이 되고자 하는 열망이다. 바로 이것 때문에 핍은 인생의 더 큰 그림을 볼 수 있고 진정한 행복에 더 가까이 갈 수 있는 것이다.

디킨즈는 피상적이고 이기적인 욕망들로 가득 찬 세상을 보며 도덕성에 기반하지 않은 야망은 위험함을 경고한다. 디킨즈에게는 자기만을 생각하고 다른 곳에는 눈을 돌리지 않는 부유한 신사들보다는 미천하고 연약한 핍이 진실된 인간이다. 고아나 다

름없는 핍이 상류계급의 신사가 되려는 욕망을 채워나가는 과정을 보면 역사적으로 어느 사회에서나 기존의 신분제도나 부의 장벽을 뛰어넘는 것이 쉬운 일이 아님을 알 수 있다. 하지만 핍은 그 넘을 수 없을 것 같은 사회적 장벽들을 넘으려 했으며 여기서 그치지 않고 도덕성과 양심의 장벽마저도 극복하려 했다. 그리고 그는 마침내 좌절과 실패를 통해 인생과 사회를 더 깊고 더 넓게 이해하는 정신적 성숙을 얻는다.

제5장 결론

　이 작품의 도덕적인 주제는 아주 단순하다. 그것은 사랑, 충정, 그리고 양심이 신분상승, 부, 계급보다도 더 중요하다는 것이다. 디킨즈 자신의 어린 시절을 빼어 닮은 어린 핍은 사회 불의에 항거하거나 더 나은 삶을 주도적으로 추구하기에는 너무 연약한 낭만적 이상주의자다. 디킨즈는 성장과정에서 어쩔 수 없이 물질만능과 계급차별 등의 사회적 악폐에 오염되고 언제나 정직하지도 못하며 진실과 환상 사이에서 갈피를 잡지 못한 채 헤매면서도 마침내 스스로의 결단과 노력으로 주어진 도전을 극복해 내는 핍을 보여줌으로써 인간에 대한 무한한 신뢰를 드러낸다.

이와 함께 디킨즈는 부에 따라 사회적 신분이 결정되는 모순을 고발함으로써 당시로서는 생경했던 '사회구조(social structure)'라는 개념을 독자들에게 희미하게나마 인식시키려고 노력한다. 디킨즈는 이전 작품들에서는 사회제도의 모순을 고발하는 데 그쳤었지만 『위대한 유산』에서는 이에서 한 발 더 나아가 도덕적인 성찰을 촉구한다. 핍의 사회적 신분상승은 도덕적 추락을 수반한다. 위대한 유산에 대한 기대가 무너지고 나서야 비로소 온전한 의미에서의 신사가 되는 핍을 그림으로써 디킨즈는 당시 사회적인 기정사실에 반기를 들어 사회적 특권과 도덕적 가치, 그리고 사법적 질서와 개인적 양심은 전혀 별개의 문제임을 웅변하고 있다.

더불어 그는 인간이 나름의 원대한 계획이나 포부를 세우고 분투해도 그 결과는 애초의 꿈과는 전혀 다르다는 것, 즉 "계획은 인간이 해도 그 성취는 신이 정한다(Man proposes, God disposes)"는 진리를 다시 한 번 상기시킨다. 그래서 『위대한 유산』은 한계와 가능성을 함께 지니고 있는 보통 사람의 사람됨을 선언하는 민중소설이다. 1870년 디킨즈가 세상을 떠났다는 말을 듣고 대부분 서민층인 그의 독자들은 주막에서 그리고 거리에서 '우리의 친구가 죽었다'며 비통해 했다고 한다.

참고문헌

Brown, Julia Prewitt. *A Reader's Guide to the Nineteenth-Century English Novel*. London: Collier Macmillan Publishers, 1985.

Chesterton, G. K. *Appreciations and Criticisms of the Works of Charles Dickens*. London: J. M. Dent & Sons, 1911.

Collins, Philip. *Dickens and Education*. London: Macmillan, 1963.

Dickens, Charles. *Great Expectations*. London: Chapman and Hall, 1861.

John, Juliet. *Dickens's Villains: Melodrama, Character, Popular Culture*. Oxford: Oxford University Press, 2001.

Jordan, John O. Ed. *The Cambridge Companion to Charles Dickens*. Cambridge: Cambridge University Press, 2001.

Leavis, F. R., and Q. D. Leavis. *Dickens the Novelist*. London: Chatto and Windus, 1970.

Lindsay, Jack. *Charles Dickens: A Biographical and Critical Study*. London: Andrew Dakers, 1950.

Manning, Sylvia Bank. *Dickens as Satirist*. New Haven: Yale University Press, 1971.

Paroissien, David. Ed. *A Companion to Charles Dickens*. Oxford: Blackwell Publishing, 2008.

Wilson, Angus. *The World of Charles Dickens*. London: Secker & Warburg, 1970.

Wilson, Edmund. *The Wound and the Bow: Seven Studies in Literature*. Revised ed. London: Allen, 1952.

Part 02

Dickens' *Great Expectations*

본문 해설

Great Expectations
by Charles Dickens
1861

1946년 작 영화 <위대한 유산>의 포스터

Chapter ONE

In the Churchyard

My name is Philip Pirrip, but as a child I could not say my name.[1] I called myself Pip, and that has been my name ever since.[2]

---

[1] 이 소설의 주인공인 핍은 등장인물(character)이면서 서술자(narrator)의 역할을 겸한다. 이 소설의 모든 과정을 겪고 난 성인이 된 '서술자 핍'은 소년과 청년, 그리고 장년이 되어 가는 '주인공 핍'의 감정과 문제를 세밀하게 회고하며 그 밖의 필요한 모든 정보를 독자들에게 제공한다.

[2] ever since=continuously since the time mentioned 그때부터 줄곧

I never knew my mother and father. They both died when I was a baby. I was brought up[3] by my only sister, who was married[4] to a blacksmith,[5] Joe Gargery.

My story begins on a cold, grey winter afternoon in the churchyard[6] where my parents are buried.[7] I would[8] often go to their graves[9] and look down at the words on their gravestone:[10] Philip Pirrip and Georgiana, Wife of the Above.[11] I was a sensitive[12] and lonely child and was often sad.

---

[3] to bring sb. up=to care for a child, teaching him or her how to behave, etc. brought-brought 양육하다

[4] to marry=to become the husband or wife of sb.; to get married to sb.; to find a husband or wife for sb. (…와) 결혼하다; …에게 결혼시키다

[5] blacksmith=a person whose job is to make and repair things made of iron, esp. horseshoes 대장장이

[6] churchyard=an area of land around a church, often used for burying people in 교회 경내 (흔히 묘지로 쓰임)

[7] to bury=to place a dead body in a grave (시신을) 묻다, 매장하다

[8] "would" - used for talking about things that often happened in the past (과거에 종종 일어났던 일을 말함) …하곤 했다

[9] grave=a place in the ground where a dead person is buried 무덤, 묘

[10] gravestone=a stone that is put on a grave in a vertical position, showing the name, etc. of the person buried there 묘비

[11] the above=the person or the thing mentioned above 위의/위에서 언급한 사람/사물

[12] sensitive=easily offended or upset 예민한; 민감한

The marshes[13] beyond[14] the churchyard were grey. The river beyond the marshes was a darker line of grey. A bitter[15] wind was blowing across the marshes from the sea. The graveyard was a dark and frightening[16] place.[17]

I shivered.[18] Cold and afraid,[19] I began to cry.

"Quiet,[20] you little devil!"[21] cried a terrible[22] voice. "Keep still[23]—or I'll cut your throat!"[24]

---

[13] marsh=an area of low land that is always soft and wet because there is nowhere for the water to flow away to 습지

[14] beyond=on or to the further side of sth. …너머의

[15] bitter=extremely cold and unpleasant (기상 조건이) 혹독한, 매서운

[16] to frighten=to make sb. suddenly feel afraid 겁먹게/놀라게 만들다

[17] 이곳 늪지대는 핍의 집 근처의 침침하고 안개 낀 곳으로 그의 일생에서 어둡고 불확실하며 위험을 잉태하고 있는 신비스런 시기를 상징한다. 이는 회색, 강, 바람, 무덤 등과 함께 이 작품 전체의 분위기를 설정한다.

[18] to shiver=to shake slightly because you are cold, frightened, excited, etc. (추위/두려움/흥분 등으로) 가볍게 몸을 떨다

[19] Cold and afraid=As I was cold and afraid

[20] quiet=making very little noise (소리가 거의 없이) 조용한

[21] devil=a person who behaves badly, esp. a child (특히 아이) 말썽꾸러기

[22] terrible=very unpleasant; making you feel very unhappy, upset or frightened 끔찍한, 소름 끼치는

[23] still=not moving; calm and quiet 가만히 있는, 고요한, 정지한.
"Keep still"="Don't move" 꼼짝 마, 움직이지 마

[24] throat=a passage in the neck through which food and air pass on their way into the body; the front part of the neck 목구멍, 목

A rough-looking[25] man had taken hold of me.[26] He held me tightly by[27] the neck.[28]

"Oh, don't cut my throat, sir!"[29] I cried. "Please, don't!"

The man's rough grey clothes were torn[30] and muddy.[31] Like me, he was shivering with[32] cold. His shoes were old and broken. He had a torn piece of cloth tied round his head. And his eyes were wild and terrible.

"Tell me your name", the man growled.[33] "Tell me. Quick!"

"Pip, sir. Pip", I answered.

"Show me where you live",[34] the terrible man demanded.

---

[25] rough=not gentle or careful; violent (행동이) 거친/난폭한

[26] to catch/get/grab/take (a) hold of sb./sth.=to have or take sb./sth. in your hands 붙잡다; 움켜쥐다

[27] "by" – used to show the part of sb./sth. that sb. touches, holds, etc. 신체의 접촉 부분을 나타냄 (바로 다음에 the를 씀)

[28] to hold=to carry sth.; to have sb./sth. in your hand, arms, etc. *held-held* (손/팔 등으로) 잡고/쥐고/들고/안고/받치고 있다/가다/다니다

[29] "sir" – used as a polite way of addressing a man whose name you do not know, for example in a shop/store or restaurant, or to show respect 선생님 (이름 모르는 남자에 대한 경칭)

[30] to tear=to damage sth. by pulling it apart or into pieces or by cutting it on sth. sharp; to become damaged in this way *tore-torn* 찢다, 뜯다; 찢어/뜯어지다

[31] muddy=full of or covered in mud(=wet earth that is soft and sticky) 진창인, 진흙투성이인

[32] with=because of; as a result of …때문에; …의 결과로

[33] to growl=to make a low sound in the throat, usually as a sign of anger 으르렁거리다; 으르렁거리듯 말하다

I pointed[35] towards our village, which was about a mile[36] away from the churchyard.

The man stared[37] at me for a moment. Then, with a sudden movement,[38] he picked me up and turned me upside down. A piece of bread fell out of my pocket. The man pushed me onto[39] a gravestone. Then he grabbed[40] the bread and began eating greedily.[41]

I sat on the gravestone where he had put me, shivering and crying with fear.[42]

"Now, tell me, where's your mother?" the man in grey[43] asked suddenly.

---

[34] to show sb. sth.=to point to sth. so that sb. can see where or what it is (방향/위치를) 알려/가리켜 주다

[35] to point=to stretch out your finger or sth. held in your hand towards sb./sth. in order to show sb. where a person or thing is (손가락 등으로) 가리키다

[36] mile=a unit for measuring distance equal to 1609 metres 약 1.6km

[37] to stare=to look for a long time 빤히 쳐다보다, 응시하다

[38] movement=an act of moving the body or part of the body (몸/신체 부위의) 움직임

[39] "onto" – used with verbs to express movement on or to a particular place or position (이동을 나타내는 동사와 함께 쓰여) …위로/위에

[40] to grab=to take or hold sb./sth. with your hand suddenly, firmly or roughly (와락/단단히) 붙잡다/움켜잡다

[41] greedy=wanting more money, power, food, etc. than you really need 탐욕스러운; 욕심 많은

[42] shivering and crying with fear=and I shivered and cried with fear

[43] in grey=wearing grey clothes 회색 옷을 입은

"There, sir", I answered, pointing over his shoulder to my mother's grave.

The man looked behind him and started to run.

"I mean—she's buried there, sir. That's my mother. 'Georgiana, Wife of the Above.'"[44]

"Oh, I see", the man said, limping[45] slowly back. "And is that your father there buried[46] with your mother?"

"Yes, sir", I replied.[47]

"Then who do you live with?" the man asked. "That is,[48] if I let you live",[49] he said roughly.

"With my sister, sir—Mrs Joe Gargery—wife of Joe Gargery, the blacksmith, sir."

---

[44] 디킨즈는 어린 핍이 묘비에 적혀 있는 그대로 외워서 자신의 어머니를 소개하는 장면을 의도적으로 삽입하여, 이 다소 희극적인 요소로써 전체적으로 암울하고 엄숙한 분위기가 주는 과도한 긴장을 완화한다.

[45] to limp=to walk slowly or with difficulty because one leg is injured 절뚝거리다

[46] there buried=who are buried there 거기 묻혀 있는

[47] to reply=to say or write sth. as an answer to sb./sth. 대답하다; 답장/답신을 보내다; 응하다, 대응하다

[48] "that is" – used to say what sth. means or to give more information 즉; 말하자면

[49] 갑자기 나타난 이 괴한은 '만약 살려준다면'이라고 말을 덧붙임으로써 위협의 기세를 누그러뜨리지 않고 있다.

"A blacksmith, is he?" the man muttered,[50] looking down at his leg. There was a thick band[51] of iron[52] round his ankle, with a broken chain hanging from the band.

The man came nearer. He took hold of my arms and tipped[53] me back over the gravestone as far as I could go. His terrible eyes stared into mine.

"Now, look here", he said. "Do you know what a file[54] is?"

"Yes, sir."

"Then you get[55] me a file. And you get me some food. Do you understand?"

"Yes, sir."

"Bring me, early tomorrow morning, a file and some food", the man repeated[56] slowly. "Bring them to the Old Fort,[57] over

---

[50] to mutter=to speak or say sth. in a quiet voice that is difficult to hear, esp. because you are annoyed about sth. (특히 기분이 나빠서) 중얼거리다

[51] band=a thin flat strip or circle of any material that is put around things, for example to hold them together or to make them stronger 묶는 것/띠; 굴레; 수갑, 족쇄

[52] iron=a hard strong metal that is used to make steel and is also found in small quantities in blood and food 철, 쇠; 철분

[53] to tip=to move so that one end or side is higher than the other; to move sth. into this position 기울이다, 젖히다

[54] file=a metal tool with a rough surface for cutting or shaping hard substances or for making them smooth (무엇을 매끈하게 다듬는 데 쓰는) 줄

[55] to get=to go to a place and bring sb./sth. back *got-got* (어디에 가서) 가져/데려/불러오다

there, by the river. Say nothing to no one[58] and maybe I'll let you live.

"But if you tell anyone about me", the terrible man said slowly, "your heart and liver will be torn out! Torn out, roasted[59] and ate."[60]

"Now,[61] I'm not alone", he went on. "There's a young man near here, listening to every word I say. He has a secret way of finding a boy, wherever he is. Even if a boy is warm in bed, behind a locked door, that young man will find him. What do you say to that?"[62]

---

[56] to repeat=to say or write sth. again or more than once (말/글로) 반복하다, 한 번 더/거듭 말하다/쓰다

[57] fort=a building or buildings built in order to defend an area against attack 보루, 요새. 여기서 'the Old Fort'는 고유명사로 두 사람 다 알고 있는 강가의 특정한 요새를 가리킨다.

[58] 'Say nothing to no one'은 'Say nothing to anyone'이라 해야 문법적으로 옳다. 티킨즈는 이 사람이 세련되지 못한 표현을 쓰게 함으로써 배우지 못했음을 간접적으로 나타낸다.

[59] to roast=to cook food, esp. meat, without liquid in an oven or over a fire; to be cooked in this way (특히 고기를 오븐 속이나 불 위에 대고) 굽다; (이런 식으로) 구워지다

[60] 여기서 'ate'는 과거분사인 'eaten'을 잘못 쓴 것으로 이 사람이 세련되지 않음을 보여준다.

[61] "Now" – used to get sb.'s attention before changing the subject or asking them to do sth. (화제를 바꾸거나 부탁을 하기 전에 남의 관심을 끌기 위해 하는 말) 자!

[62] "What do/would you say (to sth./doing sth.)?"="What do you think about sth./to do sth.?"; "Would you like sth./to do sth." 어떻게 생각해?; (…은/…하는 건) 어때요?

I promised[63] I would bring him the file and the food very early in the morning.

"Lord strike me dead if I don't—say it!"[64] the man growled.

"Lord strike me dead if I don't", I repeated.

The man lifted[65] me down from the gravestone. Then he held his arms around his shivering body.

"Goodnight, sir", I whispered.[66]

"Nothing much good about it", the man replied, looking across at wet and windy marshes. "I wish I was a frog—or a fish!"[67]

He limped off through the churchyard, towards the marshes. He turned once to look back at me.

I began to run home as fast as I could.

---

[63] to promise=to tell sb. that you will definitely do or not do sth., or that sth. will definitely happen 약속하다

[64] "Lord strike me dead if I don't"는 "내가 안 하면 주께서 벌을 내려 죽게 하시리라"는 서약으로 기독교 성경의 사무엘상 25:22를 인용한 것이다.

[65] to lift=to take hold of sb./sth. and move them/it to a different position (다른 위치로 옮기기 위해) 들어올리다/내다

[66] to whisper=to speak very quietly to sb. so that other people cannot hear what you are saying 속삭이다, 소곤거리다, 귓속말을 하다

[67] 현재 사실에 반대되는 가정인 가정법 과거로 날씨가 이렇게 축축하고 추우니 "개구리나 물고기라면 좋겠다"는 뜻이다.

When I got[68] home, the forge[69] was shut up. Joe had finished work for[70] the day. I opened the door of the house. I crept[71] quietly into the warm kitchen and saw Joe, sitting alone by[72] the fire[73], smoking[74] his pipe.[75]

Joe Gargery was a huge, fair-haired[76] man with kind blue eyes. He looked at me sadly.

---

[68] to get=to arrive at or reach a place or point *got-got* (장소/위치에) 도착하다, 이르다

[69] forge=a place where objects are made by heating and shaping pieces of metal, esp. one where a blacksmith works 대장간

[70] "for" – used to show that sth. is arranged or intended to happen at a particular time (정해진 날짜/시간을 나타내어) …에 해당하는/하도록 되어 있는

[71] to creep=to move slowly, quietly and carefully, because you do not want to be seen or heard *crept-crept* (사람/동물이) 살금살금 움직이다

[72] by=near=at the side of=beside …옆/가에

[73] fire=a pile of burning fuel, such as wood or coal, used for cooking food or heating a room 불, 난롯불

[74] to smoke=to suck smoke from a cigarette, pipe, etc. into your mouth and let it out again (담배를) 피우다

[75] sitting alone by the fire, smoking his pipe=who sat alone by the fire and smoked his pipe

[76] fair=pale in colour (피부/머리카락이) 옅은 색의; 금발의

"Mrs Joe has been out[77] looking for you,[78] Pip", Joe told me. "She's out there now, Pip. And she's got[79] Tickler[80] with her."

This was very bad news. Tickler was a stick that I had often felt[81] on my thin body.

For[82] although I had food, clothes and shelter,[83] my sister was a hard[84] and angry woman and would often beat me. Her husband, Joe, was my only friend.

"Has she been out long, Joe?" I asked nervously.[85]

"Well", said Joe, looking up at the clock, "this time, she's been out about five minutes."

---

[77] out=away from or not at home or their place of work (사람이) 집에 있지 않은, (직장 등에서 자기) 자리에 없는, 출타/외출 중인

[78] to look for=to search for sb./sth., either because you have lost them/it, or because you need them/it 찾다

[79] she's got=she has

[80] to tickle=to move your fingers on a sensitive part of sb.'s body in a way that makes them laugh (장난을 치느라고 손가락으로) 간지럼을 태우다/간질이다. 'Tickler'는 '매(rod)'의 속어인 'tickle tail'에서 온 말로 추정된다.

[81] to feel=to notice or be aware of sth. because it is touching you or having a physical effect on you *felt-felt* (촉감으로) 느끼다

[82] "for" – used to introduce the reason for sth. mentioned in the previous statement 왜냐하면 …니까

[83] shelter=the fact of having a place to live or stay, considered as a basic human need (인간 생활의 기본 요소 중) 주거지

[84] hard=showing no sympathy or affection 냉정한, 매정한

[85] nervous=anxious about sth. or afraid of sth. 불안해하는; 두려워하는

"And I hear her coming back, Pip old chap",[86] Joe added. "Get[87] behind the door!"

My sister pushed open the door with a bang.[88] She soon saw where I was hiding[89] and beat me until I cried. Then she threw me angrily across the kitchen to where Joe was sitting. Joe quietly placed[90] me in the corner near the fire and protected[91] me with his own powerful body.

My sister was twenty years older than me. She was tall and thin, with a hard face and sharp black eyes. The rough red skin on her bony[92] hands and face made her always look[93] angry.

---

[86] chap=a man (used to talk about him in a friendly way) 녀석, 친구 (남자를 친하게 이르는 말). 'Pip old chap'은 '오랜 친구 핍'이란 뜻으로 매형 가저리가 핍을 정답게 부르는 말이다.

[87] to get=to move to or from a particular place or in a particular direction, sometimes with difficulty; to make sb./sth. do this *got-got* (때때로 힘들게) 가다/이동하다; 가게/이동하게 하다

[88] bang=a sudden loud noise 쾅/쿵/탁 (하는 소리)

[89] to hide=to go somewhere where you hope you will not be seen or found *hid-hidden* 숨다

[90] to place=to put sb./sth. in a particular place …을 (조심스럽게) 놓다/두다, 설치/배치하다

[91] to protect=to make sure that sb./sth. is not harmed, injured, damaged, etc. 보호하다, 지키다

[92] bony=very thin so that the bones can be seen under the skin (사람/신체 부위가) 뼈가 다 드러나는/앙상한

[93] to look=to seem; to appear …해/처럼 보이다, (보기에) …한 것 같다

"Where have you been, you young monkey?"[94] Mrs Joe cried, stamping[95] her foot. "Tell me what you've been doing all this time!"[96]

"I've been in the churchyard", I answered, crying.

"Churchyard?" Mrs Joe repeated sharply. "You'd have been in the churchyard long ago, if it hadn't been for me.[97] Who brought you up? Tell me that!"

"You did", I sobbed.[98]

"And why I did, I don't know", my sister exclaimed.[99] "It's[100] bad enough looking after this blacksmith, without being your mother too![101] One of these days,[102] you'll drive me to the graveyard, the pair of you."[103]

94　monkey=a child who is active and likes playing tricks on people 장난꾸러기(아이)
95　to stamp=to walk with loud heavy steps 쾅쾅거리며 걷다
96　all this time=all the while 지금껏 내내
97　가정법 과거완료로 '내가 아니었더라면 너는 그 무덤에 오래 전에 묻혔을 거다'라는 뜻이다.
98　to sob=to cry noisily, taking sudden, sharp breaths (흑흑) 흐느끼다, 흐느껴 울다
99　to exclaim=to say sth. suddenly and loudly, esp. because of strong emotion or pain 소리치다, 외치다
100　"it" – used when you are talking about a situation 상황/사정에 대해 이야기할 때 씀
101　without=if it were not for '…이 아니더라도'라는 뜻의 가정이 함축되어 있다.
102　one of these days=before a long time has passed 머지않아
103　가저리 부인이 핍에게 뿐만 아니라 남편에게도 험한 말을 서슴지 않는 모습을 통해 손상된 가정의 모습을 보여준다.

Joe said nothing. He was a simple, gentle man and he never complained[104] about Mrs Joe's bad temper.[105] But he protected me when he could and I loved him for it.

It was Christmas Eve and Mrs Joe was very busy. She was making the food for the Christmas meal next day. She made me stir[106] the mixture[107] for the Christmas pudding[108] for an hour and then I was allowed[109] to sit by the fire with Joe.

As I sat by the warm fire, I thought of the man on the cold, wet marshes. I remembered my promise to him. I thought of the young man who would find me and kill me if I broke that promise.[110]

---

[104] to complain=to say that you are annoyed, unhappy or not satisfied about sb./sth. 불평/항의하다

[105] temper=a tendency to get angry very quickly (걸핏하면 화를 내는) 성질

[106] to stir=to move a liquid or substance around, using a spoon or sth. similar, in order to mix it thoroughly 젓다, (저어 가며) 섞다/넣다

[107] mixture=a substance made by mixing other substances together (여러 재료를 섞어서 만든) 혼합 재료

[108] Christmas pudding=a hot pudding like a dark fruit cake, traditionally eaten in Britain at Christmas 크리스마스 푸딩 (영국에서 전통적으로 크리스마스에 먹는 검은 색 푸딩)

[109] to allow=to let sb./sth. do sth.; to let sth. happen or be done (무엇을 하도록) 허락하다; 용납하다

[110] 핍은 늪지대에서 만났던 괴한에 대해 연민과 공포를 함께 느끼고 있다.

The silence[111] of the quiet night was suddenly broken by loud noises[112] that seemed[113] to come from the sea.

"Are those the great guns, Joe?" I asked.

Joe nodded.[114]

"Another convict's[115] escaped",[116] he said. "One got away[117] last night and the guns were fired for[118] him. Now they're[119] giving warning that a second one has escaped."

"Who's firing[120] the guns?" I asked.

"Ask no questions and you'll be told no lies",[121] my sister snapped[122] in reply.

---

[111] silence=a complete lack of noise or sound 고요, 적막, 정적
[112] noise=a sound, esp. when it is loud, unpleasant or disturbing (듣기 싫은/시끄러운) 소리, 소음
[113] to seem=to give the impression of being or doing sth. (…인/하는 것처럼) 보이다, …인/하는 것 같다
[114] to nod=to move your head up and down to show agreement, understanding, etc. (고개를) 끄덕이다, 끄덕여 나타내다; (고개가) 끄덕여지다
[115] convict=a person who has been found guilty of a crime and sent to prison 기결수; 재소자
[116] to escape=to get away from a place where you have been kept as a prisoner or not allowed to leave 달아나다, 탈출하다.
Another convict's escaped=Another convict has escaped
[117] to get away=to succeed in leaving; to escape *got-got* 빠져나가다; 탈출하다
[118] "for" – used to show a reason or cause (이유/원인) …(으)로 해서
[119] they=people in authority or experts 당국; 전문가들
[120] to fire=to shoot bullets from a gun 사격/발사/발포하다
[121] Ask no questions and you'll be told no lies.=If you ask me that, my answer might not be the truth. 진실을 말해주지 않을 것이니 묻지 마라

"Mrs Joe", I said politely, "I really should[123] like to know, if you don't mind,[124] where the firing comes from."

"From the Hulks,[125] the Hulks", my sister answered.

"And, please, what are the Hulks?"

"Hulks are prison ships, moored[126] on the other[127] side of the marshes", Mrs Joe explained[128] impatiently.[129]

"I wonder[130] who's put into prison ships and why they're put there", I said.

Mrs Joe leapt[131] up and grabbed me by the ear.

---

[122] to snap=to speak or say sth. in an impatient, usually angry, voice (보통 화난 목소리로) 딱딱거리다; 톡 쏘다

[123] "should" – used with I and we in polite requests. I와 we 뒤에 써서 정중한 요청을 나타냄

[124] to mind=to be upset, annoyed or worried by sth. 언짢아하다, 상관하다, 개의하다

[125] 'the Hulks'는 감옥으로 개조된 노후선(老朽船, hulk)의 이름이다.

[126] to moor=to attach a boat, ship, etc. to a fixed object or to the land with a rope, or anchor it (배를) 잡아매다, 계류하다, 정박시키다

[127] the other=a place, direction, etc. that is the opposite to where you are, are going, etc. 반대쪽

[128] to explain=to tell sb. about sth. in a way that makes it easy to understand 설명하다

[129] impatient=annoyed or irritated by sb./sth. 짜증난, 안달하는

[130] to wonder=to think about sth. and try to decide what is true, what will happen, what you should do, etc. 궁금하다; …이 어떨까 생각하다

[131] to leap=to move or do sth. suddenly and quickly *leaped-leaped; leapt-leapt* (높이/ 길게) 뛰다, 뛰어오르다/넘다

"People are put in the Hulks because they murder[132] and rob[133] and do all kinds of bad things", she said. "And they all begin by asking questions!"[134]

Mrs Joe pulled my ear hard[135] as she spoke and gave me a push.

"And now go off[136] to bed!" she added.

I went slowly up the dark stairs, thinking about the terrible prison ships. I had begun by asking questions. And, in a few hours, I was going to steal[137] from Mrs Joe!

I slept very little that night. I was afraid of Mrs Joe. I was afraid of the convict on the marshes. And, most of all, I was afraid of the terrible young man.[138]

---

[133] to rob=to steal money or property from a person or place (사람/장소를) (…를/…에서) 털다/도둑질하다
[134] 일반적인 상황이나 진리를 말할 때는 단순현재형 동사를 쓴다.
[135] hard=with great force 세게, 강력하게
[136] to go off=to leave a place, esp. in order to do sth. *went-gone* (특히 무엇을 하러) 자리를 뜨다
[137] to steal=to take sth. from a person, shop/store, etc. without permission and without intending to return it or pay for it *stole-stolen* 훔치다, 도둑질하다
[138] 집 밖 늪지대의 안개와 어둠과 대비되는 집안의 모습은 험악한 가저리 부인에도 불구하고 핍에게는 안식처임을 보여준다. 핍이 현실을 거부하고 미지의 세계로 나가는 모습은 이 소설에서 계속 등장하는 모티프(motif)다.
[139] dawn=the time of day when light first appears 새벽, 여명, 동이 틀 무렵
[140] to dress=to put clothes on yourself/sb. 옷을 입다/입히다

At last, the grey light of dawn[139] came into the sky. I got up and dressed.[140] Quietly and carefully, I crept downstairs to the pantry.[141]

I found some bread, a piece of cheese and a large bone with some meat on it. There was a bottle with a little brandy[142] in it and I took that too. Last of all, on the top shelf,[143] I found a beautiful, round meat pie.[144]

---

[139] dawn=the time of day when light first appears 새벽, 여명, 동이 틀 무렵
[140] to dress=to put clothes on yourself/sb. 옷을 입다/입히다
[141] pantry=a cupboard/closet or small room in a house, used for storing food 식료품 저장실
[142] brandy=a strong alcoholic drink made from wine 브랜디
[143] shelf=a flat board, made of wood, metal, glass, etc., fixed to the wall or forming part of a cupboard/closet, bookcase, etc., for things to be placed on 선반, 시렁; 책꽂이, .(책장의) 칸
[144] pie=meat, vegetables, etc. baked in a dish with pastry on the bottom, sides and top (고기, 채소 등을 다진 것을 속에 넣고 만든) 파이

A door in the kitchen led[145] into the forge. I unlocked[146] the door and looked for a file among Joe's tools.[147] Then, locking[148] the door behind me, I walked back through the kitchen.

Turning the big key, I opened the house door carefully. In[149] a few moments, I was running as fast as I could towards the Fort on the misty[150] marshes.

It was a frosty[151] morning and very damp[152] and cold. The grass was wet and water dripped[153] from the trees. The mist was so thick over the marshes that I could only see a few feet[154]

---

[147] tool=an instrument such as a hammer, screwdriver, saw, etc. that you hold in your hand and use for making things, repairing things, etc. 연장, 도구, 공구

[148] to lock=to fasten sth. with a lock; to be fastened with a lock (자물쇠로) 잠그다/잠기다

[149] in=after a particular length of time (일정 시간) …후에/있으면

[150] misty=with a lot of mist(=a cloud of very small drops of water in the air just above the ground, that make it difficult to see) (엷은) 안개가 낀/자욱한

[151] frosty=extremely cold; cold with frost(=the thin white layer of ice that forms when the temperature drops below 0°C) 서리가 내리는, 몹시 추운/차가운

[152] damp=slightly wet, often in a way that is unpleasant 축축한, 눅눅한

[153] to drip=to fall in small drops (액체가) 방울방울/뚝뚝 흐르다/떨어지다/듣다

[154] foot=a unit for measuring length equal to 12 inches or 30.48 centimetres 피트. feet은 foot의 복수형임

[155] 안개와 늪은 이 소설의 초입에서 전체 이야기의 분위기를 보여주는데 주인공인 핍의 미래가 불확실성과 위험으로 가득 차 있음을 암시한다.

[156] terror=a feeling of extreme fear (극심한) 두려움, 무서움, 공포(심)

[157] almost=not quite 거의

[158] to lose way=to become lost=to not know where you are or how to get to where you want to go *lost-lost* 길을 잃다

ahead of me. As I ran, trees, cows and gates seemed to lean out of the mist to stop me.[155]

I knew the Fort well, but in my terror,[156] I almost[157] lost my way.[158] I had just crossed a ditch[159] when I saw the man in grey. He was sitting on the ground with his back to me. I walked up to him quietly and touched his shoulder. He jumped up and turned to face[160] me. It was not the same man!

But he was dressed in the same rough clothes as the man I had met. He too had an iron[161] on his leg. It was the young man, waiting to tear my heart and liver out![162]

---

[155] 안개와 늪은 이 소설의 초입에서 전체 이야기의 분위기를 보여주는데 주인공인 핍의 미래가 불확실성과 위험으로 가득 차 있음을 암시한다.
[156] terror=a feeling of extreme fear (극심한) 두려움, 무서움, 공포(심)
[157] almost=not quite 거의
[158] to lose way=to become lost=to not know where you are or how to get to where you want to go *lost-lost* 길을 잃다
[159] ditch=a long channel dug at the side of a field or road, to hold or take away water (들판/도로 가의) 배수로
[160] to face=to be opposite sb./sth.; to have your face or front pointing towards sb./sth. or in a particular direction …을 마주보다/향하다
[161] iron=chain or other heavy object made of iron, attached to the arms and legs of prisoners, esp. in the past (과거 죄인에게 채우던) 쇠사슬/족쇄
[162] 순진한 핍은 어제의 괴한이 또 한 명의 젊은이가 있는데 약속을 안 지키면 심장과 간을 도려내어 구워서 먹을 거라고 협박한 말을 사실로 믿고 있다. 이것은 전체적으로 긴장이 고조된 험악한 분위기에 더해지는 '디킨즈적인' 해학이다. 이렇게 핍의 어린 시절에 대한 희비극적인 묘사를 보면 그가 재미있기도 하고 사랑스럽기까지 하지만 이를 곱씹어 보면 비극적인 요소가 저변을 흐르고 있는 것을 발견할 수 있다.

With a cry, I ran on[163] until I had reached[164] the Fort. And there was my convict. He was swinging[165] his arms and walking up and down to keep[166] warm.

The man grabbed the food from my hand and began eating in great mouthfuls[167] like a dog. When he drank the brandy, he shivered so violently[168] that his teeth nearly broke the bottle.

As he started to eat the pie, I spoke to him.

"I'm glad[169] you're enjoying it, sir", I said.

"Thank you, my boy. I am, I am",[170] he replied.

"Aren't you leaving[171] anything for him?" I asked anxiously.[172]

---

[163] "on" – used to show that sth. continues (쉬지 않고) 계속하여
[164] to reach=to arrive at the place that you have been travelling to …에 이르다/닿다/도달하다
[165] to swing=to move backwards or forwards or from side to side while hanging from a fixed point; to make sth. do this *swung-swung* (전후/좌우로) 흔들리다(흔들다)
[166] to keep=to stay in a particular condition or position; to make sb./sth. do this *kept-kept* (특정한 상태/위치를) 유지하다/유지하게 하다; (특정한 상태/위치에) 계속 있다/있게 하다
[167] mouthful=an amount of food or drink that you put in your mouth at one time (음식) 한 입, 한 모금
[168] violent=very strong and sudden 극심한, 지독한, 끔찍한
[169] glad=pleased; happy 기쁜/반가운
[170] I am=I am enjoying
[171] to leave=to make sth. happen or remain as a result *left-left* (어떤 결과를) 남기다/(남겨) 주다
[172] anxious=feeling worried or nervous 불안해하는, 염려하는

"Him? Oh, the young man. He doesn't need any food", the convict replied.

"Doesn't he? I thought he looked hungry", I said.

"Looked? When did you see him?"

"Just now", I answered.

"Where?"

"Over there", I said, pointing. "I thought he was you", I explained. The man stopped eating and grabbed my jacket.

"What did the man look like?" he asked me fiercely.[173]

"He...he was dressed like you and...he had an iron on his leg", I answered. "And there was a long scar[174] on his face."

"Was there?" the convict cried. "So he's escaped from the Hulks, has he? I thought I heard the guns last night. Where is he? I must find him. Curse[175] this iron on my leg. Give me that file, boy. And tell me where you saw him."

I pointed to where I had seen the young man. The convict stared through the mist. Then, sitting down on the wet grass, he began to file[176] at the heavy iron on his leg.

---

[173] fierce=angry and aggressive in a way that is frightening 사나운, 험악한
[174] scar=a mark that is left on the skin after a wound has healed (피부에 생긴) 흉터
[175] to curse=to use a magic word or phrase against sb. in order to harm them 저주를 내리다

The sky was lighter[177] now and I dared[178] not stay[179] any longer. My sister and Joe would soon be awake.[180] They would be looking for me. I began to walk quietly away.

When I looked back, the convict was bent[181] over, filing at the iron on his leg. When I looked back again, I could see nothing through the thick mist. But I could still[182] hear the sound of the file as it cut through the heavy leg-iron.[183]

---

[176] to file=to cut or shape sth. or make sth. smooth using a file (줄로) 다듬다
[177] light=full of light; having the natural light of day (날이) 밝은; (빛이) 밝은/환한
[178] to dare=to be brave enough to do sth. …할 용기가 있다, 감히 …하다, …할 엄두를 내다
[179] to stay=to continue to be in a particular place for a period of time without moving away (다른 곳에 가지 않고) 계속/그대로 있다/머무르다/남다
[180] awake=not asleep (esp. immediately before or after sleeping) (아직) 잠들지 않은, 깨어 있는
[181] to bend=move sth. so that it is no longer straight *bent-bent* 굽히다/굽혀지다
[182] still=continuing until a particular point in time and not finishing 아직(도) (계속해서)
[183] 두려움 때문이기도 하지만 탈옥수임을 알면서도 약속을 지키는 핍의 모습에서 어린 핍의 순수한 도덕적 감수성을 엿볼 수 있는데 이 경험으로 핍은 내내 죄의식을 안고 살게 된다.

Chapter TWO

Christmas Day

When I got home, Mrs Joe was too busy preparing our Christmas dinner to ask me questions. I sat down quietly by Joe.

Our dinner[1] was to be[2] at half past one. Long before that, I was scrubbed[3] clean by Mrs Joe and dressed in my best clothes. It was my job to open the door to our guests—three of our neighbours, and Uncle Pumblechook.

---

[1] dinner=the main meal of the day, eaten either in the middle of the day or in the evening (하루 중에 먹는 가장 주된) 식사; 정식
[2] to be to=to be going to …로 예정되다
[3] to scrub=to clean sth. by rubbing it hard, perhaps with a brush and usually with soap and water 문질러 씻다; 청소하다

Uncle Pumblechook was a fat, stupid man with hair that stood up on his head. He greatly admired[4] my sister but thought very little of Joe and myself.[5] He had brought two bottles of wine and he gave them to Mrs Joe with a bow and a smile.[6]

Everyone was soon eating and drinking happily. Everyone except me. I was terrified.[7] Was Mrs Joe going to serve[8] the pie today? When would she discover[9] it was missing?[10]

Dinner seemed to be finished, when my sister suddenly spoke to Joe.

---

[4] to admire=to respect sb. for what they are or for what they have done 존경하다; 칭찬하다

[5] to think poorly/little of sb./sth.=to have a very poor/little opinion of sb./sth. …을 무시/경시하다

[6] bow=the act of bending your head or the upper part of your body forward in order to say hello or goodbye to sb. or to show respect 절, (고개 숙여 하는) 인사

[7] to terrify=to make sb. feel extremely frightened (몹시) 무섭게/겁먹게 하다

[8] to serve=to give sb. food or drink, for example at a restaurant or during a meal (식당 등에서 음식을) 제공하다; (음식을 상에) 차려 주다/내다

[9] to discover=to find out about sth.; to find some information about sth. (무엇에 대한 정보를) 찾다/알아내다

[10] missing=that cannot be found or that is not in its usual place, or at home (제자리나 집에 있지 않고) 없어진/실종된

"Fetch[11] clean plates!" she ordered.[12] I held on tight to[13] the table leg. I knew what was going to happen.[14]

My sister smiled at her guests.

"And now you must all taste[15] another gift from Uncle Pumblechook", she said. "It's a delicious[16] meat pie!"

"Well, Mrs Joe, this has been a wonderful meal", Uncle Pumblechook said happily. "But I think I could[17] eat a slice[18] of that meat pie!"

My sister hurried[19] into the pantry and Uncle Pumblechook picked up his knife and fork.

---

[11] to fetch=to go to where sb./sth. is and bring them/it back (어디를 가서) 가지고/데리고/불러오다

[12] to order=to use your position of authority to tell sb. to do sth. or say that sth. must happen 명령/지시하다

[13] to hold on to sth./sb.=to keep holding sth./sb. …을 계속 잡고 있다

[14] to happen=to take place (일이) 있다/일어나다/발생하다/벌어지다

[15] to taste=to eat or drink food or liquid 먹다; 마시다

[16] delicious=having a very pleasant taste or smell 아주 맛있는, 냄새가 좋은/구수한

[17] "could" – used to show that sth. is or might be possible …일/할 수 있다 (가능성이 있음을 나타냄)

[18] slice=a thin flat piece of food that has been cut off a larger piece (음식을 얇게 썬) 조각

[19] to hurry=to move quickly in a particular direction (특정 방향으로) 급히/서둘러 가다

"You shall[20] have a slice of pie, Pip", Joe whispered to me. I could not sit there any longer. Did I cry out or not? I can't remember. But I jumped up and ran towards the front door. At the same moment, Mrs Joe came back from the pantry.

"What's happened to the meat pie?" she cried.

I opened the door and ran—straight into[21] a group of soldiers.[22] Their leader, a sergeant,[23] was holding out[24] a pair of handcuffs![25]

"Now then, young man!" the sergeant said sharply, as he marched[26] into our kitchen.

---

[20] "shall" – used to talk about or predict the future ···일/할 것이다 (미래에 대해 말하거나 미래를 예측함을 나타냄)

[21] to run into sb./sth.=to crash into sb./sth.; to meet sb. by chance *ran-run* ···을/에 들이받다/충돌하다; ···를/와 우연히 만나다/마주치다

[22] soldier=a member of an army, esp. one who is not an officer 군인, 병사

[23] sergeant=a member of one of the middle ranks in the army and the air force, below an officer 부사관

[24] to hold out=to put your hand or arms, or sth. in your hand, towards sb., esp. to give or offer sth. *held-held* 내밀다

[25] handcuffs=a pair of metal rings joined by a chain, used for holding the wrists of a prisoner together 수갑

[26] to march=to walk somewhere quickly in a determined way (단호한 태도로 급히) 걸어가다

"Excuse[27] me, ladies and gentlemen", he went on. "We're chasing[28] escaped convicts and we need the blacksmith."

"What do you want him for?" my sister asked in surprise.

"Well, I'd like to stay and talk to his charming[29] wife", the sergeant replied. "But today we're busy with[30] the King's business.[31] We need the blacksmith to do a little job for us."

Joe stood up and the sergeant held out[32] the handcuffs.

"There's something wrong with these, blacksmith", the sergeant said. "We need them today, so I'd like you to mend[33] them."

Joe took the handcuffs in his great hand.

---

[27] to excuse=to forgive sb. for sth. that they have done, for example not being polite or making a small mistake (무례나 작은 실수 등을) 용서하다/봐주다

[28] to chase=to run, drive, etc. after sb./sth. in order to catch them 뒤쫓다; 추적하다

[29] charming=very pleasant or attractive 매력적인, 멋진

[30] busy with sth./busy doing sth.=spending a lot of time on sth.; having a lot to do; perhaps not free to do sth. else because you are working on sth. (…하느라) 바쁜, (…에) 열심인; (할 일이 많아) 바쁜

[31] King's business=public service 공무

[32] to hold sth. out=to put your hand or arms, or sth. in your hand, towards sb., esp. to give or offer sth. *held-held* 내밀다

[33] to mend=to repair sth. that has been damaged or broken so that it can be used 수리하다, 고치다

"I'll have to light³⁴ the fire in the forge", he said. "This job will take³⁵ about two hours."

"That'll be all right", the sergeant answered. "We're sure that the convicts are still on the marshes. We'll capture³⁶ them before it's dark. No one has seen them, I suppose?"³⁷

Everyone except me shook their heads.³⁸ No one thought of asking me.

Joe took off³⁹ his coat and got ready⁴⁰ for work. With the soldiers' help, the forge fire was soon burning fiercely. As Joe hammered the white-hot⁴¹ iron, we all stood round and watched him.

---

34 to light=to make sth. start to burn 불을 붙이다/켜다
35 to take=to need or require a particular amount of time *took-taken* (얼마의 시간이) 걸리다
36 to capture=to catch a person or an animal and keep them as a prisoner or in a confined space 포로로 잡다, 억류하다; 포획하다
37 to suppose=to think or believe that sth. is true or possible (based on the knowledge that you have) (이미 알고 있는 지식에 의거하여 …일 것이라고) 생각/추정/추측하다
38 to shake your head=to turn your head from side to side as a way of saying "no" or to show sadness, disapproval, doubt, etc. (부정/반대/의혹 등의 의미로) 고개를 흔들다/젓다
39 to take off=to remove sth., esp. a piece of clothing from your/sb.'s body *took-taken* (옷 등을) 벗다/벗기다
40 ready=fully prepared for what you are going to do (사람이) 준비가 (다) 된
41 white-hot=so hot that it looks white (금속 등이) 백열 상태의

Mrs Joe gave the soldiers some beer. Uncle Pumblechook poured[42] out wine for the sergeant and then poured some for everyone else. Even I got a little wine.

We stood in the forge, laughing and talking. I thought sadly of the two convicts, cold and hungry[43] on the marshes.

At last the handcuffs were mended. Joe asked the sergeant if he could follow[44] the soldiers while they searched for the convicts.

"Certainly,[45] blacksmith. Bring the boy with you, if you like", the sergeant answered.

"Well", my sister said sharply, "if he gets his head shot off, don't ask me to mend it."[46]

Joe lifted me up onto his broad shoulders. As we began to follow the soldiers, I whispered in his ear.

"I hope, Joe, that we don't find them!"

---

[42] to pour=to make a liquid or other substance flow from a container in a continuous stream, esp. by holding the container at an angle (특히 그릇을 비스듬히 기울이고) 붓다/따르다

[43] cold and hungry=who were cold and hungry

[44] to follow=to come or go after or behind sb./sth. (…의 뒤를) 따라가다/오다

[45] certainly=of course (질문에 대한 대답으로) 그럼요; 물론이지요

[46] 핍이 "총을 맞아 머리가 날아가더라도 날더러 수선해 달라고 하지는 말라"는 말로 가저리 부인의 험한 성격을 잘 보여준다.

And Joe whispered back. "Let's hope they've got away, Pip old chap."[47]

It was dark now. On our way[48] to the marshes, the bitter wind blew icy rain into our faces.

The group of soldiers moved quickly. We went at a fast pace,[49] sometimes stumbling[50] on the rough ground, sometimes falling. At last we were on the marshes, splashing[51] in and out of the ditches full of icy water.

Suddenly, we heard a shout.[52] We stopped and listened. The shout was repeated and then we heard another.

The sergeant sent us to the right. On we ran, even faster, splashing through ditches, up and down steep[53] banks.[54]

---

[47] 가저리와 핍은 심정적으로 약자의 편을 드는 선량한 사람들임을 보여주는 장면으로 바로 앞의 가저리 부인의 위협적인 농담과 대비가 된다.
[48] on your/the/its way=going or coming 가는/오는 (중인)
[49] pace=the speed at which sb./sth. walks, runs or moves (걸음/달리기/움직임의) 속도
[50] to stumble=to hit your foot against sth. while you are walking or running and almost fall 발이 걸리다; 발을 헛디디다
[51] to splash=to move through water making drops fly everywhere (물 속에서) 첨벙거리다
[52] shout=a loud cry of anger, fear, excitement, etc. 외침, 고함 (소리)
[53] steep=rising or falling quickly, not gradually (경사면/언덕 등이) 가파른; 비탈진
[54] bank=the side of a river, canal, etc. and the land near it 둑, 제방

And now we could hear that two men were shouting.[55]

"Murder!"[56] one cried.

"Convicts! This way for the escaped convicts!" shouted the other.

The two men were fighting at the bottom of a ditch. They were splashing in the muddy water. The men were cursing[57] and hitting out[58] at each other.

When the soldiers pulled the men from the ditch, both of the convicts were torn and bleeding.[59]

My convict wiped[60] the blood from his face with his torn sleeve.[61]

"I caught this man! I'm giving him to you!" he cried. "Don't forget that. I caught him for you!"

---

[55] to shout=to say sth. in a loud voice; to speak loudly/angrily to sb. 외치다, 소리/고함치다; 소리 지르다, 큰 소리로 말하다
[56] murder=the crime of killing sb. deliberately 살인
[57] to curse=to swear 욕(설)을 하다
[58] to hit out=to direct blows forcefully and vigorously *hit-hit* 맹공격하다
[59] to bleed=to lose blood, esp. from a wound or an injury *bled-bled* 피를 흘리다; 피가 나다
[60] to wipe=to remove dirt, liquid, etc. from sth. by using a cloth, your hand, etc. (어디에 묻은 먼지/물기 등을) 닦다/훔치다
[61] sleeve=a part of a piece of clothing that covers all or part of your arm 소매

"That won't help you", the sergeant answered, as the two convicts were handcuffed.[62]

"I don't expect it to help me. I caught him and that's enough for me", my convict answered.

The other convict's clothes were torn and his face was bloody. But I could still see the scar on his cheek.[63]

"He tried[64] to murder me, sergeant!" the young man said.

"Tried?" my convict repeated. "Do you think I would try and not succeed?[65] No, I caught him and held him here. I could have escaped, but I wouldn't let this gentleman[66] get away. He tricked[67] me once. I'll not let him trick me again!"

"He tried to murder me", the other man repeated weakly.

---

[62] to handcuff=to put handcuffs on sb. or to fasten sb. to sth./sb. with handcuffs 수갑을 채우다

[63] cheek=either side of the face below the eyes 볼, 뺨

[64] to try=to make an attempt or effort to do or get sth. 노력하다, 애를 쓰다, (애를 써서) 하려고/이루려고 하다

[65] to succeed=to achieve sth. that you have been trying to do or get; to have the result or effect that was intended (하려던 일에) 성공하다

[66] gentleman=a man who is polite and well educated, who has excellent manners and always behaves well 신사

[67] to trick=to make sb. believe sth. which is not true, esp. in order to cheat them 속이다; 속임수를 쓰다

"He's lying. He always was a liar",[68] my convict answered. "We were put on trial[69] together and he lied at the trial. He was scared of me then and he's scared of me now.[70] Look at him! Look at the gentleman convict, shaking with fear!"

"That's enough!" the sergeant said. "Light the torches[71] there!" he shouted to the soldiers.

It was very dark now. There was no moon. In the light of the torches, my convict turned and saw me for the first time.[72]

"Wait a minute", my convict said to the sergeant. "I wish to say something. I don't want anyone to be blamed[73] for what I did. A man must eat. I took drink and food from the village. I took bread, cheese, brandy and a meat pie. From the blacksmith's house."

"Has a pie been stolen from you?" the sergeant asked Joe.

---

[68] liar=a person who tells lies 거짓말쟁이
[69] trial=a formal examination of evidence in court by a judge and often a jury, to decide if sb. accused of a crime is guilty or not 재판
[70] to be scared of=to be afraid of 두려워하다, 겁내다
[71] torch=a long piece of wood that has material at one end that is set on fire and that people carry to give light 횃불
[72] 핍과 매그위치는 이제 공범자로서 죄의식과 함께 인간적 유대로 엮이게 된다.
[73] to blame=to think or say that sb./sth. is responsible for sth. bad …을 탓하다; …의 책임으로 보다

"Yes, my wife found out it was missing—at the very moment you came in", Joe answered. "That's right, isn't it, Pip?"

"Then I'm very sorry[74] I ate your pie, blacksmith", the convict said, not looking at me.

"You're welcome[75] to it, poor miserable[76] fellow", Joe said kindly. "We don't know what you've done, but we wouldn't want you to starve,[77] would we, Pip?"

The convict wiped his torn sleeve across his eyes and turned away. Joe and I watched as the two men were led away towards the sea and the prison ships.[78]

Days later, when I saw Joe looking for his file in the forge, I nearly told him the truth. But I was a coward[79] and too afraid of what he would think of me.[80]

---

[74] sorry=feeling sad and ashamed about sth. that has been done 유감스러운, 남부끄러운, 미안한

[75] welcome=accepted or wanted somewhere 환영 받는

[76] miserable=very unhappy or uncomfortable 비참한

[77] to starve=to suffer or die because you do not have enough food to eat; to make sb. suffer or die in this way 굶주리다, 굶어 죽다; 굶기다, 굶겨 죽이다

[78] 핍과 탈옥수의 조우와 더불어 두 번째 탈옥수에 대한 언급을 통해 이제 붙잡혀 사라지는 그들이 언젠가 핍의 삶 가운데로 다시 찾아올 것임을 예시한다.

[79] coward=a person who is not brave or who does not have the courage to do things that other people do not think are esp. difficult 겁쟁이; 비겁자

[80] 이렇게 디킨즈는 어린 핍이 소극적인 거짓말을 하고 죄의식에 시달리는 모습을 그린다. 이 죄와 벌의 주제는 후일 핍이 갖게 되는 신분상승의 욕구와 도덕적 의무감 사이의 갈등으로 계속된다.

Chapter THREE

At Miss Havisham's

One evening, about two years later, Joe and I were sitting together by the fire. Mrs Joe had gone to town with Uncle Pumblechook in the pony-cart.[1]
I had learnt to read and write a little and Joe was very proud of me.[2] I was trying to teach him the alphabet. But the only letters he could recognise[3] were J, O, and E.[4]

---

[1] pony-cart=a cart with an underslung axle and two seats 이인승 마차

[2] proud=feeling pleased and satisfied about sth. that you own or have done, or are connected with 자랑스러워하는; 자랑스러운

[3] to recognise=to know who sb. is or what sth. is when you see or hear them, because you have seen or heard them or it before 누구/무엇인지 (알아보다)

"I think it's too late for me to learn, Pip old chap", Joe said sadly. "I never went to school. My mother wanted me to go to school but my father would not let me. He was a hard man, Pip. My father was a blacksmith. He kept me away from school and made me work for him.[5] He was cruel[6] to my mother and often beat[7] her."

"That's why I let your sister do what she wants", Joe explained. "She's hard on[8] you, I know, Pip, but she has a good heart. She looked after[9] you when your mother and father died. She was looking after you when she agreed[10] to marry me. 'Bring the poor little child,' I told her. 'There's room[11] at the forge for him.'"

---

4 일자무식의 가저리가 어린 처남이 글을 깨친 것을 자랑스럽게 여기는 이야기를 통해 당대의 서민들의 실상과 함께 핍이 곧 품게 될 자기개선에의 욕망을 암시한다.

5 to work for sb.=to be employed by sb. …에게 고용되다

6 cruel=having a desire to cause pain and suffering 잔혹한, 잔인한

7 to beat=to hit sb./sth. many times, usually very hard *beat-beaten* (아주 세게 계속) 때리다/두드리다

8 to be hard on sb./sth.=to treat or criticise sb. in a very severe or strict way …을 심하게 대하다/나무라다

9 to look after=to be responsible for or to take care of sb./sth. …을 맡다, 돌보다/건사하다

10 to agree=to have the same opinion as sb.; to say that you have the same opinion 동의하다

11 room=empty space that can be used for a particular purpose (특정 목적을 위한) 자리/공간

I began to cry and to thank Joe for his kindness. I knew what a good friend he was to me.

It was now eight o'clock and dark outside. Joe put more coal on the fire. We stood by the door and listened for the sound of Uncle Pumblechook's pony-cart.

Not long afterwards, my sister and Uncle Pumblechook arrived. They stood and warmed themselves by our kitchen fire. As Mrs Joe took off her bonnet[12] and shawl,[13] she looked at me sharply.

"Well, this boy should be grateful[14] to me now", she cried.

Joe and I looked at each other in surprise.

"Quite right, quite right", Uncle Pumblechook replied. "He should be grateful for the opportunity[15] she's giving him!"

Joe and I were even more surprised.

"Well, what are you staring at?" Mrs Joe snapped. Her face was redder than ever with the cold.

---

[12] bonnet=a hat tied with strings under the chin, worn by babies and, esp. in the past, by women 보닛 (아기들이나 예전에 여자들이 쓰던 끈을 턱 밑에서 묶게 되어 있는 모자)

[13] shawl=a large piece of cloth worn by a woman around the shoulders or head, or wrapped around a baby 숄

[14] grateful=feeling or showing thanks because sb. has done sth. kind for you or has done as you asked 고마워하는

[15] opportunity=a time when a particular situation makes it possible to do or achieve sth. 기회

"A 'she' was mentioned..."[16] Joe began politely.

"Miss Havisham isn't a 'he,' I suppose", my sister answered sharply.

"Miss Havisham who lives in town?" Joe asked in surprise. "How does Miss Havisham know Pip? She never leaves[17] her house, does she?"

"She doesn't know Pip, but she does know Uncle Pumblechook", Mrs Joe explained impatiently. "She wants a boy to go to her house and play. Uncle Pumblechook kindly mentioned this boy here. So he's going back to town with Uncle Pumblechook tonight. And tomorrow he'll play at Miss Havisham's, or I'll play with him!"[18]

Without another word, Mrs Joe grabbed hold of me with her bony hands. She washed and scrubbed me until I could hardly[19]

---

[16] to mention=to write or speak about sth./sb., esp. without giving much information (말/글로 간단히) 말하다, 언급/거론하다

[17] to leave=to go away from a person or a place *left-left* (사람/장소에서) 떠나다/출발하다

[18] "내일 해비샴의 집에 가서 놀지 않으면 나와 함께 놀게 될 것이다"라는 말은 "내가 벌을 주겠다"는 위협조의 농담이다.

[19] "hardly" – used esp. after *can* or *could* and before the main verb, to emphasise that it is difficult to do sth. (특히 can/could와 본동사 사이에 쓰여) 거의 …할 수가 없다/…하기가 무척 어렵다

breathe.[20] Then I was dressed in my best clothes and given to Uncle Pumblechook.

"Goodbye, Joe!" I cried, as I was pushed out of the door by Mrs Joe.

"Goodbye and God bless you, Pip old chap!" Joe answered. In a moment, I was sitting in Uncle Pumblechook's pony-cart and we were on our way to town.[21]

At ten o'clock the next morning, Uncle Pumblechook drove me to Satis[22] House where Miss Havisham lived.[23]

---

[20] to breathe=to take air into your lungs and send it out again through your nose or mouth 호흡하다, 숨을 쉬다

[21] 가저리 부인과 펌블축 삼촌은 부유한 귀부인인 해비샴과의 인연에 사뭇 들떠 있으나 정작 핍 자신은 자신에게 어떤 일이 벌어질지 또 그것이 앞으로의 삶에 어떤 영향을 미치게 될 지도 전혀 모른다. 또한 디킨즈는 여기서 야망과 자기만족에 사로잡혀 있는 두 사람과는 대조적으로 가난하지만 단순하고 정직하게 사는 가저리의 모습을 함께 보여줌으로써 사회계급의 문제를 거론하기 시작한다.

[22] 'Satis'는 '충분하다(enough)'는 뜻이다.

[23] 핍은 해비샴과의 만남으로 자신을 둘러싸고 있는 암울한 현실로부터 벗어나 신분의 상승을 이루고자 하는 열망을 품게 되는 운명적인 계기를 맞는다.

The house was very big and gloomy.²⁴ The tall iron gates in front of the house were locked. Uncle Pumblechook rang the bell and we waited.

In a few minutes, a beautifully dressed girl came across the paved²⁵ courtyard²⁶ towards us. She was very pretty and she looked very proud.²⁷

"What name?" the young lady asked.

"Pumblechook. And this is Pip", Uncle Pumblechook answered politely.²⁸

"This is Pip, is it?" the girl said, looking at me scornfully.²⁹

"Come in, Pip."

---

24 gloomy=nearly dark, or badly lit in a way that makes you feel sad 어둑어둑한; 음울한
25 to pave=to cover a surface with flat stones or bricks (돌/벽돌 등으로) 포장하다
26 courtyard=an open space that is partly or completely surrounded by buildings and is usually part of a castle, a large house, etc. (성/저택 등에서 건물에 둘러싸인) 뜰; 마당
27 proud=feeling that you are better and more important than other people 오만한, 거만한
28 polite=having or showing good manners and respect for the feelings of others 예의 바른, 공손한, 정중한
29 scornful=showing or feeling usually shown by the way you speak that sb./sth. is stupid or not good enough 경멸하는

The girl was carrying a large bunch[30] of keys. She unlocked the gate with one of them and held[31] the gate open. I went in and Uncle Pumblechook started to follow. But the girl stopped him.

"Do you wish to see Miss Havisham?" she asked.

"If Miss Havisham wishes to see me..." Uncle Pumblechook began.

"But she doesn't", the girl said sharply. "Come along,[32] boy."

She locked the gate and led me across the courtyard. It was clean, but grass grew between the stones, as though no one ever walked there. I saw now that the girl was about my age. But she was so beautiful and so proud that she seemed much older.

The big front door had chains across it. We walked on to a side door and the girl opened it.

Inside the house everything was dark. The curtains were drawn[33] and the shutters[34] were closed on all the windows. The girl picked

---

[30] bunch=a number of things of the same type which are growing or fastened together 다발, 송이, 묶음

[31] to hold=to keep sb./sth. in a particular position *held-held* (일정한 위치/상태에 그대로) 두다

[32] to come along=to hurry or to try harder (명령형으로) 서둘러; 힘 내

[33] to draw=to open or close curtains, etc. *drew-drawn* (커튼 등을) 걷다, 열다; 치다, 닫다

[34] shutter=one of a pair of wooden or metal covers that can be closed over the

up a burning candle and this was our only light. She led me along several dark passages[35] and up a wide staircase.[36] At last, we came to a door where the girl stopped.

"Go in", she said.

"After you,[37] miss",[38] I whispered politely.

"Don't be silly, I'm not going in!" the girl answered. And she walked away, taking the candle with her.

Feeling very afraid, I knocked at the door.

"Come in", a woman's voice said quietly.

I opened the door slowly and went inside. I looked around me in the greatest surprise.

The room was large and full of furniture.[39] But heavy curtains shut out[40] the daylight[41] and the room was lit[42] only by candles.

---

outside of a window to keep out light or protect the windows from damage 덧문, 셔터

[35] passage=a long narrow area with walls on either side that connects one room or place with another 통로, 복도

[36] staircase=a set of stairs inside a building including the posts and rails that are fixed at the side (건물 내부에 난간으로 죽 이어져 있는) 계단

[37] After you.=Please go first. 먼저 가세요.

[38] "miss" – used esp. by men to address a young woman when they do not know her name (남자가 이름을 모르는 젊은 여자를 부를 때) 아가씨

[39] furniture=objects that can be moved, such as tables, chairs and beds, that are put into a house or an office to make it suitable for living or working in 가구

[40] to shut out=to prevent sb./sth. from entering a place shut-shut ⋯을 못 들어가게 하다; 차단하다

I saw that I was in a lady's dressing-room.⁴³ And at the dressing-table⁴⁴ sat the strangest lady I had ever seen.

She was dressed richly,⁴⁵ in satin⁴⁶ and lace⁴⁷ clothes, and everything she wore⁴⁸ was white. A long white wedding veil⁴⁹ hung⁵⁰ down from her head. I saw with surprise that the lady's hair was white, too. She wore bright jewels and there were other jewels⁵¹ lying⁵² on the table in front of her. One of her shoes lay on the floor.⁵³ The other one was lying on the dressing-table.

---

41 daylight=the light that comes from the sun during the day (낮의) 햇빛, 일광
42 to light=to make sth. start to burn *lit-lit* 불을 붙이다/켜다
43 dressing-room=a small room next to a bedroom in some large houses, in which clothes are kept and people get dressed (침실 옆에 딸린) 옷방
44 dressing-table=a piece of bedroom furniture like a table with drawers and a mirror on top 화장대
45 richly=in a beautiful and expensive manner 호화롭게, 화려하게
46 satin=a type of cloth with a smooth shiny surface 새틴
47 lace=a delicate material made from threads of cotton, silk, etc. that are twisted into a pattern of holes 레이스
48 to wear=to have sth. on your body as a piece of clothing, a decoration, etc. *wore-worn* (옷/모자/장갑/신발/장신구 등을) 입고/쓰고/끼고/신고/착용하고 있다
49 veil=a covering of very thin transparent material worn, esp. by women, to protect or hide the face, or as part of a hat, etc. 베일, 면사포
50 to hang=to fall loosely *hung-hung* (느슨하게) 내려오다/처지다
51 jewel=a precious stone such as a diamond, ruby, etc. 보석
52 to lie=to be or remain in a flat position on a surface *lay-lain* 놓여 있다
53 floor=all the rooms that are on the same level of a building (건물의) 층

Her elbow[54] was on the dressing-table and she was resting[55] her face on her hand.

Trunks[56] full of clothes were placed about the room. Each one contained[57] many silk[58] and satin dresses. But the dresses were faded[59] and torn.

And then I saw that everything that had once been white was now faded and yellow. The fair[60] young bride[61] was now an old woman whose skin was yellow and wrinkled. Only her dark eyes showed that she was alive.[62]

Then the lady moved and those dark eyes stared at me.

"Who is it?" she asked.

"Pip, ma'am.[63] Mr Pumblechook's boy. I've come to play."

---

[54] elbow=the joint between the upper and lower parts of the arm where it bends in the middle 팔꿈치

[55] to rest=to support sth. by putting it on or against sth.; to be supported in this way (어떤 것에) 받치다/기대다; 받쳐지다/기대지다

[56] trunk=a large strong box with a lid used for storing or transporting clothes, books, etc. 트렁크 (옷, 책 등을 담는 큰 가방)

[57] to contain=to have sth. inside or as a part (무엇의 안에 또는 그 일부로) …이 들어/함유되어 있다

[58] silk=a type of fine smooth cloth made from silk thread 비단

[59] to fade=to become or to make sth. become paler or less bright (색깔이) 바래다/희미해지다; 바래게/희미해지게 만들다

[60] fair=beautiful 어여쁜

[61] bride=a woman on her wedding day, or just before or just after it 신부

[62] alive=living; not dead 살아 있는

[63] "ma'am" – used as a polite way of addressing a woman (여성을 정중히 부르는 말) 부인

"Come here. Let me look at you", the lady said.

I moved nearer, but I was afraid to look at her. Then I saw that a watch on the dressing-table had stopped at twenty to nine.

"Are you afraid to look at me?" the lady asked me slowly. "Are you afraid to look at a woman who hasn't seen the sun shine since before you were born?

"Look here", Miss Havisham whispered, touching her heart. "My heart is broken, broken. And I am so tired...[64] But I thought I would like to see a child play...So play, boy, play!"

I stood there, unable to move, not knowing what to do.

"Call Estella", Miss Havisham said at last. "Go to the door and call her."[65]

I was afraid, but I had to do what she asked. So I opened the door. I called out[66] several times, then I saw the girl walking towards me, the candle in her hand.

---

[64] tired=feeling that you would like to sleep or rest; needing rest 피로한, 피곤한, 지친

[65] 해비샴과 그녀의 집의 괴이한 모습을 묘사하는 이 부분이 대표적으로 희비극적(tragi-comic)이며 괴이한(grotesque) '디킨즈적인' 표현이다. 디킨즈는 웅장한 새티스 하우스의 묘사를 통해 핍뿐만 아니라 당시 서민층이 가지고 있는 상류사회에 대한 낭만적 인식을 보여준다. 더불어 그가 보여주는 그 저택의 거주자인 해비샴과 에스텔라의 괴이하고 잔인한 실상은 변화를 거부한 채 죽음과 부패를 안고 살아가는 당대의 지배계급 전체를 상징한다.

[66] to call out=to ask sb. to come, esp. to an emergency (특히 위급한 상황에서) …를 부르다; 호출하다

Miss Havisham smiled as the beautiful girl came into the room. She held a jewel against Estella's pretty brown hair.

"My jewels will be yours one day", Miss Havisham said quietly. "Now I want you to play cards with this boy."

"This boy? But he's so common!"[67] Estella exclaimed. "Look at his clothes. He's just a common working boy!"

"Never mind", Miss Havisham whispered. "You can break his heart, can't you?"

So I played cards with Estella. When I made mistakes,[68] she laughed at[69] me and so, of course, I made more.

"What rough hands this boy has!" Estella exclaimed, as I held the cards. "And what heavy boots he's wearing!"

"Why don't you answer her, Pip?" Miss Havisham said at last. "She says cruel things about you. What do you think of her?"

---

[67] common=typical of sb. from a low social class and not having good manners 천한; 저속한

[68] mistake=an action or an opinion that is not correct, or that produces a result that you did not want 실수, 잘못

[69] to laugh at sb./sth.=to make sb./sth. seem stupid or not serious by making jokes about them/it …을 비웃다/놀리다

"I don't want to say", I replied.[70]

"Whisper to me", Miss Havisham said, bending down.

"I think she is very proud", I said quietly.

"Yes, and what else?"

"I think she is very pretty", I went on.

"Anything else?"

"I think she is very rude.[71] And please", I added, "I should like to go home now."

"Finish your game of cards first", Miss Havisham said.

When Estella had won[72] the last game, she threw the cards down with a scornful smile.

"Come here again in six days, Pip", Miss Havisham said as I was leaving. "Take him downstairs, Estella. Give him something to eat and drink before he goes."[73]

---

[70] 여기서 핍은 에스텔라의 조롱에 대답하지 않겠다고 함으로써 그녀의 말에 동의한다. 이제 그는 계급의 차이를 분명한 현실로 받아들이고 신분상승을 꿈꾸기 시작한다.

[71] rude=having or showing a lack of respect for other people and their feelings 무례한, 예의 없는, 버릇없는

[72] to win=to be the most successful in a competition, race, battle, etc. *won-won* 이기다

[73] 여기서 디킨즈는 본격적으로 사회계급, 야망, 자기개선 등의 주제를 전면에 부각한다. 부모의 묘비 근처를 맴돌던 모습에서 볼 수 있었던 핍의 낭만적 감수성은 이제 새티스 하우스를 중심으로 전개되는데 아름답지만 잔인하고 왜곡된 성품의 에스텔라와 정체를 알 수 없는 해비샴의 기괴한 외양은 이 소설의 전개 방향을 암시해 준다.

I followed Estella down the gloomy stairs and along the dark corridors.[74] She opened the side door and the bright daylight hurt[75] my eyes and confused[76] me.

Estella told me to wait in the courtyard. In a few minutes, she returned with some meat and bread. She placed the food on the ground, as though I was a dog. Tears[77] came into my eyes. I turned my head away, so that Estella would not see me crying. But when she had gone, I cried aloud and kicked the wall with the heavy boots she had laughed at.

After a time, Estella returned with her keys and unlocked the iron gate.

"Why aren't you crying?" she asked me with a smile.

"Because I don't want to", I replied.

"Yes, you do", she said. "Your eyes are red with crying.[78] You are nearly crying now."

---

[74] corridor=a long narrow passage in a building, with doors that open into rooms on either side 복도, 회랑

[75] to hurt=to cause physical pain to sb./yourself; to injure sb./yourself hurt-hurt 다치게/아프게 하다

[76] to confuse=to make sb. unable to think clearly or understand sth. (사람을) 혼란케 하다

[77] tear=a drop of liquid that comes from your eye when you cry 눈물, 울음

[78] with=because of; as a result of …때문에, …의 결과로

She laughed, pushed me outside the gate and locked it behind me.

I went straight[79] back to Uncle Pumblechook's, but he was not at home. So I began the long walk back to the forge alone.

As I walked along, I thought about the strange things I had seen.

I thought of Estella and her scorn.[80] She had made me ashamed of my clothes, my boots and most of all, myself. I wished I had never seen her.[81] But then I remembered how beautiful she was.[82]

---

[79] straight=by a direct route; immediately 곧장, 곧바로
[80] scorn=a strong feeling that sb./sth. is stupid or not good enough, usually shown by the way you speak 경멸/멸시(감)
[81] 가정법 과거완료로 후회를 나타낸다.
[82] 핍은 에스텔라의 미모와 신분상승에 대한 막연한 기대로 해비샴이 자신에게 고통을 안겨주기 위해 에스텔라를 이용한다는 것을 모르고 있다.

Chapter FOUR

The Pale Young Gentleman

When I got home, my sister made me sit on a stool[1] and began asking me questions.

"Tell me what Miss Havisham looks like", my sister demanded.[2] "What did she say to you? What did you do?"

---

[1] stool=a seat with legs but with nothing to support your back or arms (등받이와 팔걸이가 없는) 의자
[2] to demand=to ask for sth. very firmly 요구하다; 따지다

"Miss Havisham's very tall and dark", I answered quickly. "She was sitting in a black velvet³ coach.⁴ There was a girl with her. She gave us cake on gold plates!"

"Gold plates!" Mrs Joe repeated slowly. Then she added, "I hope you pleased⁵ her. She wanted you to play. Did you?"

"Oh, yes. We played with...with flags", I said. "And then we shouted and waved our swords!"

"Swords?"

"Yes. The girl—Estella—got them from a cupboard.⁶ And there was no daylight in the room, only candles!"

Joe's eyes opened very wide.

Why was I telling all these lies? I do not know. Perhaps the truth was too strange. My visit to Miss Havisham had confused and frightened me.

---

⁴ coach=a large closed vehicle with four wheels, pulled by horses, used in the past for carrying passengers 대형 사륜마차

⁵ to please=to make sb. happy (남을) 기쁘게 하다, 기분/비위를 맞추다

⁶ cupboard=a space in a wall with a door that reaches the ground, used for storing things (문이 바닥까지 닿는) 벽장

⁷ 핍은 새티스 하우스의 경험을 통해 사회계급을 인식하게 되면서 신분상승을 갈망한다. 이전에는 늪지대에서 우연히 만난 탈옥수를 무서워하면서도 불쌍하게 여겨 위험을 무릅쓰고 도와줬지만 이제는 자신을 사랑하는 가저리마저 부끄럽게 생각한다.

⁸ to follow=to come after sth./sb. else in time or order; to happen as a result of sth. else (시간/순서상으로) 뒤를 잇다; (결과로) 뒤따르다

And Estella's words had hurt me. She had called me a common working boy. What would she think of Joe? How heavy his boots were!⁷

The following⁸ week, I walked to Miss Havisham's alone. As before, Estella unlocked the gate and took me into the house.

"Am I pretty?" she said suddenly, holding up⁹ the candle.

"Yes, very pretty", I answered.

"Am I rude?"

"Not so rude as last time."

"Not so rude?" Estella repeated angrily. And she slapped¹⁰ my face hard.

"What do you think now?" she asked.

---

7 핍은 새티스 하우스의 경험을 통해 사회계급을 인식하게 되면서 신분상승을 갈망한다. 이전에는 늪지대에서 우연히 만난 탈옥수를 무서워하면서도 불쌍하게 여겨 위험을 무릅쓰고 도와줬지만 이제는 자신을 사랑하는 가저리마저 부끄럽게 생각한다.

8 to follow=to come after sth./sb. else in time or order; to happen as a result of sth. else (시간/순서상으로) 뒤를 잇다; (결과가) 뒤따르다

9 to hold up=to support sb./sth. and stop them from falling *held-held* (쓰러지지/떨어지지 않도록) …을 떠받치다/떠받들다

10 to slap=to hit sb./sth. with the flat part of your hand (손바닥으로) 철썩 때리다/치다

"I won't tell you", I said.

"Then why don't you cry, you horrid,[11] common boy?"

"I'm not crying. I'll never cry for[12] you again!" I answered. But I was crying as I spoke. And, God knows,[13] I cried for Estella many, many times afterwards.[14]

As we were going upstairs, we passed[15] a tall man with sharp eyes and thick black eyebrows. His large hands were very clean and white.

"Who's this?" the man asked, staring at me.

"Only a boy", Estella answered.

The man held my chin[16] in his hand and stared into my eyes.

"Why are you here?" he asked.

"Miss Havisham asked me to come", I whispered.

"Did she? Then behave yourself!"[17] the man said, as he went on down the stairs.[18]

---

[11] horrid=very unpleasant or unkind 진저리 나는, 지독한
[12] for=because of …로 해서/때문에
[13] "God/goodness/Heaven knows" – used to emphasise the truth of what you are saying …임을 신은 안다
[14] afterwards=at a later time; after an event that has already been mentioned 나중에, 그 뒤에
[15] to pass=to move past or to the other side of sb./sth. 지나가다; 통과하다
[16] chin=the part of the face below the mouth and above the neck 턱
[17] to behave (yourself)=to do things in a way that people think is correct or polite 예의 바르게 행동하다

Miss Havisham was sitting in her dressing-room. She was wearing the same torn dress as before. Everything in the room was the same.

"So you're back again", Miss Havisham said. "Are you ready to play today?"

I was too frightened to answer.

"Well, if you can't play, can you work?" Miss Havisham asked.

"Yes, ma'am."

"Then go into the room on the other side of the corridor. Wait there till I come."

The room I entered was very big. In the middle of the room was a long table. By the light of the fire and the many candles, I saw that the torn table-cloth was covered[19] with dust.[20]

---

[18] '복선(伏線, foreshadowing)'이란 이야기의 나중에 일어날 사건에 대해 독자들이 준비가 되도록 미리 제공하는 단서다. 이를테면 비극적인 사건이 일어나기 전에 어두운 배경을 그린다거나, 후에 중요한 역할을 담당하게 될 인물에 대한 특별한 인물 묘사를 통해 그에 대한 강한 인상을 심어주는 것이다. 디킨즈는 이 소설에서 복선을 많이 사용하는데 이야기의 초입에 나오는 무덤의 장면 묘사라든지 이 부분에서 갑자기 나와 점잖게 행동하라는 말을 남기고 사라지는 낯선 사람 같은 경우가 그 예다. 이를 통해 독자들은 이와 관련된 무슨 일이 일어날 것 같다는 생각을 하게 된다.

[19] to cover=to place sth. over or in front of sth. in order to hide or protect it (감추거나 보호하기 위해) 씌우다/가리다

[20] dust=a fine powder that consists of very small pieces of sand, earth, etc. (흙)먼지

There was something tall and white on the table too. It was covered with dust and fat black spiders were running all over it.

Miss Havisham came into the room and stood behind me. She placed her hand on my shoulder and pointed at the table with a walking stick.

"Look, Pip", she said. "Can you see my wedding-cake? Eaten by mice and spiders. Ruined!"[21]

Miss Havisham held my shoulder hard with her thin hand.

"Help me walk, Pip", she said.

We walked slowly round and round the long table, the strange old lady leaning[22] on my shoulder.

"Today is my birthday, Pip", Miss Havisham said. "Many years ago, it should have been my wedding-day.[23] The dress I am wearing now was new then and I was young. Everything is old and ruined now. Time has ruined me too and broken my heart."

What could I say? We stood there, very quiet, in the candlelight.

---

[21] to ruin=to damage sth. so badly that it loses all its value, pleasure, etc.; to spoil sth. 망치다; 엉망으로 만들다

[22] to lean=to rest on or against sth. for support 기대다; 의지하다

[23] 가정법 과거완료로 과거에 이루어지지 않은 일을 나타낸다.

"Call Estella", Miss Havisham said at last. "Play with her again. I want to see her beat you at cards again!"[24]

So Estella and I played cards. She won every game. Miss Havisham smiled and held bright jewels against Estella's hair. How beautiful the proud girl looked!

Miss Havisham was soon tired and I was sent downstairs. When I had eaten, I walked sadly through the courtyard and into an overgrown[25] garden. No one had looked after the garden for years. Weeds[26] grew everywhere.

Turning a corner, I came face to face with a fair-haired boy of my own age.[27]

"Hello", said this pale[28] young gentleman. "Who let you in?"[29]

"Miss Estella", I answered.

"Oh, did she? Then let's fight!"

---

[24] to beat=to defeat sb. in a game or competition *beat-beaten* (게임/시합에서) 이기다
[25] overgrown=covered with plants that have been allowed to grow wild and have not been controlled (풀/잡초 등이) 마구/제멋대로 자란
[26] weed=a wild plant growing where it is not wanted, esp. among crops or garden plants 잡초
[27] face to face=involving people who are close together and looking at each other 서로 얼굴을 맞대고
[28] pale=having skin that is almost white; having skin that is whiter than usual because of illness, a strong emotion, etc. (사람/얼굴 등이) 창백한; 핼쑥한
[29] to let in=to allow to enter *let-let* 들어오게 하다; 통하게 하다

I stared at the boy in surprise. Then, suddenly, he pulled my hair and hit me hard in the stomach with his head.

I was so surprised, that I hit him hard.

"So you do want to fight, do you?" the pale young gentleman cried. "Come on, then!" Then he raised his fists[30] like a boxer and began waving[31] them in front of my face.

I hit him again and he fell backwards onto the ground. When he got up, his nose was bleeding. A minute later, I had hit him in the eye.

"You've won", he said weakly. "Shake hands."

So we shook hands and the young gentleman walked quietly away.[32]

Estella was waiting for me at the gate. Her eyes were bright and shining. I knew she had been watching the fight.

"You can kiss me if you like", she said.

I was confused but happy. I kissed her gently on the cheek. A few minutes later, I began my long walk home.

---

[30] fist=a hand when it is tightly closed with the fingers bent into the palm 주먹
[31] to wave=to move your hand or arm from side to side in the air in order to attract attention, say hello, etc. (손/팔을) 흔들다
[32] 이 핼쑥한 어린 신사와의 우연한 만남도 문학적 장치로서의 복선이다.

From that day onwards,[33] I visited Miss Havisham three times a[34] week. I did not see the pale young gentleman again, but Estella was always there.

On every visit, I pushed Miss Havisham round and round those two rooms in a wheelchair. She did not walk with me again. Instead[35] I pushed her in her chair. As I walked behind her, Miss Havisham questioned[36] me. I told her I was going to be apprenticed[37] to Joe, when I was old enough. I told her that I knew nothing, but wanted to know everything. I told her I wanted to be educated. I told her how I wanted to be a gentleman. Perhaps I hoped that Miss Havisham would pay for my education. But she never suggested it.[38]

---

[33] from...onwards=continuing from a particular time (특정 시간부터) 계속

[34] a=per …에/마다

[35] instead=in the place of sb./sth. 대신에

[36] to question=to ask sb. questions about sth. 질문하다, 심문하다, 설문조사하다

[37] to apprentice=to make a young person work for an employer for a fixed period of time in order to learn the particular skills needed in their job 견습생으로 삼다

[38] to suggest=to put forward an idea or a plan for other people to think about (아이디어/계획을) 제안/제의하다

Sometimes Estella was kind to me, but, more often, she was rude and cruel. I could not understand this proud, beautiful girl who made me so unhappy.[39]

---

[39] 핍은 자신이 해비샴의 무모한 복수의 대상임을 깨닫지 못하고, 또 한편 에스텔라의 모욕에 길들여지면서 순진하게도 해비샴이 자신에게 신분상승의 기회를 줄 것이라는 막연한 기대를 품는다.

Chapter FIVE

"I Must Become a Gentleman!"

My life went on without change for two or three years. One day Miss Havisham looked up at me, and said, "You are getting tall, Pip. What is the name of your brother-in-law,[1] the blacksmith?"

"Joe Gargery, ma'am", I answered.

"It is time for you to be apprenticed to him", Miss Havisham said. "Bring him with you one day. Bring him soon!"[2]

---

[1] brother-in-law=the brother of your husband or wife; your sister's husband; the husband of your husband or wife's sister 시아주버니; 시동생; 처남; 매부; 자형; 동서

[2] to bring=to come to a place with sb./sth. *brought-brought* 가져오다; 데려오다

So, two days later, Joe put on[3] his Sunday clothes[4] and boots. Looking very awkward[5] and uncomfortable, he walked with me to Satis House, where Miss Havisham lived.

Estella opened the gate for us. She smiled scornfully at Joe and I felt ashamed[6] of him.

Joe was so afraid of Miss Havisham that he refused[7] to look at her. He stood near the door, turning his hat round and round in his strong hands.[8]

Miss Havisham picked up a little bag from her dressing-table. She held it out to Joe.

"It is time Pip became your apprentice",[9] she said. "Pip has earned his premium[10] and here it is.

---

[3] to put on=to dress yourself in sth. …을 입다/쓰다/끼다/걸치다
[4] Sunday clothes/Sunday best=best clothes 나들이옷
[5] awkward=feeling embarrassed 어색한
[6] ashamed=feeling shame or embarrassment about sb./sth. or because of sth. you have done 부끄러운; 창피한
[7] to refuse=to say that you will not do sth. that sb. has asked you to do 거절/거부하다
[8] 이것은 가저리가 지체 높은 사람들을 만나는 어색한 자리에서 하는 행동으로 소설의 뒷부분에서도 같은 행동의 묘사가 나온다.
[9] 'It is time that...'은 가정법 과거로 '…할 때가 되었다'는 뜻이다. that 다음에는 과거동사나 should+원형동사가 나와야 한다.
[10] premium=an amount of money that you pay once to the craftsman to be his apprentice (중세 서구에서) 도제가 되기 위해 장인에게 지불하는 수련비

"There are twenty-five guineas[11] in this bag, Pip", she said to me. "Give them to Joe Gargery. He is your master[12] now. Goodbye."

And she turned away.

I looked at Miss Havisham and Estella in despair.[13]

"But don't you want me to come again, Miss Havisham?" I asked.

"No, Pip. Gargery is your master and you must work for him.

"Pip has been a good boy here", Miss Havisham said to Joe. "This money is his reward.[14] You are an honest man and will not expect more. Let them out,[15] Estella."

Bitterly disappointed, I led Joe from that strange room. He walked like a man in a dream.

And so I became a blacksmith. From that day, I lived in fear. Fear that Estella might see me at work with my dirty face and dirty hands. In my mind, I saw her beautiful face, with its hard, scornful smile.[16]

---

[11] guinea=an old British gold coin or unit of money worth 21 shillings, or £1.05 기니 (영국의 구 금화로 21실링, 즉 1.05파운드에 해당)

[12] master=an employer of workers or servants 장인(匠人)

[13] despair=the feeling of having lost all hope 절망

[14] reward=a thing that you are given because you have done sth. good, worked hard, etc. 보상

[15] to let out=to release/allow to go out *let-let* 내보내다

A year passed.[17] I still thought about Estella every day. I longed to see Estella again.[18] So I decided to go to Satis House.[19] I asked Joe for a holiday and he agreed to close the forge for a day.

When I reached Satis House, the gate was opened by a servant.[20]

"I hope you want nothing more, Pip. You'll get no more money from me", Miss Havisham said when she saw me.

"That is not why I am here, Miss Havisham", I replied. "I want you to know I am doing well in my apprenticeship,[21] that is all.[22] I shall always be grateful to you."

---

16 해비샴의 도움으로 대장장이로 훈련을 시작하게 된 핍은 이를 자신의 인생 최초의 실망과 좌절로 받아들인다. 새티스 하우스의 경험을 통해 기준이 달라진 그는 이제 가저리마저도 부끄럽게 생각하며 대장장이일 수밖에 없는 자신의 처지를 비관한다.

17 to pass=to go by (시간이) 흐르다, 지나가다

18 to long=to want sth. very much esp. if it does not seem likely to happen soon (특히 곧 있을 것 같지 않은 일을) 간절히 바라다

19 to decide=to think carefully about the different possibilities that are available and choose one of them 결정하다

20 servant=a person who works in another person's house, and cooks, cleans, etc. for them 하인, 종

21 apprenticeship=a period of time working as an apprentice; a job as an apprentice 견습 기간; 견습직

22 That is all.=That is all there is to it. 그게 전부다

"Well, Pip, you can[23] come and see me sometimes", Miss Havisham answered. "Come every year on your birthday. As you see, I am alone now."

"I...I hope Estella is well",[24] I said.

"Estella is very well", Miss Havisham replied. "And she is more beautiful than ever. She is in France, being educated to be a lady.

"Do you feel that you have lost her, Pip?" she added, with a cruel smile.

I could not answer. Miss Havisham laughed. I said goodbye to her and walked sadly home.

When I reached the forge, I was surprised to see a crowd[25] of people outside.

I ran into the kitchen. Joe was there, and the doctor. My poor sister, Mrs Joe Gargery, was lying quiet and still on the floor.

Someone had attacked Mrs Joe when she was alone in the house. She was not dead, but terribly injured,[26] unable to walk or speak.

---

[23] "can" – used to show that sb. is allowed to do sth. …해도 좋다/된다
[24] well=in good health 건강한
[25] crowd=a large number of people gathered together in a public place, for example in the streets or at a sports game 무리; 군중
[26] to injure=to harm yourself or sb. else physically 부상을 입다/입히다

My sister lay in bed for many weeks. At last she was able to sit downstairs. But her sharp voice was quiet for ever. She never spoke again. From that day onwards someone had to look after Mrs Joe all the time. And so Biddy came into our lives.[27]

Biddy was the same age as me. But she was not beautiful like Estella. How could she be beautiful? She was only a common girl from the village. But Biddy's eyes were bright. She had a sweet smile and was sensible[28] and kind.

The years passed. I visited Satis House every year, on my birthday. I never saw Estella, but I did not forget her. I longed to be educated, like Estella. I wanted Estella to think well[29] of me and to like

---

[27] 여기서 비디는 에스텔라와 대조적인 인물로 등장한다. 그녀의 단순하고 정직하며 친절한 성품은 에스텔라의 냉정한 아름다움과 부정직, 그리고 잔인함과 정반대로 나타난다. 핍은 비디의 자연적인 매력에 이끌리기도 하나 에스텔라에 대한 열정이 너무도 큰 나머지 비디는 그저 좋은 친구로, 때로는 목적을 위한 수단으로만 여기게 된다.

[28] sensible=able to make good judgements based on reason and experience rather than emotion; practical 분별/양식 있는; 합리적인

[29] well=in a good, right or acceptable way 잘; 좋게; 제대로

me. I wanted Estella's respect[30] and admiration.[31] How stupid I was!

It was summer. One Sunday afternoon, Biddy and I went for a walk on the marshes. There were ships on the river, sailing slowly towards the sea. I remembered Estella, far away in another country. I began, as usual, to dream of my plans[32] for the future.

We sat down by the river and watched[33] the water flow slowly by.

"Biddy, I am going to tell you a secret", I said. "You must never speak of it to anyone."

Biddy looked at me in surprise. She promised to tell no one.

"Biddy", I went on, "I hate[34] being a blacksmith like Joe. I want to be a gentleman."

Biddy smiled and shook her head.

"Oh no, Pip", she answered. "That wouldn't be right at all."

---

[31] admiration=a feeling of respect and liking for sb./sth. 감탄, 존경

[32] plan=a set of things to do in order to achieve sth., esp. one that has been considered in detail in advance (목표 달성을 위해 고려되는 일련의) 계획/방안/방침

[33] to watch=to look at sb./sth. for a time, paying attention to what happens (시간과 관심을 기울이며) 보다; 주시하다

[34] to hate=to dislike sth. very much 몹시 싫어하다; 질색하다

[35] reason=a cause or an explanation for sth. that has happened or that sb. has done 이유

[36] to respect=to be careful about sth.; to make sure you do not do sth. that sb. would consider to be wrong 존중하다

"But I have important reasons[35] for wanting to be a gentleman", I told her.

"Don't you think you are happier as you are, Pip?" Biddy said gently.

"Happy?" I repeated. "I can never be happy here, Biddy. Someone I admire and respect[36] very much said I'm stupid and common. I must[37] become a gentleman. I must."

"Who called you stupid and common?" Biddy asked. "That was not a true or a polite thing to say."

"A young lady I met at Miss Havisham's", I replied. "The young lady is beautiful and I love her very much. She is the reason why I must become a gentleman."

"Do you want to be a gentleman to hurt her or to make her respect you?" Biddy asked me quietly.

"I don't know."

"I think you should forget her", Biddy said. "She has been rude and cruel to you. The young lady is not worth[38] your respect."

---

[35] reason=a cause or an explanation for sth. that has happened or that sb. has done 이유

[36] to respect=to be careful about sth.; to make sure you do not do sth. that sb. would consider to be wrong 존중하다

[37] "must" – used to say that sth. is necessary or very important (sometimes involving a rule or a law) (필요성/중요성을 나타내어) …해야 하다

[38] worth=important, good or enjoyable enough to do sth. …할 가치가 있는, …해 볼 만한

"You may be right, Biddy", I said, "I believe you are. But I love her very, very much."

Tears came into my eyes. I threw myself[39] on the ground in despair.

Biddy touched my hair gently.

"Thank you for telling me this, Pip", she said. "I will always keep your secret."

I sat up.

"And I will always tell you everything, Biddy dear",[40] I said.

"Yes, I'm sure you will, Pip", Biddy replied. She smiled sadly.

But I had not told Biddy everything. I believed that Miss Havisham had plans for me. I hoped that she would give me money for my education, money to make me a gentleman. If I had money and education, Estella would love me as I loved her. I hoped that Miss Havisham would make it possible for me to marry Estella.[41]

---

[39] to throw sth./yourself=to move your body or part of it quickly or suddenly
threw-thrown 몸이나 몸의 일부를 갑자기 내던지다시피 하다

[40] dear=loved by or important to sb. 사랑하는, 소중한

[41] 핍은 자신이 해비샴의 사악하고 무모한 복수의 연습 상대라는 것도 모르고 오히려 그녀가 자신을 도울 것이라는 허무맹랑한 상상을 계속한다. 콤피슨의 죄가 해비샴에게로 또 에스텔라에게로 옮겨가 결국은 핍도 그 희생양이 되고 있는 것이다.

Chapter SIX

Great Expectations

The months and years went by. I had been Joe's apprentice for four years.

One evening, Joe and I were sitting in the village inn.¹ A stranger² came in, a big, tall man, with heavy eyebrows. The man had large, very clean white hands. To my surprise, I recognised the man. I had seen him at Miss Havisham's, many years before. He had frightened me then. He frightened me a little now.³

---

¹ inn=a pub, usually in the country and often one where people can stay the night (보통 시골 지역에 있는 숙박이 가능한) 주막

² stranger=a person that you do not know 낯선/모르는 사람

"I think there is a blacksmith here—name of[4] Joe Gargery", the man said in his loud voice.

"That's me!" Joe answered. He stood up.

"You have an apprentice, known as Pip", the stranger went on. "Where is he?"

"Here!" I cried, standing beside Joe.

"I wish to speak to you both. I wish to speak to you privately,[5] not here", the man said. "Perhaps[6] I could go home with you."

We walked back to the forge in silence. When we were in the sitting-room,[7] the man began to speak.

"My name is Jaggers", he said. "I am a lawyer in London, where I am well-known.[8] I have some unusual business[9] with

---

3 핍이 우연히 새티스 하우스에서 마주쳤던 키 크고 손이 고왔던 그 사람이다. 그는 핍의 턱을 만지며 점잖게 행동하라고 말한 뒤 사라졌었다.

4 (by the) name of=who is called …라는 이름의/…라 불리는

5 private=where you are not likely to be disturbed; quiet (장소가 남의 방해를 받지 않고) 따로/조용히 있을 수 있는

6 "Perhaps" - used when making a polite request, offer or suggestion (정중히 요청/제의/제안을 할 때) 아마; 어쩌면

7 sitting/living room=a room in a house where people sit together, watch television, etc. 거실

8 well-known=known about by a lot of people 유명한; 주지의

9 business=important matters that need to be dealt with or discussed (논의하거나 처리해야 할) 일; 안건

young Pip here. I am speaking for[10] someone else, you understand. A client[11] who doesn't want to be named.[12] Is that clear?"[13]

Joe and I nodded.

"I have come to take your apprentice to London", the lawyer said to Joe. "You won't stop him from coming, I hope?"[14]

"Stop him? Never!" Joe cried.

"Listen, then. I have this message[15] for Pip. He has—great expectations!"[16]

Joe and I looked at each other, too surprised to speak.

"Yes, great expectations", Mr Jaggers repeated. "Pip will one day be rich, very rich. Pip is to change[17] his way of life at once.[18] He will no longer be a blacksmith. He is to come with me to

---

[10] for=as a representative of …을 대표/대신하여
[11] client=a person who uses the services or advice of a professional person or organization (전문가의 서비스를 받는) 의뢰인; 고객
[12] to name/identify=to say the name of sb./sth. 이름을 대다/밝히다
[13] clear=easy to understand and not causing any confusion 알아듣기/보기 쉬운; 분명한
[14] to hope=to want sth. to happen and think that it is possible 바라다; 기대하다
여기서 'I hope'은 바로 앞에서 한 단정적인 말을 부드럽게 해주는 효과가 있다.
[15] message=a written or spoken piece of information, etc. that you send to sb. or leave for sb. when you cannot speak to them yourself (글/말로 된) 전갈/용건
[16] expectations=prospects of inheritance 유산 (상속의 가망)
[17] 이 단락에서 사용되는 *be to*+동사원형의 표현은 '예정'이나 '운명'을 나타낸다. 즉 *be going to*+동사원형이나 *be destined to*+동사원형으로 바꾸어 쓸 수 있다.
[18] at once=immediately; without delay 즉시, 당장; 지체 없이

London. He is to be educated as a gentleman. He will be a man of property."[19]

And so, at last, my dream had come true.[20] Miss Havisham —because Mr Jaggers' client must[21] be Miss Havisham—had plans for me after all.[22] I would be rich and Estella would love me![23]

Mr Jaggers was speaking again. "There are two conditions",[24] he said, looking at me. "First, you will[25] always be known[26] as Pip. Secondly", Mr Jaggers continued, "the name of your benefactor[27] is to be kept secret. One day, that person will speak

---

[19] property=a thing or things that are owned by sb.; a possession or possessions 재산; 소유물

[20] to come true=to become reality *came-come* 이루어지다, 실현되다

[21] "must" - used to say that sth. is likely or logical (추정/논리성을 나타내어) …일 것이다, …임에 틀림없다

[22] after all=despite what has been said or expected (예상/언행과 달리) 결국에는

[23] 핍은 유산을 받게 될 것을 기뻐하는데 그치지 않고 이 모든 것이 자신을 신사로 만들어 에스텔라와 결혼하게 하려는 해비샴의 계획이라고 믿는다. 이는 단순히 사춘기의 자만심뿐만이 아니라 새로운 것을 접할 때마다 자신과 비교해 보고 개선의 욕구를 갖도록 했던 그의 낭만적 이상주의의 특질에 기인하는 것으로 본질적으로 비현실적인 것이다.

[24] condition=a rule or decision that you must agree to, sometimes forming part of a contract or an official agreement (요구) 조건

[25] "will" - used for ordering sb. to do sth. (무엇을 하라고 명령함) …을 하라; …해야 한다

[26] to know=to give sb./sth. a particular name or title (명칭/직함과 관련하여) …을 (…으로) 알다

[27] benefactor=a person who gives money or other help to a person or an organization such as a school or charity (개인/학교/자선단체 등의) 후원자

to you, face to face. Until then, you must not ask any questions. You must never try to find out this person's name. Do you understand? Speak out!"[28]

"Yes, I understand", I answered. "My benefactor's name is to remain[29] a secret."

"Good", Mr Jaggers said. "Now, Pip, you will come into your property[30] when you come of age[31]—when you are twenty-one. Until then, I am your guardian.[32] I have money to pay for your education and to allow you to live as a gentleman. You will have a private[33] teacher. His name is Mr Matthew Pocket and you will stay at his house."

---

[28] to speak out=to state your opinions publicly 공개적으로 말하다/밝히다
[29] to remain=to continue to be sth.; to be still in the same state or condition 계속/여전히 …이다
[30] to come into sth.=to be left money by sb. who has died (유산으로) …을 물려받다
[31] to come of age=to reach the age when you have an adult's legal rights and responsibilities 성년이 되다
[32] guardian=a person who is legally responsible for the care of another person, esp. a child with no parents (특히 부모가 없는 아동의) 후견인
[33] private=given by a teacher, etc. to one person or a small group of people for payment (교습이) 개인적인

I gave a cry of surprise. Some of Miss Havisham's relations[34] were called Pocket. Mr Jaggers raised his eyebrows.[35]

"Do you not want to live with Mr Pocket? Have you any objection[36] to this arrangement?"[37] he said severely.[38]

"No, no, none at all", I answered quickly.

"Good. Then I will arrange everything", Mr Jaggers went on. "Mr Pocket's son has rooms[39] in London. I suggest you go there.[40] Now, when can you come to London?"

I looked at Joe.

"At once, if Joe has no objection", I said.

"No objection, Pip old chap", Joe answered sadly.

---

[34] relation=a person who is in the same family as sb. else 친척

[35] to raise eyebrows=to show that you disapprove of or are surprised by sth. (불만/놀람의 표시로) 눈썹을 치켜 올리다

[36] objection=a reason why you do not like or are opposed to sth.; a statement about this 이의; 반대 (이유)

[37] arrangement=an agreement that you make with sb. that you can both accept 합의(안)

[38] severe=not kind or sympathetic and showing disapproval 엄한; 엄격한

[39] rooms=a set of two or more rooms that you rent to live in (주방, 거실 등이 딸린) 셋방

[40] 주절의 동사 *suggest*가 제안의 뜻을 가지므로 목적절의 동사는 원형동사 또는 *should*+원형동사가 나온다.

"Then you will come in one week's time", Mr Jaggers said, standing up. "You will need new clothes. Here is some money to pay for them. Twenty guineas."

He counted out[41] the money and put it on the table.

"Well, Joe Gargery, you are saying nothing", Mr Jaggers said to Joe sternly.[42] "I have money to give you too."

"Money? What for?" Joe asked.

"For loss[43] of your apprentice", Mr Jaggers answered. "Mr Pip has been your apprentice and now you are losing him."

Dear Joe placed his heavy hand gently on my shoulder.

"Pip must go free", Joe said "Let him go free. Let him have his good fortune.[44] No money can replace[45] the dear child. We've always been the best of friends, Pip and me. Ever the best of friends…"

Joe could not say any more. He wiped away a tear.

---

[41] to count sth. out=to count coins, etc. one by one and put them somewhere 무엇을 (어디에 놓으며) 하나씩 세다
[42] stern=serious and often disapproving; expecting sb. to obey you 엄중한; 근엄한
[43] loss=the disadvantage that is caused when sb. leaves or when a useful or valuable object is taken away; a person who causes a disadvantage by leaving (귀중한 사물/인력을 잃음으로써 생기는) 손실/손해
[44] fortune=a large amount of money 재산, 부; 거금
[45] to replace=to be used instead of sth./sb. else; to do sth. instead of sb./sth. else (다른 것의 기능을) 대신/대체하다

And so my whole life changed. How happy I was! But Biddy and Joe were sad and quiet. This upset[46] me. Why were they not pleased at my good fortune?[47]

The next few days passed slowly for me. I bought new clothes, boots and a hat. I decided to say goodbye to Miss Havisham before I left for London.

"How smart[48] you look, Pip!" Miss Havisham said when she saw me. "You look like a gentleman. Why is this?"

"I have had good fortune since I last saw you, Miss Havisham", I said with a smile. "I am so grateful, Miss Havisham, so grateful."

---

[46] to upset=to make sb. feel unhappy, anxious or annoyed *upset-upset* 속상하게 만들다/하다

[47] 예기치 않게 막대한 유산을 상속 받아 자신의 낭만적 이상을 실현하게 된 핍은 자신의 가정과 가족에 대해서 복잡한 심경을 느끼고 그들에게 어떻게 행동해야 할지 갈피를 잡지 못한다. 아직 세상사의 복잡성을 이해하지 못하는 핍은 인간 본연의 사랑과 충절에 대해 깊이 숙고해 보지 못한 채 그저 부유한 신사가 된다는 꿈에 부풀어 있다. 선량한 본성을 지닌 핍이 보여주는 이런 속물 근성과 오도된 우월감은 사실 핍이 자신이 처한 복잡한 정서적 상황을 단순화하는 나름의 방식인 듯하다.

[48] smart=looking clean and neat; well dressed in fashionable and/or formal clothes 맵시 좋은, 말쑥한

"I know, I know. I have seen Mr Jaggers, Pip", Miss Havisham answered. "He tells me you have great expectations. You now have a rich benefactor and you are leaving for London tomorrow."[49]

"Yes, Miss Havisham."

"Well, be good then, Pip, and do what Mr Jaggers tells you. Goodbye, Pip. You must keep[50] the name of Pip, you know."[51]

"Goodbye, Miss Havisham."

Miss Havisham smiled and held out her hand. I bowed and kissed it.[52]

On my last evening at the forge, Biddy cooked a special supper and I wore my new clothes.

The London coach left the town at six o'clock the next morning. I told Biddy and Joe that I wanted to walk to the town alone. Was I ashamed to be seen with them there? I'm afraid[53] I was.

---

[49] 예정된 가까운 미래의 사건은 현재진행형으로 쓴다.
[50] to keep=to continue to have sth. and not give it back or throw it away *kept-kept* (돌려주거나 버리지 않고 계속) 가지고 있다
[51] "you know" – used to show that what you are referring to is known or understood by the person you are speaking to (상대방이 알고 있는 대상에 대해 언급할 때) 알지/알잖아/거 왜 있잖아?
[52] 이렇게 핍은 해비샴이 유산을 물려주었다고 생각하는 것을 알지만 막상 그녀는 이 오해를 바로잡아 주지 않는다.
[53] "I'm afraid" – used as a polite way of telling sb. sth. that is unpleasant or disappointing, or that you are sorry about (유감스러운 내용을 말할 때 예의상 덧붙이는 표현) …할/인 것 같다; (유감이지만) …이다

I said goodbye to Mrs Joe, then to Biddy and Joe. Biddy and Joe were both in tears as I waved goodbye for the last time.

I walked on and then my own tears began to fall. As I got nearer to the town, the morning mist disappeared[54] and the sun shone.[55] I was on my way to London. I was a young man with great expectations![56]

---

[54] to disappear=to become impossible to see (눈앞에서) 사라지다, 보이지 않게 되다
[55] to shine=to produce or reflect light; to be bright *shone-shone* 빛나다, 반짝이다
[56] 왁자지껄한 기쁨과 희망의 장도가 아니라 사랑하는 이들의 배웅도 사양한 채 어둠과 안개와 눈물을 뒤로하고 새 출발하는 핍의 모습에서 어떤 슬픔과 불안을 보게 된다.

Chapter SEVEN

Learning to Be a Gentleman

The journey took six hours and it was after midday[1] when I reached London. I was amazed and frightened when I saw the city. London was crowded[2] with hundreds of people and its streets were dirty.[3]

---

[1] midday=12 o'clock in the middle of the day; the period around this time 정오, 한낮

[2] to crowd=to fill a place so there is little room to move (어떤 장소를) 가득 메우다

[3] 핍은 고향 켄트의 늪지대를 떠나 이제 런던 생활을 시작한다. 황량하지만 아름다운 자연을 그대로 간직하고 있는 고향과 사람으로 넘치는 화려하면서도 지저분한 런던의 주변 환경은 여러 면에서 극적인 차이를 보인다.

I had the address[4] of Mr Jaggers' office in Little Britain, Cheapside.[5] After asking the way, I started to walk along the narrow crowded streets. At last, I found a door with "Mr Jaggers" written on it.[6]

The open door led into a small office. A clerk[7] was working there. He looked up as I walked in.

"Is Mr Jaggers here?" I asked nervously.

"Mr Jaggers is in court.[8] He won't be long",[9] the clerk answered. "You are Mr Pip, I think.[10] My name's Wemmick. Come and wait in Mr Jaggers' room."

---

[4] address=details of where sb. lives or works and where letters, etc. can be sent 주소

[5] '칩사이드'는 런던 동쪽의 금융 중심지인 시티(the City)의 한 구역이다. '리틀 브리튼'은 칩사이드의 한 대로로 서점, 금은방, 의류점 등이 모여 있었는데 재거즈의 사무실도 여기 있었다.

[6] 환경은 바뀌었지만 어린 핍은 런던에서도 사회적 계급의 상승을 꿈꾸면서도 동시에 죄와 벌의 문제에 사로잡혀 살게 된다. 지금 핍은 아직 신사라고 할 수 없는 처지인지라 모든 것에 적응하지 못하고 있다. 또한 탈옥수를 도운 것에 대해 죄의식을 갖고 있던 핍은 런던에서도 자기 유산을 관리하는 변호사부터 만나는 등 사법 및 징벌 제도를 늘 느끼며 살게 된다.

[7] clerk=a person whose job is to keep the records or accounts in an office, shop/store etc. 사무원, 직원; 점원

[8] court=the place where legal trials take place and where crimes, etc. are judged 법정, 법원

[9] sb./sth. won't be long=sb. will arrive or be back soon; sth. will happen soon (사람이) 곧 도착할/돌아올 것이다; (일/사건이) 곧 발생할/일어날 것이다

[10] 'I think'는 앞서 단정적으로 말한 것을 완화하기 위해 덧붙이는 말이다.

Mr Jaggers' room was a dark, gloomy place. Its small window was very dirty and no light came through it. There was a big black chair for Mr Jaggers and a smaller one, on which I sat.

Mr Wemmick, the clerk, went on with his work.[11] Mr Jaggers' clerk was a short, neat[12] man about fifty years old. He had a square face and a wide, thin mouth. His black eyes were very bright. On his fingers, he wore four or five silver and black rings.

By the time Mr Jaggers came back, several poorly-dressed people were waiting for him. They all began talking at once.[13] They wanted him to speak for[14] them in court.

Mr Jaggers spoke to them all in a stern and angry way. When they had gone, he came in to see me.

"Here is your allowance,[15] Pip", he said. "I think it's too much money but that's nothing to do with me.[16] You'll get into debt, of course, all young men get into debt",[17] he added severely.

---

[11] to go on (with sth.)=to continue an activity, esp. after a pause or break (잠시 쉬었다가 하던 일을) 계속하다

[12] neat=tidy and in order; carefully done or arranged 정돈된, 단정한, 말쑥한

[13] at once=at the same time 한꺼번에, 동시에

[14] to speak for=to state the views or wishes of a person or a group; to act as a representative for sb. …를 대변하다; …대신 말하다

[15] allowance=an amount of money that is given to sb. regularly or for a particular purpose 용돈; (특정 목적을 위한) 비용/수당

[16] to be/have nothing to do with sb./sth.=to have no connection with sb./sth. …과 아무 관련이 없다

"You are going to live at Barnard's Inn with Mr Herbert Pocket. Wemmick will take[18] you there."

"Wemmick!" Mr Jaggers then called out.[19] "Walk with Pip to young Mr Pocket's rooms."

Wemmick gave me a wide smile. He led me through the busy streets, always looking straight in front of him.

"Here we are,[20] Barnard's Inn", Wemmick said, turning down a narrow street into a little square.[21] He led me to the corner building and pointed up some steep stairs.

"Up there, top floor", he added. "As I look after your allowance I expect we shall meet often. Goodbye, Pip."

I found Herbert's name on a door at the top of the stairs. Under his name, there was a piece of paper. It said, "Back[22] soon."

---

17 debt=the situation of owing money, esp. when you cannot pay (특히 갚을 수 없을 정도로) 빚을 진 상황, 채무상태

18 to take=to go with sb. from one place to another, esp. to guide or lead them took-taken (사람을) 데리고 가다; 데려다 주다/안내하다

19 to call out=to shout or say sth. loudly to attract sb.'s attention (큰 소리로) 부르다; 외치다/말하다

20 Here we are.=We've arrived. 도착했다, 다 왔다

21 square=an open area in a town, usually with four sides, surrounded by buildings 광장

22 back=to or into the place, condition, situation or activity where sb./sth. was before (이전의 장소/상태로) 다시; 돌아가/와

I waited. A few minutes later, I heard quick footsteps on the stairs. A pale young man appeared, carrying a basket of strawberries.

"Mr Pip, isn't it?"[23] the young man said, with a smile. "I went to the market for some fruit. My father tells me you are to be my companion.[24] I hope you will like living here. I'm sure[25] we shall be friends."

As the young man unlocked the door, I stared at him in surprise. Then he began to stare at me.

"Why, you are the boy I fought in Miss Havisham's garden!" Herbert exclaimed.

"And you are the pale young gentleman!" I answered.

We both laughed cheerfully[26] and shook hands.

---

[23] "isn't it?"은 (네 이름이) 그렇지 않냐고 확인하는 말이다.
[24] companion=a person or an animal that travels with you or spends a lot of time with you 동반자, 동행
[25] sure=confident that you know sth. or that you are right 확신하는, 확실히 아는
[26] cheerful=happy, and showing it by the way that you behave 발랄한, 쾌활한

"It all seems so long ago", Herbert said. "Miss Havisham is my father's cousin. She's a very strange woman. You met Estella, of course. Miss Havisham adopted[27] her to take revenge."[28]

"Revenge? For what? What do you mean?" I asked.

"Don't you know?" Herbert replied. "It's a very strange[29] story. Mr Jaggers is your guardian, isn't he? He's Miss Havisham's lawyer too, and he knows all her secrets."

While we ate dinner, Herbert told me all he knew.[30]

"Miss Havisham's father died. She and her brother were very rich", Herbert said. "But the brother spent his money carelessly[31] and was soon in debt.

---

[27] to adopt=to take sb. else's child into your family and become its legal parent(s) 입양하다

[28] revenge=sth. that you do in order to make sb. suffer because they have made you suffer 복수, 보복

[29] strange=unusual or surprising, esp. in a way that is difficult to understand 이상한

[30] 이 소설에서 해비샴의 이야기는 사회계급, 낭만적 고뇌, 범죄 등의 주제를 담고 있다. 이제 초반에서 그녀의 환경과 행동을 통해 암시된 바 있는 그녀의 신비로운 삶이 드러나기 시작하는데 이전의 의문이 풀림과 동시에 그녀를 이용한 범인은 누구며, 그녀와 에스텔라와는 어떻게 인연이 되었는가 하는 또 다른 의문이 생기게 된다. 디킨즈는 아직은 작품 구성 상 일정한 신비감을 유지하며 이야기를 전하고 있다.

[31] careless=not giving enough attention and thought to what you are doing, so that you make mistakes 부주의한, 조심성 없는

"Miss Havisham's brother had a very wicked[32] friend. He was dishonest and he was a liar. Miss Havisham fell in love with this man. My father tried to warn[33] Miss Havisham, but she would[34] not listen. The two young people decided to get married and all the arrangements[35] were made for the wedding.[36] But on the wedding-day the bridegroom[37] did not come. He sent Miss Havisham a letter saying he could not marry her."

"And did Miss Havisham receive that letter at twenty minutes to nine, as she was dressing herself for the wedding?" I asked.

"Exactly at that time", Herbert said. "As you know, everything in the house stopped at that moment. Miss Havisham has not seen the daylight since."[38]

"When did she adopt Estella?" I asked.

---

[32] wicked=morally bad 못된, 사악한

[33] to warn=to tell sb. about sth., esp. sth. dangerous or unpleasant that is likely to happen, so that they can avoid it 경고하다, 주의를 주다, 조심하라고 하다

[34] "will" – used for showing that sb. is willing to do sth. (의지를 나타내어) …할 것이다; …하려고 하다

[35] arrangement=a plan or preparation that you make so that sth. can happen 준비, 마련, 주선

[36] wedding=a marriage ceremony, and the meal or party that usually follows it 결혼식, 혼례

[37] bridegroom=a man on his wedding day, or just before or just after it 신랑

[38] since=from a time in the past until a later past time, or until now 그(때) 이후로 (과거 어느 시점까지/지금까지)

"I don't know", Herbert replied. "As long as I have known Miss Havisham, Estella has been at Satis House."

"Miss Havisham wants to take revenge on all men", he went on. "Miss Havisham has brought up Estella to break men's hearts, because her own heart was broken."

The next day, Herbert took me to his father's house in Hammersmith,[39] to begin my education as a gentleman. I was to live there while I was studying. I also had my own room at Herbert's. We got on well together.[40] Herbert taught me how to dress in smart London clothes. He also showed me how to behave like a gentleman. I was able to help Herbert pay for his rooms with my allowance.

Herbert had little money and no expectations. His rooms were almost empty and not very comfortable. I had the idea of buying carpets and some more furniture. But to get these things I needed more money. Feeling a little afraid,[41] I went to Mr Jaggers.

---

[39] '해머스미스'는 런던 중심에서 서쪽으로 8km 정도 떨어진 템즈 강 바로 북쪽의 구역이다.

[40] to get on/along with sb.=to have a friendly relationship with sb. …와 잘 지내다

"How much do you want?" said Mr Jaggers sharply.

"Well..." I began.

"Come, you must have an idea", Mr Jaggers went on in his stern way. "Shall[42] we say[43] fifty pounds?"

"Oh, not nearly so much as that", I said quickly.

"Five pounds then?" Mr Jaggers suggested.

"Oh, more than that!" I exclaimed.

"More than five", Mr Jaggers said slowly. "How much more? Twice five? Three times?[44] Four times five? Will that do?"[45]

I told Mr Jaggers that twenty pounds would do very well.

"Wemmick!" Mr Jaggers cried, as he left the office. "Give Mr Pip twenty pounds!"

"I don't think I understand Mr Jaggers", I said to Wemmick when we were alone.

---

[41] Feeling a little afraid=As I felt a little afraid 두려움을 느껴서

[42] "shall" – used in questions with I and we for making offers or suggestions or asking advice I와 we를 주어로 하는 의문문에서 제의/제안/조언/요청을 나타냄. "Shall we say"="Let's say"

[43] to say=to suggest or give sth. as an example or a possibility (예를 들거나 가능성을 제시할 때) 아마 …이다; …를 예로 들다; …라고 가정하다

[44] times=multiplied by …으로 곱한, …배/곱절의

[45] to do=to be suitable or be enough for sb./sth. *did-done* 적절하다, 충분하다

"He doesn't expect you to understand him. He doesn't want you to", Wemmick replied. "No one understands him—that's why he's so successful.[46] Here's your money, Mr Pip."

———

Another young man was studying with Mr Matthew Pocket. His name was Bentley Drummle. He came from a good family and he was very rich. Bentley Drummle was a gentleman but he did not behave like one. He was a big, awkward, clumsy[47] young man. And he was proud and bad-tempered.[48]

Mr Jaggers took an interest[49] in Matthew Pocket's young gentlemen. One day he invited[50] us all to his house for dinner.

---

[46] successful=having become popular and/or made a lot of money (부/명예 등을 얻어) 성공한, 출세한

[47] clumsy=moving or doing things without skill or in a way that offends people (말/행동이) 세련되지 못한, 서투른

[48] 드러믈은 이 소설에서 그리 중요하지 않은 부차적인 인물이지만 핍과 대비되면서 계급차별의 허구성을 드러내준다. 핍은 결국 드러믈을 통해서 사회계급과 지적 능력, 도덕적 가치는 무관함을 깨닫고 자신이 무시했던 가저리와 매그위치의 인격에 경의를 표하게 된다.

[49] interest=the feeling that you have when you want to know or learn more about sb./sth. 관심, 흥미, 호기심

[50] to invite=to ask sb. to come to a social event 초대/초청하다

The food was good and we had plenty[51] to drink. Mr Jaggers liked to watch us talking and arguing. He was interested[52] to see how much Drummle and I hated each other.

Dinner was served by Mr Jaggers' housekeeper.[53] She was a tall woman of[54] about forty. Her face was very pale, and her eyes were dark. Her long dark hair lay over her shoulders.

When the woman brought in the food, she looked only at Mr Jaggers. She was breathing quickly, as though she was afraid.

As he drank his wine, Bentley Drummle became more and more bad-tempered. He kept saying[55] how strong he was. Very soon he and I had taken off our jackets to show how strong our arms were.[56]

---

[51] plenty=a large amount; as much or as many as you need 풍부한 양; 충분한 양

[52] to interest=to attract your attention and make you feel interested; to make yourself give your attention to sth. …의 관심/흥미를 끌다; (…에) 관심/흥미를 보이다

[53] housekeeper=a person, usually a woman, whose job is to manage the shopping, cooking, cleaning, etc. in a house or an institution 가정부, 식모

[54] "of" – used with measurements and expressions of time, age, etc. 시간, 나이 등을 나타낸다.

[55] to keep doing=to continue doing sth.; to do sth. repeatedly *kept-kept* …을 계속하다; 반복하다

[56] 출신 계급은 낮지만 유산상속을 통해 곧 부유한 귀족인 드러믈과 대등한 사회적 위치를 얻게 되리라는 확신이 있는 핍은 여러 장면에서 드러믈에게 기죽지 않고 맞서는 모습을 보여준다. 이렇게 디킨즈는 혈통보다는 현실적으로 돈이 있고 적절한 교육수준만 된다면 누구든 신사계급으로의 신분이동이 가능하게끔 전통적 계급구조가 점차 변화하고 있음을 강조한다.

At that moment, the housekeeper came in to take the plates from the table. Mr Jaggers suddenly caught hold of one of her arms. He looked at us all and then spoke.

"If you want to see strength", Mr Jaggers said, "look at this woman's wrists. Molly, let them see your wrists—both of them."

"Master,[57] no", the woman whispered, staring at Mr Jaggers with her strange, dark eyes.

"Show them, Molly", Mr Jaggers said.

He held Molly's wrists down on the table.

"There's power in those wrists", Mr Jaggers said. "Few men have the strength this woman has. She has used it too. She was wild once, but I have broken her."

"That'll do,[58] Molly", Mr Jaggers said at last, letting go[59] of his housekeeper's wrists. "We have seen you. You can go."

Mr Jaggers filled our wine glasses again. Very soon, Drummle and I were shouting at each other. We both stood up, ready

---

[57] master=a man who has people working for him, often as servants in his home (흔히 하인/종의) 주인

[58] "that will do" – used to order sb. to stop doing or saying sth. 그만 해; 그만하면 됐어

[59] to let go of=to stop holding sb./sth. let-let (쥐고 있던 것)을 놓다; …에서 손을 놓다

to fight. But Mr Jaggers made us be quiet and told us it was time to go home.

I was ashamed of my behaviour.[60] As we were leaving his house, I turned and apologised[61] to Mr Jaggers.

"It's nothing, Pip", Mr Jaggers replied. "But be careful of that young man, Drummle. He's bad-tempered and cruel. He could[62] be dangerous.[63] Take care, Pip. Bentley Drummle will make[64] a bad enemy."[65]

I followed[66] Mr Jaggers' advice.[67] I was pleased when Drummle completed his studies[68] and left Mr Pocket's house.

---

[60] behaviour=the way that sb. behaves, esp. towards other people 처신, 행위, 행동
[61] to apologise=to say that you are sorry for doing sth. wrong or causing a problem 사과하다
[62] "could" – used to show that sth. is or might be possible (가능성이 있음을 나타내어) …일/할 수도 있다
[63] dangerous=likely to injure or harm sb., or to damage or destroy sth. 위험한
[64] to make=to become or develop into sth.; to be suitable for sth. (성장/발달하여) …이 되다
[65] enemy=a person who hates sb. or who acts or speaks against sb./sth. 적
[66] to follow=to accept advice, instructions, etc. and do what you have been told or shown to do (충고/지시 등을) 따르다/따라하다
[67] advice=an opinion or a suggestion about what sb. should do in a particular situation 조언, 충고
[68] studies=a particular person's learning activities, for example at a college or university 학업

I was so busy learning[69] to be a gentleman, that I did not write to Joe and Biddy. They were part of my old life, a life I wanted to forget. I was a gentleman now. I did not want to remember that I had been a poor, uneducated blacksmith.

Then one day I received a letter.

My dear Mr Pip,

I am writing to you at the request[70] of Mr Gargery. He is going to London and will call on[71] you at nine o'clock on Tuesday morning. Your poor sister, Mrs Joe, is still not well. Mr Gargery and I talk about you every night.

Your servant and friend,

Biddy

The letter arrived on Monday. I did not wish to see Joe, but I prepared a big breakfast for him. Herbert and I were ready and waiting long before nine o'clock.

---

[69] to be busy doing=spending a lot of time on sth. (…하느라) 바쁜, (…에) 열심인
[70] request=the action of asking for sth. formally and politely (격식을 차려 정중히 하는) 요청/신청
[71] to call (on)=to make a short visit to a person or place …에게 들르다, …를 찾아가다

At last I heard Joe's heavy step on the stairs. I heard him stop and slowly read my name on the door. Then he knocked.

"Joe, how are you, Joe?" I cried, as I opened the door.

"Pip old chap, how are you?" Joe answered, taking my hand in his.

Joe's honest face shone with joy. He shook my hand so much that I thought he would never stop.

Joe looked awkward and uncomfortable in his best clothes. He took off his hat and twisted it round and round in his great hands.[72] He stared around the room and stared at my brightly-coloured dressing-gown.[73]

"Well, what a gentleman you are, Pip!" he exclaimed.

"And you look well too, Joe", I answered. "Let me take[74] your hat." But Joe held his hat all through the meal.

"Tea or coffee, Mr Gargery?" Herbert asked politely.

---

[72] 소설의 초반에서 가저리는 해비샴에 집을 방문했을 때도 어색한 나머지 같은 행동을 했다. 핍은 이런 가저리의 모습에 대한 반감을 겨우 감추고 마지못해 그를 맞이한다. 이에 성숙한 서술자 핍은 자신의 어린 시절인 주인공 핍에 대해 부정적으로 묘사한다.

[73] dressing-gown=a long loose piece of clothing, usually with a belt, worn indoors over night clothes, for example when you first get out of bed 가운, 실내복

[74] to take=to put your hands or arms around sb./sth. and hold them/it; to reach for sb./sth. and hold them/it *took-taken* (손/팔을 뻗쳐) 잡다/집다/안다

"Thank you kindly, sir.[75] I'll take whatever you'll be taking yourself", Joe answered.

"Coffee then", Herbert said cheerfully. But Joe looked so unhappy that, with a kind smile, Herbert gave him some tea.

Joe was uncomfortable and awkward with us and this made me angry. I was too stupid to see that it was my fault.[76] I should not have been ashamed of him.[77] I was glad when Herbert left us to go to work.

"Now we are alone,[78] sir...Joe began, but I interrupted[79] him angrily.

"Why do you call me 'sir,' Joe?" I asked.

"Now we are alone, sir", Joe repeated slowly, "I must tell you why I am here, in the home of a gentleman."

I said nothing.

"Well, sir—Pip", Joe went on, "Miss Havisham asked to see me. She has a message for you. And the message is that Estella has come home and would be glad[80] to see you."

---

[75] Thank you kindly.=Thank you very much.
[76] fault=the responsibility for sth. wrong that has happened or been done 잘못, 책임
[77] 가정법 과거완료로 과거의 사실에 대한 후회를 나타낸다.
[78] alone=without any other people 혼자; 다른 사람 없이
[79] to interrupt=to say or do sth. that makes sb. stop what they are saying or doing (…의 말/행동을) 방해하다/중단시키다/가로막다

At the sound of Estella's name, my heart began to beat very fast. I did not answer Joe. I could only think of Estella.

Joe stood up, twisting his hat in his hand.

"Don't leave, Joe", I said. "You must stay[81] to dinner."

"No, Pip old chap", Joe answered. "You are a gentleman now. It's not right for me to be here in London. But if you ever come back and visit us at the forge, you will be very welcome. Until then, I'll say goodbye. Goodbye and God bless you, Pip old chap."

And before I could answer, Joe had gone.

I sat at the table, excited and confused. Miss Havisham had plans for Estella and me, that was clear. Miss Havisham had made me a gentleman, so that Estella could marry me. With joy in my heart, I began to prepare for my journey.[82]

---

[80] glad=very willing 기꺼이 …하려는

[81] to stay=to continue to be in a particular place for a period of time without moving away (다른 곳에 가지 않고) 계속/그대로 있다/머무르다/남다

[82] journey=an act of travelling from one place to another, esp. when they are far apart (특히 멀리 가는) 여행/여정/이동

Chapter EIGHT

Young Men in Love

I left London early next morning. When I got to Satis House, I rang the bell as usual and a servant opened the gate. Taking a candle, I walked along the dark and gloomy corridors and up the stairs. I knocked on the door of Miss Havisham's dressing-room.

"That's Pip's knock. Come in, Pip", I heard Miss Havisham say.

When I opened the door, Miss Havisham was sitting by the dressing-table as usual. Beside her, was an elegant[1] young woman who I had not seen before.

"Well, Pip?" Miss Havisham said.

"I heard that you wished to see me, Miss Havisham, so I came at once", I said.

As I spoke, the elegant young lady looked up at me. It was Estella. She smiled.

"Has she changed, Pip?" Miss Havisham asked. "She used to[2] be proud and scornful. Do you remember?"

Although I was wearing my fine clothes, I felt clumsy and awkward. I was that common boy again who Estella had laughed at.[3]

"Has Pip changed?" Miss Havisham asked Estella.

"Very much", Estella answered.

As we talked, Estella's smile tore at my heart. The more I saw of[4] her, the more I loved her.

---

[1] elegant=attractive and showing a good sense of style 우아한

[2] "used to" – used to say that sth. happened continuously or frequently during a period in the past …하곤 했다; 과거 한때는/예전에는 …이었다/했다

[3] 핍은 런던에서 갈망하던바, 신분의 상승을 이뤘지만 이상하게도 자신감과 행복감은 잃고 살았다. 이제 신사가 되어 금의환향하여 새티스 하우스를 방문한 핍은 기대와는 달리 미천한 신분의 어린 시절 겪었던 굴욕이 계속됨에 고통스러워한다.

"Isn't she elegant, isn't she beautiful? Don't you admire her, Pip?" Miss Havisham whispered.

"Everyone who sees Estella must admire her", I replied.

"Then love her, love her, Pip!" Miss Havisham cried. "It does not matter[5] how she behaves towards you. If she is good to you, love her. If she tears your heart to pieces, love her, love her.

"Never forget, Pip", Miss Havisham went on, "you must give everything for real love. You must give your whole heart, as I did, as I did!"

And she fell back into her chair with a cry.

Before I left Satis House, Estella and I walked together in the garden. I reminded[6] Estella how I had once fought Herbert there.

"Herbert and I are great friends now", I said.

"Of course, with your new life, you have new friends", Estella answered. "The people who you knew before cannot be your companions now."

---

[4] to see of=to meet; to be in contact with *saw-seen* …를 만나다; …와 접촉하다
[5] to matter=to be important or have an important effect on sb./sth. 중요하다; 문제되다
[6] to remind=to help sb. remember sth., esp. sth. important that they must do 상기시키다, 다시 한 번 알려/말해 주다

I did not answer. Estella's words made me feel ashamed of Joe and Biddy. I decided not to visit them at the forge as I had planned.

We walked on and I showed Estella the place where I had cried.

Estella stopped for a minute and looked at me.

"I have not changed, Pip", she said. "If we are to[7] meet again, you must understand that. Remember, I have no love in my heart for anyone. No love in my heart at all."

I heard Estella's words, but I did not believe them. Estella and I were going to be together. Miss Havisham had planned it.

But my love for Estella did not make me happy. I was in torment[8] when I saw her and in torment when I did not see her.

---

7 여기서 be to+동사원형은 '의도'를 나타낸다.

8 torment=extreme suffering, esp. mental suffering; a person or thing that causes this (정신적인) 고통, 고뇌; 고통을 안겨 주는 사람/것, 고민거리

Back in London, I could no longer keep my feelings to myself.[9] When Herbert and I were having dinner, I made a decision.[10]

"My dear Herbert", I began, "I have something important to tell you. But it is a secret."

Herbert smiled.

"Your secret will be safe with me, Pip", he said.[11]

I took a deep breath.[12]

"Herbert! I must tell you. I love...I adore[13] Estella!"

Herbert smiled again.

"I know that, my dear Pip", Herbert said. "I believe you adored her from the first moment you saw her!"

"You are right, Herbert", I said. "And now she is a beautiful and elegant young woman."

---

[9] to keep sth. to yourself=to not tell other people about sth. ···에 대하여 남들에게 말하지 않다

[10] decision=a choice or judgement that you make after thinking and talking about what is the best thing to do 결정, 판단

[11] Your secret will be safe with me.=I will not tell your secret to anyone.

[12] breath=the air that you take into your lungs and send out again (숨을 쉴 때 입에서 나오는) 입김/숨

[13] to adore=to love sb. very much ···를 흠모/사모하다

"Then you are lucky[14] that she has been chosen for you", Herbert said cheerfully. "But has Mr Jaggers ever said that Estella is part of your expectations, Pip?"

"No, never", I said slowly.

"Then perhaps she is not part of your expectations. Perhaps you should not think of Estella so much", Herbert said. "Think of the way she has been brought up. Think of Miss Havisham. Estella has the power to make you very unhappy, Pip. Could you not forget her for a time?"[15]

I shook my head.

"No, that's impossible, quite impossible", I replied.

"Well, then, I suppose there is nothing more to say", Herbert said kindly.

"But you are not the only one in love, Pip", Herbert added. "I have a secret of my own.[16] And my secret is—I am engaged[17] to be married!"

---

[14] lucky=having good luck 운이 좋은, 행운의

[15] time=a period of time, either long or short, during which you do sth. or sth. happens (어느 정도 기간의) 시간/동안/때/시기

[16] a secret of my own=my own secret 나만의 비밀

[17] to be engaged=to promise to marry 약혼하다

"Congratulations,[18] Herbert", I said. "May I know the lady's name?"

"Her name is Clara. She lives with her father, who is an invalid.[19] As I have no expectations and she is poor, we cannot marry yet. Not until I make my fortune!

"That means hard[20] work", Herbert went on. "One day I shall have enough money to marry and then how happy Clara and I will be!"

How lucky Herbert was! He was poor, but Clara loved him. I was in love with a beautiful woman and I had great expectations. But Estella was proud and had no love in her heart for me.

Would Estella ever forget her pride[21] and love me?

---

[18] "Congratulations!" – used when you want to tell sb. that you are pleased about their success or achievements 축하합니다!
[19] invalid=a person who needs other people to take care of them, because of illness that they have had for a long time (혼자 생활하기 어려운) 병약자
[20] hard=needing or using a lot of physical strength or mental effort (육체적/정신적으로) 힘든
[21] pride=the feeling that you are better or more important than other people 자만심, 우월감

Chapter NINE

I Come of Age

I now come to a time of my life of which I am bitterly ashamed. I forgot my old friends, Joe and Biddy. I did not visit them at the forge. I spent too much money and got into debt. I thought only of the time when I would be twenty-one. The time when I would receive my fortune and be able to marry Estella.

One day, I received a message from Estella. It was a short note,[1] but it made me very happy.

---

[1] note=a short informal letter (격식을 차리지 않은 짧은) 편지, 쪽지

Satis House

*I am coming to London in two days' time. Miss Havisham wants you to meet me at the coach office in Cheapside. The coach arrives at five o'clock.*²

Yours,

Estella

I met Estella at the coach office and then took her to Richmond.³ She was more beautiful than ever. Estella was going to live in the house of an important⁴ lady. She was going to be introduced⁵ to the rich and powerful people of London society.⁶

Now that Estella was living in London, I tried to see her as often as I could. I would often go to Richmond and wait for many hours outside her house, hoping to see her.

---

² 일정, 시간표 등에선 단순 현재형을 쓴다.

³ 리치몬드는 런던 남서부의 부유한 교외지역으로 에스텔라는 한 유력한 과부 모녀와 함께 살게 된다.

⁴ important=having great influence or authority (사람이) 중요한, 영향력이 큰, 권위 있는

⁵ to introduce=to tell two or more people who have not met before what each other's names are; to tell sb. what your name is 소개하다

⁶ society=the group of people in a country who are fashionable, rich and powerful 상류 사회, 사교계

Sometimes Estella allowed me to see her and once she let me kiss her. But she was often as proud and cold as she had been in the old days.[7]

At this time I started to get more and more into debt. Living in London cost a lot of money.[8] I bought fashionable[9] clothes and expensive food and drink. Herbert and I joined a club[10] for young gentlemen, and we went to the theatre, the opera and well-known restaurants. But the allowance I received was not enough to pay all of my debts. And Herbert was poor and he did not have the expectation of a fortune. He could not pay his debts.

On my twenty-first birthday I would come of age. I would become a rich man of property. On that day I would receive my fortune. I waited anxiously[11] for that day.

---

[7] 디킨즈는 아직도 해비샴의 계획에 따라 에스텔라와 결혼하게 될 거라는 환상을 가지고 있는 핍을 보여준다. 그러나 핍과 에스텔라의 관계는 이전보다 더 악화되었다. 이전에는 놀이 친구로서 모욕을 당했을 뿐이지만 이제는 순수한 지인의 자격으로 에스텔라가 그녀의 구애자들을 만나러 가는데도 동행하고 잔심부름까지도 하게 된다.

[8] to cost=to need to pay (a particular amount of money) in order to buy, make or do it *cost-cost* (값/비용이) …이다/들다

[9] fashionable=used or visited by people following a current fashion, esp. by rich people (유행의 첨단을 걷는) 부유층이 애용하는

[10] club=an organisation and a place where people, usually men only, can meet together socially or stay (보통은 남성들만의) 사교 단체, 클럽

[11] anxious=wanting sth. very much 열망하는, 간절히 바라는

I had not seen Biddy and Joe for many months. Then one day, a letter arrived from Biddy with bad news. My sister, Mrs Joe, was dead.

I went by coach from London to the funeral[12] in the country. My sister was buried near my parents, in that lonely churchyard near the marshes.

As I stood in the graveyard beside Biddy and Joe, I thought of the convict I had met there long ago. In my mind, I saw his face and heard his terrible voice. I remembered how he had frightened me.

Now that[13] Mrs Joe was dead, Biddy was going back to the village. She was going to teach in the school.

After supper, I walked with Biddy in the garden. Biddy told me, in her quiet way, how much Joe loved me and how good he was.

"I know that, Biddy", I said quickly. "I won't forget Joe, now he's alone. I shall come here to see him often."[14]

---

[12] funeral=a ceremony, usually a religious one, for burying or cremating a dead person 장례식

[13] now that=inasmuch as; since …이므로/이기 때문에

Biddy said nothing.

"Didn't you hear what I said, Biddy?" I asked.

"Yes, Mr Pip."

"Don't call me 'Mr Pip,' Biddy", I said crossly.[15] "And why don't you answer my question?"

"Are you quite sure that you will want to come from London to see Joe?" Biddy said at last, looking at me carefully.

"What a terrible thing to say, Biddy!" I cried. "You have shocked[16] me very much."

She did not answer.

I slept badly[17] that night, for Biddy's words had upset me. When I got up in the morning, Joe was already at work[18] in the forge. I went in and shook him by the hand.[19]

"Goodbye, dear Joe! I shall be back soon and often", I said.

---

[14] to see=to visit *saw-seen* 방문하다, 보러/찾아가다
[15] cross=annoyed or quite angry 짜증난, 화가 난
[16] to shock=to surprise and upset sb. 충격을 주다, 깜짝 놀라게 하다, 경악하게 하다
[17] badly=not in an acceptable way (받아들일 만한 수준이 못 되게) 잘 못, 형편 없이
[18] at work (on sth.)=busy doing sth. 일하는 중
[19] to shake sb. by the hand.=to shake sb.'s hand=to shake hands with sb.=to take sb.'s hand and move it up and down as a way of saying hello or to show that you agree about sth. …와 악수를 하다

"Never too soon, sir, and never too often, Pip old chap", Joe replied.

I shook hands with Biddy too, although I was still a little angry with her.

But Biddy was quite right, of course. In London, my thoughts were only of Estella and my great expectations. I did not go back to see Joe as I had promised.[20]

And then, at last, it was my twenty-first birthday. Mr Jaggers called me to his office. I first shook hands with Wemmick and then went in to Mr Jaggers.

"Congratulations, Mr Pip", the lawyer said. "I expect you have some questions to ask me. I shall answer them if I can."[21]

---

[20] 가저리와 비디에 대한 핍의 죄의식은 가저리 부인의 장례식에서 극에 달한다. 누이 가저리 부인은 가저리만큼은 아니라 하더라도 실제로 핍을 키운 사람이었기 때문에 그녀의 죽음은 핍이 성인이 되어 가며 인격적으로도 성장하는데 중요한 사건이다. 그는 자신을 사랑하는 지체 낮은 사람들에 대한 지금까지의 행동을 뉘우치고 앞으로는 잘하겠다고 가저리와 비디에게 약속을 해 보지만 이들은 믿으려 하지 않는다. 그럼에도 핍은 자주 오겠다는 약속을 꼭 지키겠다고 혼자 다짐하며 런던으로 돌아오지만 결국은 그들의 불신에 이유가 없지 않다는 걸 알게 된다.

[21] to expect=to think or believe that sth. will happen or that sb. will do sth. …을 예상/기대하다

I took a deep breath and began to speak.

"Am I going to learn[22] the name of my benefactor today, Mr Jaggers?"

"No. Ask me another."[23]

"Will I know the name soon?"

"I can't answer that at the moment", Mr Jaggers said.[24] "Have you another question?"

"Have I...anything to receive, sir?"

Mr Jaggers smiled and asked me a question.

"You are in debt, I suppose?"

I said nothing.

"Come, Pip, are you in debt or not?"

"I'm afraid I am, Mr Jaggers."

"Of course. You know you are", he said. "Wemmick!" he called. "Give Mr Pip that piece of paper. Now, take it in your hand and look at it, Pip."

"This is a banknote[25] for £500", I said in surprise.

---

[22] to learn=to become aware of sth. by hearing about it from sb. else …을 알게 되다

[23] another=one more; an extra thing or person 또 하나(의); 더, 또

[24] at the moment=now; at the present time (현재형에서) 지금/마침, 바로 지금; (과거형에서) (마침) 그때

[25] banknote=note=a piece of paper money 은행권, 지폐

"Right. And that sum of money is yours, Pip. It is a small part of your expectations. You will have that sum of money each year. You will not get into debt. Later, you will learn the name of your benefactor. These are my instructions."[26]

I thought for a moment. "Is it possible that my benefactor may come to London—or ask me to go anywhere else?"[27]

"It is possible, but not yet", Mr Jaggers said. "That is all I have to say at present,[28] Pip."

As I left Mr Jaggers' office, I was already making plans. First of all, I must pay all my debts. Secondly, I wanted to help Herbert.

Herbert worked hard,[29] but he had no money and no expectations. I knew that Herbert would not accept money from me. So, with Wemmick's help, I made arrangements for him to become a partner[30] in a small business[31] in London. He would work hard

---

[26] instructions=sth. that sb. tells you to do 지시
[27] 핍은 스물한 살이 되는 생일에 성인이 되었다. 이제는 돈이 필요할 때마다 재거즈에게 가지 않아도 정기적으로 수입이 들어오게 되었고, 재거즈가 자신에게 유산을 물려준 사람이 누군지를 밝혀줄 것으로 기대했다. 핍은 그것이 해비샴이고 그녀는 또 자신과 에스텔라의 결혼도 계획하고 있음을 확인하고 싶어 했지만 재거즈는 아주 사무적으로 대하며 아무 것도 알려주지 않는다.
[28] at present=at the moment=currently 현재는, 지금은, 목하
[29] hard=with great effort; with difficulty 열심히, 힘껏; 힘들게
[30] partner=one of the people who owns a business and shares the profits, etc. (사업) 파트너, 동업자
[31] business=a commercial organisation such as a company, shop/store or factory (회사/가게/공장 등의) 사업체

and soon be able to marry Clara. My expectations would help them both.[32]

Soon after my birthday, I received a short note from Estella.

It is time for me to visit Miss Havisham. She tells me you must take me to Satis House. The day after tomorrow, if you please.[33]

Estella

Everything at Satis House was the same. We sat together by the fire in the big room. Miss Havisham looked at Estella, proud of her beauty.

Estella told Miss Havisham about all her admirers. Miss Havisham asked many questions and listened to Estella's answers with a cruel smile.

---

[32] 이제 성인이 되어 유산의 일부를 받게 된 핍은 친구 허버트가 자립할 수 있도록 돕는다. 핍은 웨믹의 도움을 받아 청년 동업자를 구하는 사업가를 물색하여 허버트가 그 사업에 투자하도록 한다. 이렇게 핍은 성인이 되어 좀더 성숙해지면서 어려운 친구를 동정하고 돕는 데서 기쁨을 찾게 된다. 재미있는 것은 핍이 자신에게 유산을 물려주는 사람이 누군지 모르는 것처럼 자신도 익명으로 허버트를 돕는다는 것이다.

[33] "if you please" – used when politely asking sb. to do sth. 정중히 요청할 때 덧붙이는 표현

As Estella was speaking, Miss Havisham held her arm tightly. But after a time, Estella moved away impatiently.

"Are you tired[34] of me, you ungrateful[35] girl?" Miss Havisham cried. "Do you have a heart of stone?"

"I am what you have made me", Estella answered, with a proud, hard look. "You have looked after me. I owe[36] you everything. What do you want from me now?"

"Love", Miss Havisham answered sadly.

Estella laughed.

"You adopted me. You became my mother", Estella said. "All that I am, all that I have, is yours. But I cannot give you what you never gave me. Love."

"I gave her love, didn't I?" Miss Havisham cried, looking at me. "I gave her all the love I had—strong, burning love! You know I'm telling the truth."

---

[34] tired=feeling that you have had enough of sb./sth. because you no longer find them/it interesting or because they make you angry or unhappy 싫증난, 물린, 지긋지긋한

[35] ungrateful=not showing or expressing thanks for sth. that sb. has done for you or given to you 감사할 줄 모르는, 은혜를 모르는, 배은망덕한

[36] to owe=to feel that you ought to do sth. for sb. or give them sth., esp. because they have done sth. for you 신세를 지고 있다; (은혜를 입었으므로) …해야 하다/한다고 생각하다

"Your love was not true love", Estella answered coldly. "Your plan has always been clear. You wanted revenge for the love you lost. I have learnt your lessons[37] well. I have always followed your teaching."

"So proud, so hard", Miss Havisham said, crying softly.

"Who taught me to be proud? Who praised[38] me when I was hard?" Estella replied.

"But not proud and hard to me! You cannot be proud and hard to me, Estella!" Miss Havisham cried, holding out her arms to the beautiful girl.

Estella looked at Miss Havisham coldly.

"I have never forgotten the wrong[39] done to you. I have behaved as you wanted me to behave", Estella said. "I am what you have made me. That is all."

Miss Havisham sank down[40] on the floor, crying bitterly. Her long white hair spread out[41] around her.

---

[37] lesson=an experience, esp. an unpleasant one, that sb. can learn from so that it does not happen again in the future (특히 불쾌한 경험을 통해 얻게 되는) 교훈

[38] to praise=to express your approval or admiration for sb./sth. 칭찬하다

[39] wrong=behaviour that is not honest or morally acceptable 나쁜 행동/짓

[40] to sink (down)=to move downwards, esp. by falling or sitting down *sank-sunk* (쓰러지듯이 맥없이) 주저앉다

[41] to spread (out)=to cover a large area *spread-spread* (넓은 범위에 걸쳐) 펼쳐지다

"But I wanted you to love me! Love me!" she cried.

Estella, tall and straight, stared at the fire. After a time, we helped Miss Havisham to her feet.[42] When I left, the two women were sitting side by side, silent in that terrible, decaying[43] room.[44]

In London, Estella had many admirers. Everywhere Estella went—to the theatre, to balls, to dinners—men fell in love with her.[45] To my horror,[46] Bentley Drummle was one of Estella's admirers. He was very rich and I thought that Estella made him believe that she liked him.

---

[42] to help sb. to feet=to help sb. to stand (up) 일어서도록 돕다
[43] to decay=to be destroyed gradually by natural processes; to destroy sth. in this way 부패하다, 썩다; 부패시키다, 썩게 만들다
[44] 핍은 에스텔라와 함께 해비샴을 방문하여 처음으로 이들 모녀가 언쟁하는 것을 목격한다. 해비샴은 에스텔라가 남자들을 농락하는 얘기를 들으며 기뻐하는데, 에스텔라는 해비샴마저도 자신을 따라다니는 남자들처럼 차갑게 대하며 이 모든 것은 해비샴에게서 배운 것이라고 하여 그녀를 절망하게 한다.
[45] to fall in love with sb.=to become enamoured of sb. …와 사랑에 빠지다
[46] horror=a feeling of great shock, fear or disgust 공포(감), 경악

One night, at a ball,[47] Drummle had been paying more attention[48] to Estella than usual.

"Why do you let[49] him near you, Estella?" I asked. "Drummle is stupid and bad-tempered. All he has is money and his important family name. But you give him looks and smiles that you never give to me."

Estella answered angrily.

"Do you want me to treat[50] you like the others?" she asked. "Do you want me to deceive[51] and entrap[52] you?"[53]

"Do you deceive and entrap Drummle then, Estella?"

"Yes. Him and many others. All of them but you, Pip. Will you never be warned?"

---

[47] ball=a large formal party with dancing (큰 규모의, 격식을 갖춘) 무도회
[48] attention=the act of listening to, looking at or thinking about sth./sb. carefully 주의, 집중, 주목
[49] to let=to allow sb./sth. to go/be somewhere let-let (어디에 가는 것을/ 있도록) 허용하다, 놔두다
[50] to treat=to behave in a particular way towards sb./sth. (특정한 태도로) 대하다, 다루다, 취급하다, 대우하다
[51] to deceive=to make sb. believe sth. that is not true 속이다, 기만하다
[52] to entrap=to put or catch sb./sth. in a place or situation from which they cannot escape 덫으로 옭아매다
[53] 핍은 에스텔라가 드러믈과 결혼한다는 말을 듣고 그가 어리석고 포악하다며 심하게 반대하는데, 에스텔라는 그와 결혼하는 것은 그를 속이고 함정에 빠뜨리는 일이며 핍에게는 그러고 싶지 않다며 대수롭지 않게 반응한다. 그러나 핍은 이 말을 듣고 자신이 이제껏 그녀에게 하찮은 존재였음을 느낄 수밖에 없게 된다.

"About what?"

"Don't fall in love with me. It will bring you nothing but sorrow."[54]

---

[54] sorrow=a feeling of great sadness because sth. very bad has happened 슬픔, 비애

Chapter TEN

Abel Magwitch

Two years passed and I was twenty-three years old. I was still living with Herbert, but we now had rooms near the river. Herbert's business was doing very well.[1] His company now had offices overseas[2] and Herbert often went away[3] on business.

---

[1] to do well=to be successful *did-done* 잘 되다, 성공적이다; 잘 하다, 성공하다
[2] overseas=to or in a foreign country, esp. those separated from your country by the sea or ocean 해외에/로, 외국에/으로
[3] to go away=to leave home for a period of time, esp. for a holiday/vacation *went-gone* (휴가/여행 등으로) 한동안 집을 떠나다

The weather had been stormy all day. The strong wind was blowing the rain hard against the windows. Herbert was in France on business, and I was alone.

A church bell struck[4] eleven. I closed the book I was reading. It was time to go to bed. But as I stood up, I heard the sound of footsteps[5] on the stairs.

For a moment, I felt afraid. Then I picked up the lamp and opened the door.

"Who's there? Who do you want?" I called.

"Mr Pip. Top floor", a rough sounding voice answered.

"That is my name", I said. "Is anything wrong?"

"Nothing's wrong", the voice replied.

I held the lamp higher.

A man was coming slowly up the stairs. He was about sixty years old. The man had long, grey hair that lay over his shoulders. His face was wrinkled[6] and brown and he was roughly-dressed.

---

[4] to strike=to show the time by making a ringing noise, etc. *struck-struck/stricken* (시간을 알리기 위해 시계가) 치다, 알리다

[5] footstep=the sound or mark made each time your foot touches the ground when you are walking or running 발소리; 발자국

[6] to wrinkle=to make the skin on your face form into lines or folds; to form lines or folds in this way (얼굴에) 주름을 잡다, 찡그리다; 주름이 지다, 생기다

To my surprise, the man was holding out his arms to greet[7] me.

"Do you wish to come in? Have you business with me?" I asked.

"Yes, I wish to come in, master", the man answered quietly. He walked slowly into the room. He looked around him with pleasure.[8]

"What do you want?" I asked.

The man took off his hat and sat down.

"Just give me a little time", he said in his rough voice. "I've come a long way and had a hard journey. You are alone here, aren't you?" he added.

"Why do you, a stranger, ask me that question?"

---

[7] to greet=to say hello to sb. or to welcome them 맞다, 환영하다
[8] pleasure=a state of feeling or being happy or satisfied 기쁨, 즐거움

"A stranger?" the man repeated. "That's a disappointing[9] word to hear, when I've come so far. But you're a brave[10] fellow,[11] I can see[12] that. Don't harm[13] me, Pip. You'll be sorry if you do."

And then I knew him. I fell back[14] against the wall. He was the convict I had helped so long ago on the marshes!

The man stood up and again held out his arms to me.

"Yes, young sir. I am the convict you helped. You were brave then, my boy", he said. "I have never forgotten it, Pip, never."

"Stop!" I cried, as he moved towards me. "That was a long time ago. I was a little child then. I am pleased you are grateful. And I hope you have changed your way of life. But you must understand…"

The man looked at me sharply.

"Understand? What must I understand?" he said.

---

[9] disappointing=not as good, successful, etc. as you had hoped; making you feel disappointed 실망스러운, 기대에 못 미치는

[10] brave=willing to do things which are difficult, dangerous or painful; not afraid 용감한

[11] fellow=a man or boy (남자나 소년을 가리켜) 녀석, 친구

[12] to see=to understand sth. *saw-seen* 알다, 이해하다

[13] to harm=to hurt or injure sb. or to damage sth. 해치다; 해를 끼치다, 손상시키다

[14] to fall back=to move or turn back *fell-fallen* 물러나다

"...understand that our lives are different now", I went on. "There is no further[15] reason for us to meet. But you are wet and you look tired. Let me get[16] you a drink before you go."

The man sat down again.

"I will have a drink before I go", he said slowly. "Hot rum and water, if you please."

I prepared the drink quickly. When I handed[17] him the glass, I saw that the old convict's eyes were full of tears.

I sat down near him with my own glass.

"I do not wish to be hard on you", I said. "Indeed, I wish you well. How have you been living?"

"I've been in Australia. I've been a sheep farmer, and I've done well, marvellously[18] well", the old convict replied.

"I am glad to hear it", I said.

"Thank you, dear boy. And I see that you have done well since I last saw you. May I ask how?"

"I...I've come into some property", I said.

"May I ask what property? May I ask whose?"

---

[15] further=more; additional 더 이상의; 추가의
[16] to get=to prepare a meal *got-got* (식사를) 준비하다
[17] to hand=to pass or give sth. to sb. 건네주다, 넘겨주다
[18] marvellous=extremely good; wonderful 기막히게 좋은, 경탄할 만한

For some reason, I began to shake[19] with fear.

"I don't know", I answered.

"Could I guess[20] your yearly income,[21] since you came of age?" the man asked quietly. "Would it be—five hundred pounds?"

My heart was beating[22] wildly now. I stood up and held tightly to the back of my chair. I stared at the man in terror.

"I suppose you had a guardian. A lawyer maybe?" the convict went on. "Did his name begin with J?"

I could not speak. I felt faint[23] and the room began to move around me.

"Do you want to know how I found you?" the convict went on. "Well, that lawyer has a clerk called Wemmick. He sent me your address."

---

[19] to shake=to make short quick movements that you cannot control, for example because you are cold or afraid *shook-shaken* (추위/무서움 등으로 몸을) 떨다, 떨리다

[20] to guess=to find the right answer to a question or the truth without knowing all the facts (추측으로) 알아맞히다/알아내다

[21] income=the money that a person, a region, a country, etc. earns from work, from investing money, from business, etc. 소득, 수입

[22] to beat=to make, or cause sth. to make, a regular sound or movement *beat-beaten* (심장이) 고동치다; (북이) 둥둥 울리다; (날개가) 퍼덕이다

[23] faint=feeling weak and tired and likely to become unconscious 실신할 것 같은, 어지러운

I could not breathe. I gave a cry and almost fell to the ground. The old convict caught hold of me and placed me gently on a chair.

"Yes, Pip, dear boy", he said. "It's me what's made a gentleman of you.[24] I swore[25] that I would make you a gentleman and I have. Every guinea I've made[26] has been for you. I've lived a poor life, so that you could live well. Yes, Pip, that starving convict you met on the marshes has made you a gentleman. I've sent money all these years for you to spend. And now I've come to see the gentleman I've made!

"Look at your clothes", he went on, "a gentleman's clothes. And these are your books", he added, looking around the room. "Hundreds and hundreds of books. You shall read them to me, dear boy, for I've had no education. But it's me what's had you educated.[27] I'm proud of you, Pip, dear boy, proud!"

And he took my cold hands and put them to his lips.

---

[24] to make sth. of sb./sth.; to make sth. sth.=to cause sb./sth. to be or become sth. *made-made* (…을 …으로/…이 되게) 만들다/하다/삼다

[25] to swear=to make a serious promise to do sth. *swore-sworn* (…을 하겠다고) 맹세하다

[26] to make=to earn or gain money *made-made* (돈을) 벌다/얻다

[27] "it's me what's had you educated"는 "it's me who's had you educated"라고 해야 문법적으로 옳다.

I felt very ill.[28] I could not speak.

"Don't try to talk, Pip", the old convict went on. "You weren't prepared for this, I see. Didn't you ever think it could[29] be me?"

"Never, no, never!" I whispered.

"Well, it was me. And no one knew about it but Mr Jaggers."

The old man smiled. "How good looking you've grown, my boy", he said. "You're in love with a beautiful girl, I'm sure. She shall be yours, if money can help you."

Estella, oh, Estella, I thought.

"Yes, you've grown to be a fine gentleman, Pip", the convict said. "I promised myself I would see you one day, and now I have. It wasn't safe[30] to come, but I came."

"Not safe? What do you mean?" I asked in surprise.

"I was transported[31] for life",[32] he answered quietly. "If you're sent as a convict to Australia, it's death to return. If I am caught, I shall be hanged,[33] hanged by the neck until I'm dead."

---

[28] ill=suffering from an illness or disease; not feeling well 아픈, 병 든; 몸/기분이 안 좋은

[29] "could" – used to show that sth. is or might be possible 가능성이 있음을 나타낼 때 씀

[30] safe=protected from any danger or harm (신체적인 위험 등으로부터) 안전한, 안심할 수 있는

[31] to transport=to send sb. to a faraway place as a punishment 귀양/유배 보내다

[32] for life=for the remainder of your life 죽을 때까지(의); 평생/종신(의); 무기의

I held my head in my hands. This wretched[34] man was my benefactor! By coming to see me, he had ruined all my dreams. And he had put his own life in danger[35] too.

I could not send him away. I stood up slowly. I closed the shutters over the windows and locked the door. I prepared the bed in Herbert's room for the man and, at last, he went to sleep.

Later, I sat by the fire, trying to think. Miss Havisham's plans for me? All a dream. Estella? She was not meant[36] for me.

And because of this man, a convict, I had forgotten Joe and Biddy. I could never undo[37] the wrong I had done them.[38]

What should I do with the man in the next room? What was going to become of him?[39] What was going to become of me?

---

[33] to hang=to kill sb., usually as a punishment, by tying a rope around their neck and allowing them to drop; to be killed in this way 교수형에 처하다; 교수형을 당하다; 목을 매달다

[34] wretched=extremely bad or unpleasant 끔찍한, 형편없는

[35] danger=the possibility of sth. happening that will injure, harm or kill sb., or damage or destroy sth. (사망/부상/손상 등의) 위험

[36] to mean=to intend sb. to be or do sth. *meant-meant* ⋯이 되게/⋯을 하게 의도하다

[37] to undo=to cancel the effect of sth. *undid-undone* 무효로 만들다, 원상태로 돌리다

[38] 핍은 겉으로는 신사의 풍모를 갖추었을지 몰라도 내면의 순수함을 잃어 감사할 줄 모르고 기고만장하던 과거를 후회하며 매형 가저리와 비디에 대해 부끄러운 마음을 갖는 사람으로 서서히 바뀌게 된다.

[39] to become of sb./sth.=to happen to sb./sth. *became-become* ⋯이 어떻게 되다

At last I fell asleep[40] by the fire. I awoke[41] to hear the church bell striking five. The room was dark. The wind was still blowing the rain hard against the windows.

I made breakfast. The old convict ate in great mouthfuls. I was disgusted[42] by him. He then lit his pipe and stood in front of the fire. He took out a wallet[43] of money and threw it onto the table.

"There, my boy, spend that", he said. "I've come back to see my boy spend money like a gentleman!"

"No, no, we must talk!" I cried. "I don't even know your name. How long are you staying in England? Where do you plan to live?"

"My name is Magwitch, Abel Magwitch", he said. "And I'm staying in England forever, though it's death by hanging if I'm caught."

---

[40] to fall asleep=to go to sleep *fell-fallen* 잠들다
[41] to awake=to wake up; to make sb. wake up *awoke-awoken* (잠에서) 깨다/깨우다
[42] to disgust=to make (sb.) feel shocked and almost ill/sick because it is so unpleasant 혐오감을 유발하다, 역겹게 만들다
[43] wallet=a small flat folding case made of leather or plastic used for keeping paper money and credit cards in 지갑

I decided that I had to speak to Mr Jaggers. Leaving[44] Magwitch alone, I locked the door of my rooms and hurried to the lawyer's office.

When he saw me, Mr Jaggers held up his hand.[45]

"Don't tell me anything—I don't want to know", he said quickly.

"I must know one thing, Mr Jaggers", I said. "I have been told something about my benefactor. Is it true?"

"You cannot have been 'told' anything. 'Told' means you have talked to that person. You cannot have talked to him. He is in Australia. You must have been 'informed,'"[46] Mr Jaggers warned me.

I understood then that Mr Jaggers knew Abel Magwitch was in England. And he knew that his client was in danger.

"'Informed,' then", I agreed, "'informed' that Abel Magwitch is my benefactor."

"That is true. Your benefactor is the man in Australia."

"But I thought that Miss Havisham..." I began.

---

[44] to leave=to make or allow sb./sth. to remain in a particular condition, place, etc. *left-left* (어떤 상태/장소 등에 계속) 있게 만들다/그대로 두다
[45] hold up one's hand=raise one's hand *held-held* 손을 올리다
[46] to inform=to find out information about sth. (…에 대해 정보를) 알아내다

"You have misunderstood.[47] Miss Havisham was never your benefactor. Your benefactor is far away. But he has plenty of money for you. You will have it soon."

I did not want the money now. I knew that Estella would never be mine. I left Mr Jaggers' office without another word.

On my way home I bought some new clothes for Abel Magwitch. But when I had cut his hair and he was dressed in the new clothes, he still looked like a convict—a murderer perhaps. The more I saw the man, the more I feared and hated him.

Herbert returned from France that afternoon. When I heard his step on the stairs, I opened the door quickly.

"Hello, Pip!" Herbert said cheerfully. Then he added, "How pale you look! What's the matter?"[48]

Then he saw Magwitch.

"Who is this?" he asked in surprise.

"Herbert, my dear friend", I said, shutting and locking the door behind him, "something very strange has happened."

---

[47] to misunderstand=to fail to understand correctly *misunderstood-misunderstood* …을 오해하다

[48] the matter=a problem when sb. is upset, unhappy, etc. (걱정/고민 등의 원인이 되는) 문제, 일

Before I could explain, Magwitch took a little black bible from his pocket and held it out to Herbert.

"Take the Holy Book[49] in your right hand, dear boy", he said to him. "Swear to God that you will never repeat what Pip is going to tell you."

"Do it, Herbert", I whispered. So Herbert took the bible and repeated the words and then the old convict shook him by the hand.

"Now you have sworn on the Bible. God has heard your promise. Sit down and listen to what Pip is going to tell you."

So I told Herbert everything.

"I need your help, Herbert", I said at last. "What should I do now?"

"My poor dear Pip", Herbert exclaimed. "I am so confused that I cannot think clearly. But the first thing is to find rooms for...Mr Magwitch. Then, I'm afraid, there is only one thing to do."

Herbert turned to Abel Magwitch, who was listening carefully.

"You must leave England", Herbert told him. "Go to France or Germany. You will be safe there. And you must go with him,

---

[49] the Holy Book=the Holy Bible/Scriptures 성서

Pip", Herbert went on. "This man's life is in danger because he came to see you. It is only right that you should get him out of danger."⁵⁰

I stared at the floor unhappily. I did not care where I went. I had no expectations now—for I could never take money from Magwitch again. My life had been ruined by this man who I hated and feared.

"Very well",⁵¹ I said at last. I turned to Magwitch.

"If I am to help you, I must know everything about you. Why were you put in prison? Who was that other man on the marshes? Tell us."

He stared at the fire for a moment and then began to speak.

"Dear boy and Pip's friend, my story can be told in a very few words", the convict began. "I don't know where I was born. I know nothing about myself but my name. The first thing I remember was stealing food to keep alive. In jail and out of jail, in jail and out. I was punished wherever I went. I had no education. I only learnt to read and write a little."

---

⁵⁰ to get sb. out of danger=to deliver sb. who is in danger 위험에 처한 사람을 구하다

⁵¹ "Very well." – used as a way of saying yes to sb. or of agreeing to do what they ask (동의를 표하는 방식으로) 좋아

Magwitch stopped for a moment and then went on.

"About twenty years ago, I met Compeyson, the man I fought on the marshes. He looked like a gentleman, but he was very wicked and very clever. He asked me to help him with his plans. And he made sure,[52] that if anything went wrong,[53] I would be blamed for it.

"Compeyson had a friend, a young man with a rich sister. The two men treated this woman very badly and stole her money."

When Herbert heard this, he looked up quickly, but he said nothing.

"Later, the young man died", Magwitch went on. "Compeyson had more and more power over[54] me. All the wicked things he planned were done by me. When we were caught, I was blamed for everything. I sold everything. I had to pay the lawyer, Mr Jaggers, to speak for me in court. But when Compeyson and me stood up in court, he was dressed like an honest gentleman and I looked wicked and dishonest. So he was sent to prison

---

[52] to make sure=to do sth. in order to be certain that sth. else happens *made-made* 반드시 (…하도록) 하다; (…을) 확실히 하다
[53] to go wrong=to experience problems or difficulties *went-gone* (일이) 잘못되다/문제를 겪다
[54] "over" – used to show that sb. has control or authority 통제/지휘권을 갖고 있음을 나타냄

for seven years. I was sent to prison for fourteen years. And we were both sent to the Hulks.

"One day, I had a fight with Compeyson and cut his face. I escaped from the Hulks onto the marshes. That's where you helped me, dear boy. When I found out that Compeyson had escaped too, I caught him and waited for the soldiers to come. So instead of escaping, I was transported to Australia for life."

"And Compeyson?" I asked quietly. "Where is he now?"

"I never heard of him again. He may be alive or dead. I don't know. But if he finds me here, it's death for me or him!"

The old convict said no more, but smoked his pipe and stared at the fire.

Herbert passed[55] a piece of paper to me. On it, he had written these words:

Miss Havisham's brother was the young man. Compeyson was the man who was going to marry her. But he stole her money and left her on her wedding-day.

I looked at Herbert, but said nothing. I was trying to think.

---

[55] to pass=to give sth. to sb. by putting it into their hands or in a place where they can easily reach it 건네주다, (무엇을 쉽게 손닿는 곳으로) 주다

If Compeyson was alive, he might find out that Magwitch had returned. Herbert was right. Magwitch was in danger in London. I had to take the old man away as soon as possible.[56]

That same day, we found a cheap room for him to stay in. Some days later, Herbert took Magwitch to the house where Clara lived with her father. The house was at Old Mill Bank, a quiet place, near the river. Magwitch could live there on the top floor. As soon as possible, we would get him out of England.[57]

We told Wemmick of our plan.[58] He promised to warn us if anyone asked about Magwitch.

Every time I went out, I thought that someone was following me. Was Compeyson alive and in London? Had he seen his old enemy? Did Compeyson know about me and Abel Magwitch?

---

[56] 매그위치의 콤피슨에 대한 이야기를 통해 핍의 삶을 규정해 왔던 두 개의 이야기 줄거리, 범죄자 매그위치 이야기와 해비샴과 에스텔라의 이야기 줄거리가 하나로 합쳐지게 된다. 핍의 내밀한 죄의식의 세계와 야망의 세계가 사실은 하나의 역사로 전개되었음이 드러나면서 갑자기 선악과 유무죄를 구분하는 경계가 위협받게 된다.

[57] 매그위치는 처음부터 핍을 아들처럼 생각했는데 이제는 핍도 매그위치를 다소 막연하게나마 아버지와 같은 인물로 생각하게 된다. 핍은 오래 전 늪지대에서 그를 처음 보았을 때 그랬던 것처럼 그에 대해 어떤 의무감을 갖게 되었지만 혐오감이나 실망감을 완전히 떨쳐 내거나 감추지는 못한다.

[58] to tell of sth.=to make sth. known; to give an account of sth. *told-told* …을 알려주다; …을 설명하다

Chapter ELEVEN

Secrets from the Past

My expectations were at end. Miss Havisham was not my benefactor. Estella could not be mine. But I had to see her again.

I found out that Estella was staying with Miss Havisham, and I decided to go to Satis House for the last time.

Once more I walked through the dark, dusty corridors of Satis House. I found Miss Havisham and Estella sitting together in the dressing-room. Estella was knitting.[1] Both women looked at me in surprise.

---

[1] to knit=to make clothes, etc. from wool or cotton thread using two long thin knitting needles or a machine (실로 옷 등을) 뜨다/짜다, 뜨개질을 하다

"Why are you here, Pip?" Miss Havisham asked.

"I have something that I must say[2] to you, Miss Havisham", I replied. "I have found out who my benefactor is, and I am very unhappy. I thought it was you. You knew that I thought this. But you did not tell me my mistake. Was that kind,[3] Miss Havisham?"

"Kind? Do you expect me to be kind, Pip?" Miss Havisham answered, hitting her stick on the floor angrily.

"I expect nothing from you, Miss Havisham", I said quietly. "I have come because I need your help, but not for myself."

"Who do you want me to help?" Miss Havisham asked. "What do you want, Pip?"

"Two years ago, I was able to help my good friend, Herbert Pocket. I paid money for him to become a partner in a business", I explained. "He does not know who did this. Now I need more money, to complete my plans for him. I cannot take money from my benefactor. Can you help me?"

At first Miss Havisham said nothing. Then she spoke.

"Have you anything else to say, Pip?" she asked.

---

[2] "I must say..." – used to emphasise an opinion 의견을 강조하는 표현으로 "이 말만은 꼭 해야겠다", "이건 분명히 하겠다"는 뜻이다.

[3] kind=caring about others; gentle, friendly and generous 친절한, 다정한

I looked at Estella. She went on knitting and did not raise her head.

"Estella", I said, "you know I love you. I have always thought that Miss Havisham wanted us to marry. I know now that this is not true. But I must tell you that I love you and always will."

"Love is a word I do not understand", Estella answered. "I tried to warn you, Pip, but you didn't listen. I am going to be married, but not to you."

"Then who...?" I began.

"Bentley Drummle", Estella said quietly.

"Estella! That can't be true!"[4] I cried. "He is stupid and cruel. You will never be happy with him."

"Do you think he will be happy with me?" Estella said, with a cold smile. "I know nothing of happiness or love. You will soon forget me, Pip."

"You are part of my life, part of every breath I take", I whispered. "I shall never forget you, Estella, never. God bless[5] you and forgive[6] you."[7]

---

[4] sth. can't be true=sb. is sure sth. is not true 일 리가 없다

[5] to bless=to ask God to protect sb./sth. (신의) 가호/축복을 빌다

[6] to forgive=to stop feeling angry with sb. who has done sth. to harm, annoy or upset you; to stop feeling angry with yourself *forgave-forgiven* 용서하다

[7] 본문은 맨 앞에 기원을 뜻하는 조동사 *may*가 생략된 형태다. 즉 "May God

I kissed her hand. I do not remember leaving the room.

I was in despair. Without waiting for the coach, I set off[8] to walk the long road to London.

It was after midnight[9] when I reached home. I climbed[10] the stairs to our rooms, desperate[11] and exhausted.[12] Fixed[13] to the door was a piece of paper.

Don't stay here tonight. Go to Old Mill Bank at eight tomorrow night. Burn this note.

The message was in Wemmick's writing.[14]

I stayed at an inn and waited for the hours to pass. At eight o'clock that night, I was outside the house at Old Mill Bank. I knocked at the door and Herbert opened it.

He took me inside and spoke quietly.

---

bless you and forgive you."라고 할 수 있다.

[8] to set off=to begin a journey *set-set* 출발하다
[9] midnight=12 o'clock at night 자정, 밤 열두 시, 한밤중
[10] to climb=to go up sth. towards the top 오르다, 올라가다
[11] desperate=feeling or showing that you have little hope and are ready to do anything without worrying about danger to yourself or others 자포자기한, 발악하는, 될 대로 되라는 식의
[12] exhausted=very tired 기진맥진한, 진이 다 빠진, 탈진한
[13] to fix=to put sth. firmly in a place so that it will not move (움직이지 않게) 고정시키다/박다
[14] writing=the particular way in which sb. forms letters when they write (개인의) 필체/서체/글씨체

"He is safe now", Herbert said, "but there is danger. Wemmick found out and warned us. Come upstairs and see Magwitch."

Abel Magwitch was sitting quietly by the window of his room. He was looking at the river below him. His face looked old and gentle now.

"I'm pleased to see you, dear boy", he said. "Compeyson is in London, looking for me. Compeyson found out that I had come to see you. But Herbert thinks I am safe here and Jaggers knows everything."[15]

"This is a good place to be, for another reason", Herbert told me. "When you and Magwitch are ready to leave, we can row[16] him down the river ourselves. You can get on board[17] a ship at the mouth[18] of the river. Compeyson will[19] not expect you to escape like this. You will soon be far away."

"When do we go?" I asked quickly.

---

[15] 콤피슨이 런던에 있다는 소식과 함께 미행되는 느낌을 갖게 되면서 갑자기 위험이 현실적으로 느껴지기 시작한다.

[16] to row=to take sb. somewhere in a boat with oars 노/배를 저어 …를 태워/데려다 주다

[17] on board=on or in a ship, an aircraft or a train 승선/승차/탑승한

[18] mouth=the place where a river joins the sea (강의) 어귀

[19] "will" – used for stating what you think is probably true …일 것이다 (무엇이 사실일 것이라는 짐작을 나타냄)

"Soon, Pip", Herbert said. "First, we'll buy a boat and row up and down the river every day. People will get used to[20] seeing us. They will think we enjoy[21] rowing on the river. Meanwhile,[22] I will come here as usual.[23] When I visit Clara, I can see Magwitch. You must not come here, Pip. Compeyson wants you to lead him to Magwitch."

We followed Herbert's plan. Herbert and I rowed on the river nearly every day.

No stranger went near Old Mill Bank, but I was unhappy. I spent many hours walking the streets alone.

One evening, I met Mr Jaggers. "Come and dine[24] with me, Pip", the lawyer said. "I have something for you."

When we were sitting in Mr Jaggers' house, he gave me a note from Miss Havisham. She wanted to see me on business. I decided to go to Satis House the next day.

---

[20] to get used to sb./sth.=to become familiar with sb./sth. …과 친숙/익숙해지다
[21] to enjoy=to get pleasure from (sth.) …을 즐기다
[22] meanwhile=while sth. else is happening (다른 일이 일어나고 있는) 그 동안에
[23] as usual=in the same way as what happens most of the time or in most cases 늘 그렇듯이, 평상시처럼
[24] to dine=to eat dinner (잘 차린) 식사를 하다, 만찬을 들다

"Well, Pip", Mr Jaggers said, as we sat down to eat, "I hear that Estella is married. She is Mrs Bentley Drummle now. There will be only one master[25] in that marriage—Mrs Bentley Drummle!"

As Mr Jaggers was speaking, Molly, his housekeeper, placed our food on the table. As she stood behind her master, Molly moved her hands nervously. She moved her hands as though she was knitting.

I looked at the woman's dark eyes, her long, dark hair and her moving fingers. Where had I seen hair and movements like that before?

I remembered the last time I had seen Estella and a strange idea came into my mind. I grew pale and my heart began to beat very fast.

I did not speak, but Mr Jaggers saw me looking at Molly. When Molly left the room he slowly nodded his head. I had not asked the question, but he had answered it.

It was true! Molly was Estella's mother! And only Mr Jaggers and I knew the truth.

---

[25] master=a person who is able to control sth. (⋯을 마음대로 할 수 있는) 주인

The next day, I went to Satis House. Miss Havisham was in the big room with the long table. She was sitting in a chair by the fire.

She agreed to help Herbert.[26] When we had finished our business, she looked at me sadly.

"Are you very unhappy, Pip?" she asked.

"Yes, Miss Havisham. I am. There are many things making me unhappy. You know about one of them."

Suddenly, Miss Havisham fell down on her knees.[27]

"Oh, what have I done? What have I done?" she cried. "Estella is married. Do you know that?"

"Yes."

"Then forgive me, Pip. Forgive me for making you unhappy."

---

[26] 핍이 매그위치에게 부드러워지는 것처럼 해비샴도 핍에게 부드러워 진다. 핍은 이제 자신도 무일푼의 신세가 됐지만 자신을 도와 달라고 하는 것이 아니라 해비샴의 친척이기도 한 친구 허버트를 도와 달라고 해비샴을 설득했고 마침내 그녀의 동의를 얻었다.

[27] to fall/go down on one's knees=to drop on/to one's knees 털썩 무릎을 꿇다

"I forgive you, Miss Havisham", I answered. "I am to blame[28] for my unhappiness too. But Estella is also unhappy. You should ask her for forgiveness.[29] You have made her what she is."[30]

"Yes, yes, I know it!" Miss Havisham cried. "I adopted her when she was a little child. I was unhappy and wanted revenge. I took away[31] love from her heart and put ice in its place.[32] If you knew my story, you would understand!"

"Miss Havisham, I do know your story", I answered. "I know why you adopted Estella and taught her to be cruel. I do not hate you, Miss Havisham. I am sorry[33] for you."

I helped Miss Havisham back into her chair by the fire. Then I left the room quietly.[34]

---

[28] to be to blame=to be responsible for sth. bad (…에 대한) 책임이 있다, 책임을 져야 하다

[29] forgiveness=the act of forgiving sb.; willingness to forgive sb. 용서

[30] 해비샴이 그간의 모든 악행을 완전히 회개하고 핍에게 무릎을 꿇고 용서를 구함으로써 강력한 미치광이 노파인 해비샴과 어리고 겁 많은 핍의 역학관계가 일거에 역전된다.

[31] to take away=to make a feeling, pain, etc. disappear *took-taken* (감정/통증 등을) 없애 주다

[32] in its place=in the natural or correct position for sth. 그 자리에, 제자리에

[33] sorry=feeling sad and sympathetic 안된, 안쓰러운, 애석한

[34] 핍은 자신을 괴롭혀 온 우월한 신분의 그녀가 죽기 전 그 영혼의 순수함을 조금이라도 회복할 수 있도록 도와준다.

I went downstairs and walked up and down in the garden. A feeling of great sadness filled my heart as I stood in that unhappy place.

I knew I would never return to Satis House. I ran upstairs quickly to see Miss Havisham for the last time. She was sitting quietly by the fire and did not move.

As I turned to go, a great flame[35] sprang up[36] suddenly from the fire. The flame leapt onto Miss Havisham's old, torn clothes. As I stood there, she ran towards me crying out in terror. Her torn clothes were burning fiercely.

I pulled off[37] my heavy coat and threw it over the screaming[38] woman, pushing her down. Then I dragged[39] the cloth from the table to cover her. The remains[40] of the ruined wedding-feast crashed down.[41] There were clouds[42] of dust, and mice and spiders

---

[35] flame=a hot bright stream of burning gas that comes from sth. that is on fire 불길, 불꽃

[36] to spring up=to appear or develop quickly and/or suddenly *sprang-sprung* 휙 나타나다; 갑자기 생겨나다

[37] to pull off=to remove sth. from a place by pulling (없애거나 치우기 위해) 뽑다/빼다/잡아당기다

[38] to scream=to give a loud, high cry, because you are hurt, frightened, excited, etc. (아픔/무서움으로) 비명을 지르다; (흥분 등으로) 괴성을 지르다/빽빽거리다

[39] to drag=to pull sb./sth. along with effort and difficulty (힘들여) 끌다/끌고 가다

[40] remains=the parts of sth. that are left after the other parts have been used, eaten, removed, etc. (사용하거나 먹거나 제거하거나 하고) 남은 것, 나머지

ran across the floor. Miss Havisham screamed and screamed with pain.

Hearing Miss Havisham's cries, the servants rushed[43] in. We laid[44] Miss Havisham on the table and covered her gently. She was badly[45] burned and could not be moved. Over and over again,[46] she repeated the same words.

"What have I done? What have I done? Forgive me, oh, forgive me!"

A servant went to fetch a doctor. But he could not help her.

Miss Havisham lay there for several[47] hours. I stayed with her, until, calm at last, she died.

My hands and arms had been badly burnt. Herbert came to Satis House and he took me back to London. There he looked after me. He was kind and gentle.

---

[41] to crash down=to fall with a very loud noise (요란한 소리를 내며) 부서지다, 붕괴하다

[42] cloud=a large mass of sth. in the air, for example dust or smoke, or a number of insects flying all together (먼지/연기/곤충 떼 등이 구름같이) 자욱한 것

[43] to rush=to move or to do sth. with great speed, often too fast 급(속)히 움직이다/하다, (너무 급히) 서두르다

[44] to lay=to put sb./sth. in a particular position, esp. when it is done gently or carefully *laid-laid* (특히 살며시 조심스럽게) 놓다/두다

[45] badly=seriously 심하게/몹시

[46] over and over again=many times; repeatedly 몇 번이고, 되풀이해서

[47] several=more than two but not very many (몇)몇의

At first, my mind was confused, but, with Herbert's help, I slowly grew stronger.

My first thoughts were for Magwitch.

"He is safe", Herbert told me. "But as soon as you are well, we must help him to escape.

"I like him better now", Herbert went on. "We have talked together many times. Did you know he once had a wife, Pip? Magwitch's wife was a wild young woman and very jealous.[48] She thought another woman wanted to steal her husband. So she fought the woman and the woman died. Magwitch's wife was put on trial for murder."

"Murder?" I repeated in horror.

"Yes, murder. She was put on trial, but Mr Jaggers was her lawyer. He spoke for her in court and she was acquitted.[49]

"Magwitch and this woman had a child, a little girl", Herbert went on. "Magwitch loved the child very much. But after the trial, the woman and the child disappeared. Magwitch never saw them again."

---

[48] jealous=feeling angry or unhappy because sb. you like or love is showing interest in sb. else 질투하는

[49] to acquit=to decide and state officially in court that sb. is not guilty of a crime 무죄를 선고하다

"Herbert", I said slowly, "how long ago did these things happen?"

"About twenty years ago", Herbert answered. "Three or four years before Magwitch saw you in the churchyard. You reminded him of the child he had lost."

I sat up slowly.

"Herbert", I said, "I have something to tell you. I am sure it is the truth. The man we are hiding,[50] Abel Magwitch, the returned convict, is Estella's father."

As soon as I was strong enough, I went to see Mr Jaggers. "We know who Estella's mother is, Mr Jaggers", I told him.

"Estella's mother, Pip?" Mr Jaggers said carefully.

"Yes. I have seen her in your house, Mr Jaggers."

The lawyer said nothing.

"I now know something more—the name of Estella's father", I went on.

Mr Jaggers looked at me sharply.

---

[50] to hide=to put or keep sb./sth. in a place where they/it cannot be seen or found hid-hidden (남이 보거나 찾지 못하게) 감추다/숨기다

"His name is Abel Magwitch", I said, "and Abel Magwitch is the man who is my benefactor."

"Why does Magwitch think this?" Mr Jaggers asked in surprise.

"He doesn't think this", I answered. "He does not know that his daughter is alive."

I told Mr Jaggers everything I knew and the things I had guessed.[51]

"Mr Jaggers", I said at last, "terrible things have happened to all these people. They must be told the truth."

Mr Jaggers thought for a time before he spoke.

"Perhaps you are right in what you have guessed, Pip. But who would be helped by knowing the truth now? Would the mother be helped? Or the father? Or the child?

"Think carefully, Pip. No one would be helped by knowing the truth, no one."

Mr Jaggers was right. I thought of Estella. She had married a rich man from a proud family. But she was the daughter of a convict. The truth would destroy[52] her. She must never know it.

---

[51] to guess=to try and give an answer or make a judgement about sth. without being sure of all the facts 추측/짐작하다

[52] to destroy=to damage sth. so badly that it no longer exists, works, etc. 파괴하다; 말살하다

Chapter TWELVE

Escape

It was now March. My burnt hands and arms had healed.[1] Herbert and I decided it was time for Magwitch to leave England. I liked the old convict very much now, though I refused to accept his money. I had to help him. I had to get him to a safe place.

We found that a ship was leaving London for Hamburg in a few days' time. The big paddle-steamer[2] would come down

---

[1] to heal=to become healthy again; to make sth. healthy again 치유되다, 낫다; 치유하다, 낫게 하다

[2] paddle-steamer=an old-fashioned type of boat driven by steam and moved forward by a large wheel or wheels at the side 외륜선 (구식 증기선)

the Thames at high tide.³ Our plan was to row down the river towards the sea. Magwitch would be dressed as a river pilot.⁴ He would carry a black bag and wear a thick cloak.⁵ The captain⁶ of the steamer needed a river pilot to guide him along the river to the sea. Magwitch and I would board⁷ the steamer and leave England for ever.

The day came for us to leave. In the evening, Herbert and I left our rooms and rowed down the river to Old Mill Bank. Magwitch was waiting for us.

He got into the boat and sat down.

"Dear boy, faithful⁸ dear boy. Thank you, thank you", he said quietly.

His voice was more gentle now. He was peaceful and quiet. For the first time in his life, people had cared for him⁹ and spoken

---

³ tide=a regular rise and fall in the level of the sea, caused by the pull of the moon and sun; the flow of water that happens as the sea rises and falls 조수, 밀물과 썰물; 조류

⁴ pilot=a person with special knowledge of a difficult area of water, for example, the entrance to a harbour, whose job is to guide ships through it 수로 안내인, 도선사

⁵ cloak=a type of coat that has no sleeves, fastens at the neck and hangs loosely from the shoulders, worn esp. in the past 망토

⁶ captain=the person in charge of a ship or commercial aircraft 선장; 기장

⁷ to board=to get on a ship, train, plane, bus, etc. 승선/승차/탑승하다

⁸ faithful=staying with or supporting a particular person, organization or belief 충실한, 충직한, 신의 있는

to him kindly. And so he was no longer the wild and terrible man I had first met.

"If all goes well, you will be a free man in a few hours", I told him.

"Well, I hope so, dear boy. The water is moving quietly and there seems to be no danger", he said. "But we don't know what will happen, today or in the future."

We rowed all night. Sometimes Herbert rowed. Sometimes I rowed. We stopped from time to time, to rest and eat. We listened for[10] the sound of another boat, but we heard nothing. No one was following us.

By the time it was light, we were a long way down the river. We moored by the bank and waited for the great paddle-steamer to pass.

When we saw the smoke of the steamer, we started rowing again. We rowed strongly towards the middle of the river.

Then, to my horror, I saw another boat moored ahead of us. When we had passed, it moved quietly out from the bank to

---

9 to care for=to look after sb. who is sick, very old, very young, etc. ⋯를 보살피다/돌보다

10 to listen (out) for sth.=to be prepared to hear a particular sound (특정한 소리가 나는지) 잘 듣다/귀를 기울이다

follow us. It was a larger and faster boat than ours. Two men were rowing together.

There were four men in the boat. Three of the men were wearing uniforms.[11] They were Customs[12] men. The fourth man sat in the back of the boat with his face covered.

The big steamer was nearer now. The shadow of the huge ship fell upon our small rowing boat. The steamer came nearer and nearer and its great paddles[13] turned in the water with a terrible noise.

Suddenly, the Customs boat leapt ahead of us.

"You have a convict from Australia there!" a man shouted. "His name is Abel Magwitch. I am here to arrest that man.[14] Stop and give him to us!"

The great steamer came nearer and nearer. The people on board shouted when they saw the two boats far below.

---

[11] uniform=the special set of clothes worn by all members of an organisation or a group at work, or by children at school 제복, 군복, 교복, 유니폼

[12] Customs=the government department that collects taxes on goods bought and sold and on goods brought into the country, and that checks what is brought in 세관

[13] paddle=a short pole with a flat wide part at one or both ends, that you hold in both hands and use for moving a small boat, esp. a canoe, through water (작은 보트, 특히 카누용의 짧은) 노

[14] to arrest=to seize (sb.) by legal authority or warrant; to take into custody 체포하다

"Stop the paddles! Stop the paddles!" they cried.

The two rowing boats were touching each other now. Suddenly, Magwitch leant across and pulled the cloak from the fourth man's face. On the man's face was a long scar.

"Compeyson! I knew it was you!" Magwitch cried. As he grabbed the man, there was another shout from the steamer. The boats turned round and round in the rough water. The paddles of the steamer were now above our heads.

Our boat overturned.[15] The water roared[16] in my ears. I was turned over and over by the crashing water from those terrible paddles.

A moment later, I was pulled roughly into the other boat. Herbert was there too. But our boat had gone. And where were Magwitch and Compeyson?

The paddle-steamer had moved on now and the Customs men were looking down into the water. Then I saw Magwitch. He was swimming, but his heavy clothes were pulling him under the water. The Customs men grabbed him and pulled him into the Customs boat. Chains were put on his wrists and ankles.

---

[15] to overturn=to turn upside down or on its side 뒤집(히)다

[16] to roar=to make a very loud, deep sound 으르렁거리다/포효하다; (크고 깊은 소리로) 울리다/웅웅거리다

Magwitch had been badly injured by the turning paddles. "I think Compeyson's gone to the bottom of the river, dear boy", he whispered to me. "I had him in my arms. Then he fought free[17] and the paddles hit him."[18]

The Customs men soon stopped looking for Compeyson. As we were rowed back to London in the Customs boat, I held the old convict's hand in mine. This rough, hard man had remembered my kindness to him long ago. He had treated me better than I had treated Joe![19]

"Dear boy", Magwitch whispered", use my money when I've gone. One thing I ask—come to the court and see me for the last time. They will hang me now."

"I will stay with you until the end", I said. "I will be as faithful to you as you have been to me."[20]

---

[17] free=away from or out of a position in which sb./sth. is stuck or trapped (고정되거나 매여 있던 것에서) 벗어나/떨어져

[18] 모든 것을 빨아들이는 악마적인 속성을 가지고 있는 강은 디킨즈가 가장 항구적이며 효과적인 상징으로 사용하는 도구다. 초자연적인 힘을 가진 강은 인간세계에서 가려내지 못했던 선과 악의 결과를 강의 결투에서 분명히 선별해 낸다.

[19] 위험을 무릅쓰고 한때는 공포의 대상이었던 매그위치에게 자유를 찾아 주기 위하여 그와 함께 템즈 강을 따라 내려가는 핍에게서 과거의 겁 많고 소심한 모습을 찾아볼 수 없다.

[20] 핍이 새티스 하우스에서 에스텔라를 처음 만난 다음 그녀가 혹시 대장간에서 일하는 자신의 모습을 보지 않을까 두려워했던 그 당시와 비교해 볼 때 사형선고를 받은 매그위치의 곁을 떠나지 않는 핍의 의연함은 분명한 질적 변화를 보여준다.

There was no hope for a returned convict. Magwitch was tried[21] and sentenced[22] to death by hanging. But he was very ill. His injuries[23] were very bad. He was taken from the court to the prison hospital. I sat with him every day.

Every day, Magwitch grew weaker. One day, when I visited him, I felt that his death was near. He was pale and very weak.

"Dear boy, God bless you", he whispered, as I sat down by the bed. "You never left me even when there was danger. You stayed near me when the dark clouds gathered.[24] This has been the best part left my life."

His breathing was very bad now. He lay back on the bed and closed his eyes. I held his hand in mine.

"Dear Magwitch, I have something to tell you", I said quietly. "Can you understand what I say?"

The old convict held my hand tightly.

---

[21] to try=to examine evidence in court and decide whether sb. is innocent or guilty (법원에서) 심리/재판하다

[22] to sentence=to say officially in court that sb. is to receive a particular punishment (형을) 선고하다

[23] injury=harm done to a person's or an animal's body, for example in an accident 부상

[24] to gather=to gradually increase in number or amount (수/양이) 서서히 많아지다/ 늘어나다

"You had a child once, who you loved and lost", I said slowly. "She lived and found rich friends. She is a lady now and very beautiful. And I love her."[25]

With the last of his strength, Abel Magwitch raised my hand to his lips. He opened his eyes and looked at me. Then he smiled and his eyes closed again—for ever.[26]

---

[25] 자신이 가저리에게 한 행동을 되씹어 보면서 매그위치가 자신에게 베푼 사랑이 얼마나 위대한가를 알게 된 핍은 이제껏 그토록 소중하게 여겨왔던 사회적 계급을 개의치 않는 사람이 되었다. 이로써 디킨즈는 세상의 부귀영화보다 사랑과 연민, 충절이 인간이라면 누구나 추구해야 할 가치가 있는 덕목임을 이 소설의 궁극적인 도덕적 교훈으로 제시한다.

[26] 이렇게 디킨즈는 매그위치가 사형이 집행되기 전에 병사하게 만들어 사회 모순의 희생양인 그에게 마지막 동정을 표한다.

Chapter THIRTEEN

Friends Together

And now followed the most terrible time of my life. Magwitch had wanted me to have his money, but when he was sentenced to death, the court took[1] his money and property. I had many debts and no money to pay them. When Magwitch died, Herbert was abroad[2] on business. I was alone.

---

[1] to take=to remove sth. without permission or by mistake (남의 허락도 없이 또는 실수로 어떤 것을) *took-taken* 가져/앗아가다
[2] abroad=in or to a foreign country 해외에(서), 해외로

I became very ill—I had a fever[3] and could neither move nor speak. In my feverish[4] dreams I remembered everything that had happened to me. My thoughts were strange and confused.

I thought I was in the river again, turning over and over in the crashing water. Then I thought I was a little child, sitting beside Joe. More and more in my dreams, the face I saw was Joe's. Joe, who had always been kind, had always been ready to help me. Joe, to whom I had been so unkind and so ungrateful.[5]

Then one day, I opened my eyes. I was very weak, but the fever had gone. And there was Joe, sitting quietly by the window, smoking his pipe and smiling at me.

"Is that really you, Joe?" I said.

"Of course it is, Pip old chap. Waiting to help you as always,[6] Pip."

"Oh, Joe, I've been so ungrateful", I said. "Why are you so good to me?"

"You and me were ever the best of friends, Pip", Joe answered.

---

[3] fever=a medical condition in which a person has a temperature that is higher than normal (의학적 이상 징후로서의) 열

[4] feverish=suffering from a fever; caused by a fever 열이 나는; 열로 인한

[5] 핍의 신체적 혼수상태는 지난날 잘못된 욕망으로 물들어 속물주의에 빠졌던 병든 본성이 죽고 새 사람으로 거듭나는 과정이다.

[6] as always=as usually happens or is expected 늘 그렇듯, 언제나처럼

"When you're well enough, we'll leave London and go back to the country, Pip old chap!"

"How long have I been ill, Joe?" I asked.

"How long?" Joe repeated slowly. "Well, it's the end of May now. Tomorrow is the first of June."

"And have you been here all this time, Joe?"

"That's right, old chap. Mr Jaggers told us you were ill. Biddy said I must come to you at once, so I did. Biddy is a very good woman. She loves you Pip and so do I. Biddy has taught me to read and write. She has told me to write to her about you."

As I grew stronger, I told Joe everything. I told him how rich I had been and that now I was poor. But Joe did not want to hear.

"Pip old chap, we've always been the best of friends", Joe said. "Why try to explain what's past?[7]

"When you were a child, I tried to save you from Mrs Joe and Tickler. Now I want to keep these troubles from you. There's no need for money to come between us.[8] It never did before."

---

[7] past=gone by in time (시간상으로) 지나간

[8] to come between sb. and sb.=to damage a relationship between two people …사이에 끼어들다; …사이를 갈라놓다

With Joe's help, I was soon able to walk a little. My fever had completely gone and I felt better every day.

But one thing worried me. As I grew stronger, Joe became more awkward and uncomfortable with me. He even began to call me 'sir.'

One night, Joe came into my room and asked me how I was. "Dear Joe, I am completely well now, thanks to you", I answered. Joe touched my shoulder with his great hand.

"Then goodnight, sir", he whispered.

In the morning, I got up and dressed. I called to Joe, but he was not in his room. His luggage[9] had gone.

Joe had left a note on the table.

As you are well again, I am leaving you. You will do better without Joe now.

Ever the best of friends, Joe

With the note, were all my bills.[10] Joe had paid all my debts. I knew what I had to do. I would go back to the forge and

---

[9] luggage=bags, cases, etc. that contain sb.'s clothes and things when they are travelling (여행용) 짐/수하물

[10] bill=a piece of paper that shows how much you owe sb. for goods or services 고지서, 청구서

ask Joe to let me live there. I would live and work there for a short time. Then I would go overseas and work for Herbert.

Later on,[11] I would marry Biddy and live with her as a poor man. It was best to forget Estella. My great expectations were at an end. I would be a happier man without them.

It was late June and the weather was very beautiful. I walked slowly along the road to our village. I was enjoying the quiet peace of the fields and paths[12] that I knew so well.

In the country I could live a simple life with Biddy. Joe would be nearby[13] at the forge. Here I would forget the past and all my foolish dreams.

The village school, where I thought I would find Biddy, was closed. I walked on to the forge, and that too was closed.

---

[11] later on=at a time in the future; after the time you are talking about 나중에; (지금 이야기 중인 시간보다) 후/뒤에
[12] path=a way or track that is built or is made by the action of people walking (사람들이 지나다녔거나 만들어서 생긴) 작은 길
[13] nearby=near in position; not far away 인근의/에, 가까운 곳의/에

But all the windows of our house were open wide. There were clean curtains at the windows and the little garden was bright with flowers.

And there, in the doorway,[14] stood Joe and Biddy, holding hands. When they saw me, they laughed with pleasure.

"My dear Biddy, how smart you look!" I said. "And you too, Joe", I added. "What's the matter?"

"It's my wedding-day, Pip!" Biddy cried. "And I'm married to Joe!"

So my last dream disappeared.[15]

"Dear Biddy, you have the best husband in the world", I said. "And you, dear Joe, have the best wife. She will make you very happy, my dear, dear, Joe.

"I have come to thank you for everything you have done for me", I said. "One day, I shall have enough money to pay you back, Joe."

"Perhaps you will have[16] a child, a little boy", I went on. "Tell him how I love and respect[17] you both. Teach him to grow up

---

14 doorway=an opening into a building or a room, where the door is 출입구
15 자신의 마지막 희망이었던 비디와의 결혼의 꿈이 깨어지자 핍은 세상이 언제까지 자기만을 기다리고 있진 않다는 교훈을 또 다시 체득하게 된다.
16 to have=to give birth to sb./sth. *had-had* (아기 등을) 낳다
17 to respect=to have a very good opinion of sb./sth.; to admire sb./sth. 존경하다

a better man than me. And forgive me, dear Joe, for the wrong I have done you."

"Pip, dear old chap, there is nothing to forgive", Joe said. "God knows, there is nothing to forgive."

"Nothing to forgive, Pip dear, nothing to forgive", Biddy whispered.[18]

A month later, I left England and went to Egypt. I worked there as a clerk for Herbert. He and his partner were doing well, and, after a few years, I became a partner too. Herbert married Clara and I paid back my debt to Joe.

I worked in Egypt for eleven long years. I did not return to England in all that time.

---

[18] 디킨즈는 런던에서 가식적이지만 나름 세련되고 고결한 삶을 살고 있던 핍이 투박하고 촌스러운 가저리 앞에서 부끄러워하게 하며 새 사람으로 변화되는 얘기를 통해서 급진적인 사회경제적인 변혁보다는 개인의 정신적이고 도덕적 변화를 강조하고 있다.

Then, one evening in December, I returned to the old forge. I opened the kitchen door quietly and looked in. There was Joe, sitting in his place by the fire. And there, sitting on a stool next to him, was a little boy.

"We called him Pip, after[19] you", Joe said. "We hoped he would grow like you, and we think he has!"

"I am very pleased, Joe", I said.

"I do not think that I shall ever marry and have children", I went on. "But I shall love young Pip as if he were my own son."

"But you will marry and have children of your own, Pip", Biddy told me, with a smile.

"That's what Herbert and Clara say", I replied. "But I shall never marry."

"Dear Pip", Biddy said softly, "Are you sure you still don't long for Estella? I'm sure you have not forgotten her."

"My dear Biddy, I have forgotten nothing of my past life", I answered. "But that dream has gone, like all the others."

---

[19] after=in the style of sb./sth.; following the example of sb./sth. …을 본 뜬/따라서

I knew that Estella's marriage had been unhappy. Her husband, Bentley Drummle, had died, but I was sure that Estella had married again.

After supper, I decided to visit the place where Estella and I had first met. I walked slowly from the forge and it was almost dark when I reached the tall iron gates. Satis House had been pulled down[20] and the old garden was completely overgrown. Only the gates and the garden wall were standing. I walked in the garden in the evening mist. The moon and a few stars shone in the sky.[21]

A woman was walking in the garden. As I got closer to her she turned and spoke my name.

"Estella", I answered quietly.

"I am surprised that you recognise me", Estella replied. "My sad life has changed me, Pip."

Estella was still beautiful. But there was a sadder, kinder look in her eyes. She touched my hand gently.

---

[20] to pull down=to destroy a building completely (건물을 완전히) 허물다/헐다
[21] 여기서 이 소설의 중심 주제가 마지막으로 정리된다. 이제 핍은 사회계급이 행복의 척도가 될 수 없으며 변화무쌍한 세상에서 선악과 유무죄를 엄격하게 규정하기는 거의 불가능함을 안다. 시간이 정지된 장소였던 새티스 하우스가 파괴된 것은 세상은 늘 변화함을 상징한다. 또한 살면서 마땅히 사랑해야 할 사람들을 사랑하며 사는 삶이 얼마나 행복한가를 경험한 서술자 핍은 주인공인 자기 자신은 매섭게 비난하지만 적들을 용서하고 친구들과 화해한다.

"It is strange that we should[22] meet here, Estella, after so many years", I said. "Do you often come back?"

"I have never returned until today. All this belongs to[23] me now. It is all I have left. You have been working overseas, I think."

"Yes", I answered. "I work hard and I am doing well."

"I have often thought of you, Pip", Estella said.

"You have always been in my thoughts", I answered.

"It is strange to be here, in the old place again", Estella said. "I have changed. I am a better person, I hope. You were kind to me all those years ago, Pip. Be kind to me now. Let us part from each other[24] as friends."

"We are friends", I answered, "friends who will never part. For now I have met you again, Estella, I will never let you go."

Estella smiled. I held her hand and we walked together out of the overgrown garden. And I knew that, this time, we would never, never part.

---

[22] "should" - used after *that* after many adjectives that describe feelings 감정을 나타내는 많은 형용사 뒤의 that 절에 씀
[23] to belong to sb.=to be owned by sb. …의 소유/것이다, …에 속하다
[24] to part from each other=to leave each other 서로 헤어지다

Part 03

Dickens' *Great Expectations*

이해 점검

Chapter 1. In the Church Yard

1. The person telling the story calls himself Pip. What is his real name?
2. At the start of the story, Pip is in a graveyard. What is he doing there? Who does he meet? What does this person ask Pip to do?
3. Who does Pip live with? Describe these people.
4. When Pip returns late to the forge, he is frightened of many things. Who and what is he frightened of?
5. When Pip returns from the churchyard, where is Mrs Joe?
6. How long has Mrs Joe been out looking for Pip?
7. What is Tickler?
8. What does Pip learn about the great guns and the Hulks?
9. Pip steals food and a file. Where does he take these things and who does he meet on his way?
10. What is unusual about the second convict's face?
11. Who does Pip think the second convict is?

Chapter 2. Christmas Day

1. What is the occasion for having dinner guests at the Gargery's?
2. Why is Pip scrubbed clean and wearing his best clothes at half past one on Christmas?
3. What do you know about Uncle Pumblechook?
4. What makes Pip uncomfortable during the Christmas dinner?
5. "What's happened to the meat pie?" Pip's sister asks. Describe what happens next.
6. Joe has to do some work that afternoon. What work is it?
7. When the two convicts are found, what are they doing?
8. What does the second convict claim the first convict tried to do to him?
9. How does Joe feel towards the first convict?
10. Who takes the blame for stealing the food from Mrs Joe?
11. Where are the convicts taken?
12. Why doesn't Pip tell Joe the truth concerning the convict and the theft?

Chapter 3. At Miss Havisham's

1. What does Pip try to teach Joe?

2. What is probably the reason that Joe married Pip's sister?

3. What is the only word that Joe can read?

4. Mrs Joe and Uncle Pumblechook bring some news from town. What is this news?

5. Who first takes Pip to Miss Havisham's house?

6. What happens when Pip reaches the gate of Satis House?

7. Who does Pip meet inside the house? What is strange about this person?

8. At what time has a watch on the dressing-table stopped in Miss Havisham's house?

9. How does Estella hurt Pip's feelings?

10. What game does Pip play with Estella?

11. What does Pip think about the people in Satis House?

12. How do you think Pip feels when he leaves Satis House?

Chapter 4. The Pale Young Gentleman

1. What does Pip tell Mrs Joe about his visit to Satis House? Why do you think he says these things?
2. On his second visit to Satis House, Pip meets a stranger. Describe this man.
3. Pip goes into a different room with Miss Havisham. What does the room look like?
4. What does Miss Havisham ask Pip to do on this visit?
5. What does Pip learn about Miss Havisham?
6. Who does Pip meet in the garden and what happens?
7. Estella was waiting for Pip at the gate. What does she say?
8. After his second visit, Pip goes to Satis House three times every week. What does he tell Miss Havisham about his hopes for the future?

Chapter 5. "I Must Become a Gentleman!"

1. "You are getting tall, Pip. What is the name of your brother-in-law, the blacksmith?" Miss Havisham asks. Why is this an important question?
2. What does an apprentice mean?
3. What does Miss Havisham pay Joe for Pip's apprenticeship?
4. How does Pip feel?
5. How does Joe embarrass Pip at Miss Havisham's?
6. "From that day, I lived in fear." What is Pip afraid of?
7. What is the reason Pip wants to return to Miss Havisham's?
8. When Pip visits Miss Havisham, what does she first say?
9. What does he learn from her about Estella?
10. When does Miss Havisham invite Pip to return?
11. What happens to Mrs Joe?
12. Who comes to live at the forge?
13. Pip tells this person a secret. What is Pip's secret?
14. What questions does this person ask Pip?
15. Pip believes that Miss Havisham has plans for him. What does he hope and believe?

Chapter 6. Great Expectations

1. Pip has been apprenticed for four years. One evening a stranger comes to find Pip and Joe. Why is Pip surprised?
2. What does the stranger want?
3. What are Pip's "great expectations"?
4. "There are two conditions", the stranger says. What are these conditions?
5. What will happen when Pip is twenty-one? What is going to happen to Pip now?
6. When Mr Jaggers offers Joe money to compensate for the loss of Pip's services, what does the blacksmith do?
7. Who does Pip believe is his benefactor?
8. Pip's life is going to change again. How do Biddy and Joe feel about this?
9. Why does Pip walk to the town alone?

Chapter 7. Learning to Be a Gentleman

1. What is Pip's impression of London?
2. Where does Pip first go when he gets to London? Who does he meet first there?
3. What does Mr Jaggers give to Pip?
4. Pip is taken to Bernard's Inn. Who takes him?
5. Who does he meet there? Why is Pip surprised to meet this person?
6. Pip's new friend tells him more about Miss Havisham. What does Pip learn about her?
7. Pip wants to become a gentleman. Who helps Pip to behave like a gentleman? Who is going to educate him as a gentleman?
8. Why does Pip ask Mr Jaggers for more money?
9. Pip goes to Mr Jaggers' house for dinner. Who is Bentley Drummle? Where did Pip meet him? What happens between Pip and Bentley Drummle at dinner?
10. "If you want to see strength", Mr Jaggers said, "Look at this woman's wrists." Who is Jaggers speaking about? What does he do?
11. Mr Jaggers warns Pip not to have much to do with one of his guests. Who is it?
12. Who writes Pip a letter?

13. Joe Gargery visits Pip in London. Why does he come?

14. How does Joe look in his best clothes?

15. What news does Joe bring Pip?

Chapter 8. Young Men in Love

1. Pip goes to Satis House. How does he feel when he meets Estella again?
2. How has Estella changed since the last time Pip saw her?
3. Miss Havisham talks to Pip about love. What does he say?
4. Why does Pip decide not to visit Joe and Biddy?
5. What does Estella say about herself?
6. Pip and Herbert tell each other their secrets. What are the secrets?
7. When does Herbert plan to marry his fiancée?

Chapter 9. I Come of Age

1. "I now come to the time of my life of which I am bitterly ashamed." Why is Pip ashamed?
2. Why does Estella come to London?
3. Where is Estella to live?
4. How does Estella behave towards Pip?
5. Why does Pip go to visit Joe and Biddy?
6. Why is Biddy going to leave the forge now?
7. What is Biddy going to do to earn a living?
8. What does Pip promise Biddy?
9. What is Biddy's response to Pip's promise?
10. What happens on Pip's twenty-first birthday?
11. What information does Pip want from Mr Jaggers?
12. How does Pip help Herbert?
13. Whom does Pip accompany back to Satis House?
14. "Who taught me to be proud? Who praised me when I was hard?" Why is Miss Havisham upset by Estella's words?
15. Back to London, Pip is hurt by Estella. How?
16. Estella admits that she deceives and entraps every suitor except one. Who is that one?

Chapter 10. Abel Magwitch

1. Two years have passed. Who visits Pip one stormy night, when Herbert is away on business?
2. Why is Pip horrified by his visitor?
3. Where has the convict been working all this time? What has he been doing?
4. Who is Pip's benefactor?
5. Where does Magwitch stay for the night?
6. How does Pip feel about the convict staying with him?
7. Pip goes to see Mr Jaggers. What does Mr Jaggers say when he hears Pip's news?
8. Herbert tells Pip that he must leave England. Why?
9. What story does Magwitch tell Pip and Herbert?
10. Who helps Pip decide what to do with Magwitch?
11. Why were Compeyson and Magwitch sentenced differently?
12. What does Herbert say in his note to Pip?
13. What do Pip and Herbert do next?

Chapter 11. Secrets from the Past

1. Why are Pip's expectations at an end?
2. Why does Pip go to see Miss Havisham?
3. "Love is a word I do not understand. I tried to warn you, Pip, but you didn't listen." Who says this to Pip?
4. What else does she tell him?
5. What confession does Pip make to Estella?
6. How does Pip get back to London?
7. When Pip returns to London he finds a message on his door. Who wrote the note?
8. What does Pip do?
9. Magwitch has some bad news for Pip. What is this news?
10. Herbert has a plan. What is the plan?
11. Where is Magwitch now living?
12. How are Pip and Herbert preparing to help Magwitch escape from London?
13. Pip goes to dinner with Mr Jaggers. What does he discover about Molly?
14. What does Miss Havisham agree to do for Pip when he goes to say goodbye to Miss Havisham?
15. What happens at Satis House when Pip goes to say goodbye to Miss Havisham?

16. How is Pip injured?

17. Where does Pip go to confirm the story about Magwitch, Molly, and Estella?

18. Does Magwitch know that his daughter is alive?

19. Will the knowledge of Estella's parents be kept a secret?

20. Why will Pip not tell Estella of the identity of her parents?

Chapter 12. Escape

1. How are Abel Magwitch and Pip going to leave England?
2. Where is the steamer going that Pip and Magwitch are planning to board?
3. What goes wrong?
4. What are Pip's feelings about Magwitch now?
5. What does Magwitch ask Pip to do?
6. Why is Magwitch happy when he dies?

Chapter 13. Friends Together

1. What happens to Pip's inheritance?
2. What happens to Pip after the death of Magwitch?
3. Who comes to care for Pip?
4. What does Joe leave in his farewell letter to Pip?
5. Where does Pip go when he gets better?
6. "So my last dream disappeared." What was Pip's last dream? Why has the dream disappeared?
7. Pip leaves England. How long is he away?
8. When Pip returns to England he goes to the forge. Who does he meet there?
9. Pip goes for a walk. Where does he walk to? Who does he meet? What do they talk about?
10. "And I knew that, this time, we would never, never part." What does Pip mean by these words?

Overall

1. In what publication was Great Expectations originally serialised?

    (a) Home and Away (b) The English Almanac
    (c) Simple Wisdom (d) All the Year Round

2. To what genre of fiction, defined by its depiction of a character's growth from childhood to adulthood, does Great Expectations belong?

    (a) *Bildungsroman* (b) *Künstlerspiegel*
    (c) Mannerism (d) Victorian paternalism

3. In what region of England are the marshes of the novel found?

    (a) Sussex (b) Wessex
    (c) Kent (d) Gloucestershire

4. Where does Pip first encounter Magwitch?

    (a) The river (b) Mrs Joe's house
    (c) The forge (d) The churchyard

5. What is the name of Miss Havisham's manor?

    (a) Satis House (b) Lockmont
    (c) Larchmont (d) Satyr House

6. The main character in this novel calls himself Pip because
   (a) he is much like his father, and Pip is short for "chip off the old block."
   (b) his real name is Philip, but he is too small to pronounce it, so he calls himself Pip.
   (c) he is an orphan, and it is the name Joe selects for him.
   (d) his sister refuses to call him Philip because she wants to keep him from growing up.

7. Before Pip finds out that he has been left money to become a gentleman, he plans to
   (a) accept Pumblechook's offer to work with him.
   (b) become a farmer on the land behind Joe's house.
   (c) become a blacksmith.
   (d) make amends with his sister.

8. Pip feels guilty for helping the convict mainly because he
   (a) feels terrible about stealing Mrs Joe's food.
   (b) knows it is wrong to help an escaped criminal who may have killed someone.
   (c) does not tell Joe the truth about his encounter with the convict.
   (d) thinks he acted cowardly by giving the convict some food.

9. Which of the following incidents from the story is an example of irony?

   (a) The two convicts in the marsh are both glad to see the prison guards who are there to take them back to the Hulks.
   (b) Miss Havisham wants revenge on all men so she makes sure Estella grows up with a cold heart. As a result, Estella cannot love anyone.
   (c) Joe Gargery, a blacksmith, is Pip's real father.
   (d) Compeyson is the man who jilted Miss Havisham.

10. When Biddy asks Pip why he wants to become a gentleman, he tells her that

    (a) he wants to make Estella respect him.
    (b) he wants to make Miss Havisham proud.
    (c) he doesn't know.
    (d) he wants to hurt Estella.

11. When Joe visits Miss Havisham's house, he

    (a) tells her she must pay Pip for his services.
    (b) is so overwhelmed that he cannot speak to Miss Havisham directly.
    (c) does not understand why Pip thinks Estella is beautful.
    (d) offers to help repair her home and grounds.

12. Pip receives word that Joe will be coming to see him in London. Pip feels

    (a) excited that he will spend time with Joe and introduce him to all of his friends.
    (b) Joe is coming to ask Pip for money.
    (c) Joe is coming to check up on his progress.
    (d) disturbed and mortified.

13. Who buys Herbert's way into business?

    (a) Pip   (b) Miss Havisham
    (c) Drummle   (d) Estella

14. Before Pip finds out who his actual benefactor is, he believes it is

    (a) Jaggers.   (b) Estella.
    (c) Miss Havisham.   (d) Mr Pocket.

15. Although Estella has a cold heart, she demonstrates at least some affection for Pip by

    (a) letting him escort her to Richmond.
    (b) letting him kiss her cheek after his fight with Herbert.
    (c) explaining to Pip that it is useless for him to love her because she is heartless and cannot love anyone.
    (d) getting him a snack after his visits with Miss Havisham.

16. Who is Pip's tutor in London?

    (a) Harold Pocket   (b) Walter Pocket
    (c) Herbert Pocket   (d) Matthew Pocket

17. Where does Estella live when she goes abroad?

    (a) France (b) Spain

    (c) Germany (d) Boston

18. Who is Estella's father?

    (a) Compeyson (b) Magwitch

    (c) Joe (d) Jaggers

19. What time does Miss Havisham's clock stop at?

    (a) Noon (b) Midnight

    (c) Twenty past nine (d) Twenty to nine

20. At what age does a boy come of age?

    (a) Nineteen (b) Twenty

    (c) Twenty-one (d) Twenty-two

21. Who tells Pip that Compeyson was Miss Havisham's fiancé?

    (a) Wemmick (b) Herbert

    (c) Estella (d) Magwitch

22. Who is the "pale young gentleman"?

    (a) Wemmick (b) Herbert

    (c) Jaggers (d) Startop

23. Whom does Estella marry?

    (a) Startop (b) Drummle

    (c) Pip (d) Herbert

24. What happens to Compeyson at the end of the novel?

   (a) He escapes with the Havisham fortune.

   (b) He is shot by the police.

   (c) He is killed by Orlick.

   (d) He disappears and is presumed drowned.

25. What accident befalls Miss Havisham before her death?

   (a) She is thrown from a horse.

   (b) She is burned in a fire.

   (c) A table crushes her legs.

   (d) She falls from a window.

Answer Key

Chapter 1. In the Church Yard

1. It is Philip Pirrip.

2. While Pip is looking at his parents' gravestone, he meets a rough-looking man. He asks Pip to bring him a file and some food.

3. He lives with his sister and her husband, Joe Gargery. Joe is a blacksmith. He is a huge, fair-haired man with kind blue eyes. His wife is tall and thin, with a hard face and sharp black eyes. Her skin is tough and red.

4. He is afraid of his sister Mrs Joe, the convict on the marshes, and the terrible young man who will come to kill him if he breaks his promise to the convict.

5. She is out looking for Pip.

6. She has been out about five minutes.

7. Tickler is a stick used by Mrs Joe to discipline Pip.

8. He learns that the guns are fired from the Hulks, prison ships, when a convict escapes.

9. Pip takes the file and the food to the Fort. On the way, he meets a second escaped convict.

10. He has a long scar on his face.

11. Pip thinks that the second convict is the young man the first convict said, who listens to every word and has a secret way of finding anyone.

Chapter 2. Christmas Day

1. It is Christmas Day.
2. Because there will be guests for dinner at half past one. Pip will open the door to them.
3. He is a fat, stupid man with hair that stands up on his head. He greatly admires Mrs Joe, but he thinks very little of Joe and Pip.
4. Pip is fearful that Mrs Joe will find the food missing.
5. Pip opens the door to run away, but he runs straight into a group of soldiers, who are chasing the escaped convicts.
6. The soldiers want Joe to mend some handcuffs.
7. The two convicts are fighting one another in a ditch.
8. The second convict says that the first convict was trying to kill him.
9. He feels that he should not starve no matter what he has done.
10. The first convict takes the blame for stealing the food.
11. The two convicts are taken back to the Hulks.
12. Pip does not tell Joe the truth because he is too afraid of what Joe will think of him.

Chapter 3. At Miss Havisham's

1. He tries to teach Joe the alphabet.

2. Joe probably married Pip's sister because he felt sympathy for Pip being treated badly by her.

3. "Joe" is the only word that Joe can read.

4. The news is that a lady called Miss Havisham wants Pip to go to her house and play.

5. Uncle Pumblechook first takes Pip to Miss Havisham's house.

6. A beautifully dressed young girl comes to the gate and asks their names. She unlocks the gate, lets Pip go in but says that Miss Havisham does not want to see Uncle Pumblechook.

7. Pip meets an old lady with white hair. All her clothes are white, old and faded and she is wearing a wedding veil.

8. It has stopped at twenty minutes to nine.

9. She calls Pip a "common working boy" and brings attention to his heavy boots and clothes.

10. He plays a card game with Estella.

11. He thinks Estella is very proud and very pretty. He also thinks she is very rude. He thinks that Miss Havisham is the strangest lady he has ever seen.

12. Pip must feel angry and ashamed, but remember Estella's beauty.

Chapter 4. The Pale Young Gentleman

1. He tells that Miss Havisham was tall and dark, and sat in a black velvet coach; a girl gave them cake on gold plates; and they played with flags and swords. Pip does not know why he says these things. He thinks perhaps the truth is too strange to tell.
2. He is a tall man with sharp eyes and thick black eyebrows. He has large hands which are very clean and white.
3. It is a big room with a long table in the middle. It is lit with many candles, and there is a fire burning. The table-cloth is torn and covered with dust. On the table is something tall and white, and fat black spiders are running over it. Miss Havisham tells Pip it is her wedding-cake.
4. She asks Pip help her walk round and round the table.
5. He learns that it is Miss Havisham's birthday, and that it should have been her wedding day on this day many years ago.
6. Pip meets a fair-haired boy of his own age, and they fight. Pip wins and they shake hands.
7. She says "You can kiss me if you like."
8. Pip tells that he wants to be apprenticed to Joe when he is old enough, and he wants to be educated and to be a gentleman.

Chapter 5. "I Must Become a Gentleman!"

1. Because Miss Havisham has decided that Pip is old enough to be apprenticed to him, and wants to see him.
2. An apprentice is someone who is bound by law to work for a master in order to learn his trade.
3. Miss Havisham pays Joe 25 guineas as his premium.
4. Pip feels bitterly disappointed, because Miss Havisham does not want him to come to her house again.
5. Pip is embarrassed because of the way Joe is dressed and because Joe will not talk directly to Miss Havisham.
6. He is afraid that Estella might see him at work.
7. Pip wants to see Estella again.
8. She says that he will get no more money from her.
9. Pip learns that Estella is in France, being educated to be a lady. Miss Havisham says she is more beautiful than ever.
10. She invites him to come and see her every year on his birthday.
11. Someone attacks her when she is alone in the house. She is terribly injured and is unable to walk or speak.
12. Biddy, a girl from the village, comes to look after Mrs Joe.
13. Pip's secret is that he hates being a blacksmith, and he wants to be a gentleman.

14. Biddy asks three questions: "Don't you think you are happier as you are?" "Who called you stupid and common?" and "Do you want to be a gentleman to hurt her or to make her respect you?"

15. Pip believes that Miss Havisham will give him money for his education. He hopes that if he has money and education, Estella will love him and will marry him.

Chapter 6. Great Expectations

1. Because he recognises the man; he has seen him at Miss Havisham's many years before.
2. He wants to speak to Joe and Pip.
3. He will be very rich one day—a man of property.
4. The conditions are that Pip will always be known by that name, and that the name of his benefactor is to be kept secret.
5. Pip will come into his property when he is twenty-one. Now he is to go to London to be educated, and to live as a gentleman.
6. Joe refuses the money and replies that no money can replace the dear child.
7. Pip believes Miss Havisham is his benefactor.
8. They are sad and quiet. They do not seem pleased at Pip's good fortune.
9. Because he was ashamed to be seen with Joe and Biddy.

Chapter 7. Learning to Be a Gentleman

1. Pip is amazed and frightened. London is crowded, and its streets are dirty.
2. He goes to Mr Jaggers' office, and meets first Mr Wemmick, Mr Jaggers' clerk.
3. Mr Jaggers gives Pip an allowance.
4. Mr Wemmick takes Pip to Bernard's Inn.
5. Pip meets Herbert Pocket there, and is surprised because he recognises him as the boy he once fought in Miss Havisham's garden.
6. Pip learns that Miss Havisham was to marry a man who was her brother's friend, but he wrote to her on the wedding-day to say that he could not marry her. Since then she has not seen the daylight. She has adopted Estella, and brought her up to break men's hearts, because she wants to take revenge on all men.
7. Herbert Pocket helps Pip to behave like a gentleman, and Matthew Pocket, Herbert's father, is going to educate him as one.
8. Pip asks Mr Jaggers for more money to buy carpets and furniture for Herbert's rooms.

9. Bentley Drummle is a very rich young man. Pip met him at Matthew Pocket's house where he is also studying. They argue and are about to fight. Mr Jaggers stops them.

10. He is speaking about Molly, his housekeeper. He catches Molly's arm and makes her show the young men her wrists.

11. Mr Jaggers warns Pip of Bentley Drummle.

12. Biddy writes Pip a letter.

13. He comes to deliver a message from Miss Havisham.

14. He looks awkward and uncomfortable.

15. Estella has returned and wants to see Pip.

Chapter 8. Young Men in Love

1. He feels clumsy and awkward. He feels again like the common boy Estella had laughed at.
2. She has become a young woman, even more beautiful than before. However, she is still distant and cool to Pip, but not hateful as before.
3. She says that he must give everything for real love. He must love Estella whether she is good to him or not.
4. Because Estella makes him ashamed of Joe and Biddy by saying that the people he knew before cannot be his companions now.
5. She says that she has not changed, and has no love in her heart for anyone.
6. Pip's secret is that he loves Estella. Herbert's secret is that he is engaged to be married to a lady called Clara.
7. He plans to marry her when he makes his fortune.

Chapter 9. I Come of Age

1. Because he did not visit Joe and Biddy, spent too much money, and got into debt.
2. Because she is going to be introduced to the rich and powerful people of London society.
3. She is to live in Richmond.
4. She is often proud and cold, as she had been years ago.
5. Because his sister has died. He goes to the country for the funeral.
6. Because it will not be proper for Biddy to stay there with only Joe.
7. Biddy is going to teach in the school.
8. Pip promises Biddy that he will return often to see Joe.
9. Biddy does not say anything to Pip's promise. She knows that Pip is only feeling guilty for Joe and that he will not return.
10. He visits Mr Jaggers' office and receives five hundred pounds.
11. He is hoping to find out who his benefactor is.
12. He makes arrangements for Herbert to become a partner in a small business in London.
13. He accompanies Estella back to Satis House.
14. Because she wanted Estella to be proud and hard with everyone else, but to love her.

15. Because she pays more attention to Bentley Drummle than she does to him.
16. It is Pip that Estella does not try to deceive and entrap.

Chapter 10. Abel Magwitch

1. An old man with long, grey hair and a wrinkled, brown face visits Pip.
2. Because he recognises him as the convict he helped on the marshes long ago.
3. He has been working in Australia as a sheep farmer.
4. Magwitch, the first convict on the marshes, is his benefactor.
5. He stays in Herbert's room for the night.
6. Pip is frightened of Magwitch and locks the door leading to his room.
7. He tells Pip that Magwitch is indeed his benefactor. What he says makes Pip understand that he must pretend that Magwitch is still in Australia.
8. Because Magwitch has risked his life by coming to visit him.
9. Magwitch tells how Compeyson—the other convict on the marshes—asked him to help with wicked plans, but made sure that when things went wrong, he was blamed. He also says that as the result of his escape from the Hulks he was transported to Australia for life.
10. Herbert helps Pip devise a plan as to what to do with Magwitch.
11. Because when Compeyson and Magwitch stood up in court, Compeyson was dressed like an honest gentleman and Magwitch looked wicked and dishonest.

12. He says that Compeyson was the man who was going to marry Miss Havisham; but he stole her money and left her on her wedding-day.

13. They find a cheap room for Magwitch to stay in, then they arrange for him to stay with Clara and her father.

Chapter 11. Secrets from the Past

1. Because Miss Havisham is not his benefactor, and Estella cannot be his.
2. Pip goes to see Miss Havisham to ask her to help him complete his plans for Herbert by giving him some money.
3. Estella says that to Pip.
4. She says that she is going to marry Bentley Drummle.
5. Pip confesses that he has loved her since he first went to Satis House.
6. Pip is so unhappy that he walks all the way back to London.
7. Mr Wemmick wrote it.
8. He stays at an inn for the night and until the next evening.
9. It is the news that Compeyson is in London looking for him.
10. The plan is that he and Pip will row Magwitch down the river, and Magwitch and Pip will board a ship at the mouth of the river far from London.
11. Magwitch is now living in the house where Clara, Herbert's fiancée, lives.
12. They start rowing up and down the river every day so that people will get used to seeing them and think they enjoy rowing on the river.
13. Pip discovers that she is Estella's mother.

14. Miss Havisham agrees to help Pip by aiding Herbert in his business.
15. Miss Havisham asks Pip to forgive her for making him unhappy. And a flame from the fire leaps onto her old clothes, and they burn. Pip throws his coat over her to put out the flames, but Miss Havisham is badly burned and she soon dies.
16. Pip's hands are burned while trying to save Miss Havisham.
17. Pip goes to Mr Jaggers to confirm the story.
18. Magwitch has no idea that his daughter is alive.
19. Pip and Mr Jaggers agree that it would do no good to anyone to release any of this information concerning Magwitch, Estella, and Molly.
20. Estella has married for money, and Drummle is from a wealthy family. The knowledge of Estella's convict father and murdering mother would not be a welcomed fact for the Drummle family. It would destroy her marriage and her life. Pip would never do anything to hurt Estella.

Chapter 12. Escape

1. They are going to row down the Thames to meet the paddle-steamer. Magwitch will pretend to be a river pilot and they will board the steamer.

2. They are planning to board a steamer bound for Hamburg, Germany.

3. Compeyson is in a boat with three Customs men, trying to arrest Magwitch. Pip's boat overturns, and Magwitch pulls Compeyson out of the other boat. Compeyson drowns, but Magwitch is injured by the paddles of the steamer and he is captured.

4. Pip now feels kindness towards Magwitch.

5. He asks Pip to come and see him for the last time in the court, and to use his money when he is gone.

6. Because Pip has told him that his daughter is alive and rich.

Chapter 13. Friends Together

1. The court takes Magwitch's money and property when he is sentenced to death.
2. He becomes very ill.
3. Joe comes to care for Pip.
4. Joe has paid all of Pip's debts and left the receipt in his farewell letter.
5. He goes to the forge to see Joe and Biddy.
6. It was the dream that he would marry Biddy. But it disappears when he finds Biddy has married Joe.
7. He is away for eleven years.
8. He meets Joe, Biddy and their son.
9. Pip walks to the place where he and Estella first met—Satis House. He meets Estella. She says her sad life has changed her, and Pip talks of his work overseas. She says she has often thought of him, and he says she has always been in his thoughts.
10. He means that they will be married.

Overall

1. (d) 2. (a) 3. (c) 4. (d) 5. (a)
6. (b) 7. (c) 8. (a) 9. (a) 10. (c)
11. (b) 12. (d) 13. (a) 14. (c) 15. (c)
16. (d) 17. (a) 18. (b) 19. (d) 20. (c)
21. (b) 22. (b) 23. (b) 24. (d) 25. (b)

작가 연보

1812	• 찰즈 디킨즈(Charles John Huffam Dickens)가 2월 7일 금요일 잉글랜드 포츠머스의 교외인 랜드포트(Landport)에서 부두에 위치한 해군경리국의 직원인 아버지 존 디킨즈(John Dickens)와 어머니 일리저벳 디킨즈(Elizabeth Dickens)의 사이에서 8남매의 두 번째이자 장남으로 태어남.
1814	• 6개월 된 막냇동생이 뇌염으로 세상을 떠남. • 아버지의 전근으로 가족 모두가 런던으로 이사함. 이후에도 당시의 미국과의 전쟁으로 아버지가 자주 전근하게 됨.
1816	• 아버지의 전근으로 가족 모두가 채텀(Chatham)으로 이사함. • 집에서 열정적으로 독서에 몰입해 온 그가 처음으로 학교 교육을 받게 됨.
1821	• 바로 집 옆에 있는 침례교 목사가 운영하는 윌리엄 가일즈 학교(William Giles' School)에 등록함. • 아버지를 따라 산책하던 중 1856년 구입하게 되는 대저택 '개즈 힐 플레이스(Gad's Hill Place)'를 처음 보게 됨. • 해군의 구조조정으로 아버지가 실직하여 가족의 수입원이 끊김.
1822	• 가족이 런던 캠든 타운(Camden Town)으로 이사함. • 런던의 학교로 전학 감.
1823	• 가정 형편 상 학교를 그만둠. • 어머니가 가사를 떠맡고 여성을 위한 사설 교육기관을 설립하였으나 학생을 하나도 받지 못함.
1824	• 2월 2일 약 40파운드의 채무를 해결하지 못한 아버지가 체포되어 마샬시(Marshalsea) 감옥에 수감되자 가족 모두가 아버지의 감방에서 함께 지내게 됨.

	• 찰즈만 가족과 떨어져 런던 중심부 체링크로스(Charing Cross)에 있는 워런즈 흑색도료공장(Warren's Blacking Factory)에서 일하게 됨.
	• 5월 28일 작은 유산을 물려받게 된 아버지가 채권자들과 합의하여 감옥으로부터 석방됨에 따라 온 가족이 다시 캠든 타운에 살게 됨.
1825	• 웰링턴 하우스 아카데미(Wellington House Academy)에 다니게 됨.
1826	• 다시 한 번 가세가 기울어 누이와 함께 학교를 그만둠. 곧이어 가족이 살던 집에서도 쫓겨남.
1827	• 학교를 그만두고 변호사 사무실(Ellis & Blackmore, Solicitors)에서 사환으로 일하기 시작하여 가족 수입의 일부를 감당함.
	• 배우의 꿈을 안고 런던의 극장가를 들락거리는 한편 신문기자가 되기로 결심하고 속기술을 익힘.
1828	• 런던의 몇몇 신문에 기고하여 호평을 받음.
1829	• 런던의 민사법원(Doctor's Commons Courts)에서 자유계약 기자로 일함.
1830	• 부유층의 딸인 머리아 비드넬(Maria Beadnell)을 만나 사랑에 빠짐.
1831	• 참정권 확대를 논의하는 개혁법(Reform Bill) 사태 기간 중 의회 담당 기자로 활동함.
1832	• 전문 배우가 되려고 코번트 가든 극장(Covent Garden Theatre)에서 열린 연기 심사에 참석하려 했으나 갑작스런 병으로 참가하지 못함.
1833	• 3편의 아마추어 연극에서 배우와 무대를 맡음.
	• 첫사랑 머리아 비드넬과 관계가 끝남.

1834	• 첫 번째 단편「포플러 웍에서의 만찬(Dinner at Poplar Walk)」 등을 익명으로『먼슬리 매거진(Monthly Magazine)』에 발표함.
• 『모닝 크로니클(Morning Chronicle)』의 신문기자로 일하면서『먼슬리 매거진』에도 계속 기고함.
• "보즈(Boz)"라는 가명을 쓰기 시작함.
• 또다시 채무 문제로 체포된 아버지를 도와줌.
1835	• 『모닝 크로니클』의 편집인인 조지 호가스(George Hogarth)의 딸 캐서린 호가스(Catherine Hogarth)와 약혼함.
1836	• 『보즈의 스케치(Sketches by Boz)』의 1부가 출판됨. 저작권료로 150파운드를 받음.
• 3월 30일『피퀵 페이퍼스(Pickwick Papers)』의 연재를 시작함.
• 4월 2일 캐서린 호가스와 결혼함.
• 『모닝 크로니클』의 기자를 그만두고『벤틀리즈 미셀러니(Bentley's Miscellany)』의 편집인이 됨.
• 12월에『보즈의 스케치』의 2부를 출판함.
• 평생 절친한 친구이며 그의 첫 번째 전기 작가가 되는 존 포스터(John Forster)를 만남.
1837	• 『올리버 트위스트(Oliver Twist)』의 집필을 시작하여 매월 자신이 편집인이 된『벤틀리즈 미셀러니』에 연재함.
• 5월에 그가 함께 살면서 무척 아꼈던 17세의 처제 메리(Mary)가 세상을 떠남. 이로 인해 크나큰 상실감을 겪음.
• 7월에 처음으로 유럽을 방문함.
• 7남 3녀의 첫째가 되는 아들 찰스(Charles)가 출생함.
• 『피퀵 페이퍼스』의 연재를 마침.

1838
- 요크셔(Yorkshire) 빈민학교의 참혹한 실상을 그린 『니콜라스 니클비(Nicholas Nickleby)』를 시작함.
- 둘째이자 장녀인 메이미(Mamie)가 태어남.

1839
- 『벤틀리즈 미셀러니』의 편집인 직을 사임함.
- 4월에 『올리버 트위스트』를 마침.
- 『니콜라스 니클비』는 10월에 마침.
- 셋째인 딸 케잇(Kate)이 태어남.

1840
- 후일 두 편의 소설로 발전하게 되는 『험프리 씨의 시계(Master Humphrey's Clock)』의 일회분이 발표됨.
- 『오래된 골동품 가게(The Old Curiosity Shop)』를 시작함.

1841
- 2월에 『오래된 골동품 가게』를 마침. 이어 『바나비 러지(Barnaby Rudge)』를 시작하여 11월에 마침.
- 넷째인 아들 월터(Walter)가 태어남.

1842
- 미국과 캐나다 전역을 여행함. 이 경험을 『아메리카 단상(American Notes)』으로 출판하여 미국에서 엄청난 반향을 일으킴.
- 캐나다 몬트리올에서 3편의 연극에서 감독과 연기를 맡음.

1843
- 『마틴 처즐윗(Martin Chuzzlewit)』을 시작함.
- 『크리스머스 캐럴(Christmas Carol)』이 12월에 출판됨.
- 런던에서 사회 문제에 대해 공개적으로 발언하기 시작함. 지식의 원천과 자유의 수호자로서의 언론과 출판의 가치를 옹호함.

1844
- 7월 가족과 함께 이태리로 가 1년 정도 머묾.
- 12월에 혼자 잠시 런던에 옴. 『차임즈(The Chimes)』가 출판됨.
- 다시 제노아(Genoa)로 간 뒤 다섯째인 아들 프랜시스(Francis)가 태어남.

1845
- 7월에 잉글랜드로 돌아옴.

- 자신의 아마추어 극단을 창단함.
- 12월에 세 번째 크리스마스 소설인 『난로 위의 귀뚜라미(The Cricket on the Hearth)』가 출판됨.
- 여섯째인 아들 알프레드(Alfred)가 태어남.

1846
- 잠시 『데일리 뉴스(Daily News)』의 편집인으로 일함.
- 『돔비와 아들(Dombey and Son)』의 연재를 시작하여 1848년 4월까지 계속함.
- 가족과 함께 로잔(Lausanne)과 파리를 여행함.
- 네 번째 크리스마스 소설인 『인생의 투쟁(The Battle of Life)』이 12월에 출판됨.
- 출판이 아닌 자신의 자녀들의 도덕 교육을 위해 성서의 복음서를 해설한 『우리 주님의 생애(The Life of Our Lord)』를 집필함. 이는 그의 장남이 세상을 떠난 1934년 출판될 때까지 그 가족만의 복음서로 남았었음.

1847
- 잉글랜드로 돌아옴.
- 윤락녀 재활 기관 유레이니어 코티지(Urania Cottage)를 설립하고 후원함.
- 일곱째인 아들 시드니(Sydney)가 태어남.

1848
- 자서전의 일부를 집필함. 이는 미완성인 상태로 남겨졌고 사후 포스터의 전기에 포함될 때까지 출판되지 않음.
- 아마추어 극단에서 감독 및 배우로 활동함.
- 다섯 번째이자 마지막 크리스마스 소설인 『귀신 들린 사람(The Haunted Man)』이 12월에 출판됨.

1849
- 『데이비드 코퍼필드(David Copperfield)』의 연재를 시작함.
- 여덟째인 아들 헨리(Henry)가 태어남.

1850	• 11월에 『데이비드 코퍼필드(David Copperfield)』의 연재를 마침.
	• 주간지 『하우스홀드 워즈(Household Words)』를 창간하고 편집인이 됨.
	• 아홉째인 딸 도라(Dora)가 태어남.
1851	• 아버지와 9개월 된 딸 도라가 세상을 떠남. 아내 캐서린이 신경쇠약에 걸림.
	• 『황량한 집(Bleak House)』의 집필을 시작함.
1852	• 『황량한 집』이 매월 연재되기 시작함.
	• 마지막이자 열 번째인 아들 에드워드(Edward)가 태어남.
1853	• 9월에 『황량한 집』의 연재를 마침.
	• 오거스터스 에그(Augustus Egg), 윌키 콜린즈(Wilkie Collins)와 함께 이태리를 여행하고 돌아옴.
	• 자신의 작품의 대중 낭독회를 시작함.
1854	• 랑카셔(Lancashire)에서의 파업을 관찰한 경험을 토대로 8월까지 『하우스홀드 워즈』에 주간으로 『고된 시기(Hard Times)』를 연재함.
	• 여름과 가을을 가족과 함께 불로뉴(Boulogne)에서 보냄.
1855	• 첫사랑 머리아 비드넬을 다시 만나게 되지만 실망함.
	• 10월에 가족과 함께 파리 여행을 함.
	• 정부의 실정과 관료의 부패를 고발한 『리틀 도릿(Little Dorrit)』이 월간으로 연재되기 시작함.
	• 행정개혁협회(Administrative Reform Association)를 공개적으로 지지하고 정부 정책의 실패로 악화된 계급 갈등의 해결을 촉구함.

1856	• 윌키 콜린즈와 연극 <프로즌 딥(The Frozen Deep)>을 제작, 공연함.
	• 어릴 적부터 열망해 왔던 대저택 "개즈힐"을 구입함.
1857	• 6월에 『리틀 도릿』을 마침.
	• 개수한 "개즈힐"에서 여름을 보냄. 그가 존경하던 작가 한스 크리스티안 안데르센(Hans Christian Anderson)이 개즈힐을 방문함.
	• 그의 극단이 여왕 앞에서 <프로즌 딥>을 공연함.
	• 젊은 배우 엘런 터난(Ellen Ternan)과 사랑에 빠짐.
1858	• 런던에서 유료로 대중 낭독회를 시작함.
	• 새커리(William Makepeace Thackeray)와 논쟁함.
	• 아내 캐서린과 별거함.
1859	• 런던에서 낭독회를 계속함.
	• 새로운 주간지 『올 더 이어 라운드(All the Year Round)』를 창간하고 편집인이 됨.
	• 위 잡지에 『두 도시 이야기(A Tale of Two Cities)』를 11월까지 연재함.
1860	• 가족과 함께 개즈힐에 들어와 살기 시작함.
	• 사적인 편지의 대부분을 태워 버림.
	• 『위대한 유산(Great Expectations)』이 주간으로 연재되기 시작함.
1861	• 대중 낭독회를 새로이 시작함.
	• 8월에 『위대한 유산』을 마침.
1862	• 대중 낭독회를 계속함.
1863	• 어머니와 인도 캘커타에 군인으로 있던 아들 월터가 세상을 떠남.

	•파리와 런던에서 대중 낭독회를 계속함.
	•새커리가 죽기 전 그와 화해함.
1864	•『우리의 공통의 친구(Our Mutual Friend)』가 월간으로 연재되기 시작함.
	•과로로 건강이 악화되기 시작함.
1865	•엘런 터난과 함께 열차 사고로 큰 충격을 받음.
	•11월에 죽기 전에 마친 마지막 소설 『공통의 친구』가 끝남.
1866	•잉글랜드와 스코틀랜드에서 대중 낭독회를 계속함.
1867	•의사의 충고를 무시하고 잉글랜드와 아일랜드에서 대중 낭독회를 계속함. 미국에서 대중 낭독회를 가짐.
1868	•미국 낭독 여행을 마침. 건강이 악화되었으나 『올 더 이어 라운드』의 업무를 계속함.
1869	•잉글랜드와 스코틀랜드, 아일랜드에서 대중 낭독회를 계속함.
	•가벼운 뇌졸중 증세를 보여 지방 낭독회 일정을 취소함.
	•『에드윈 드루드의 수수께끼(The Mystery of Edwin Drood)』의 연재를 시작함.
1870	•1월 런던에서 고별 낭독회를 12회 엶. 하루 종일의 작업을 마친 후 6월 8일 개즈힐에서 뇌출혈을 겪음. 9일 58세로 사망하여 14일 웨스트민스터 사원에 안치됨.
	•『에드윈 드루드의 수수께끼』의 예정된 12회분 중 생전에 완성한 6회분이 최종회로 9월에 발표됨.

지은이 **권정기**
우석대학교 교양학부 교수로 연세대학교 정치외교학과와 대학원 정치학과 및 영국 케임브리지 대학교 정치학과를 졸업했다.

빅토리아 시대의 사회계급과 욕망
디킨즈의 『위대한 유산』
Social Class & Desire in Victorian England

© 권정기, 2013

1판 1쇄 인쇄__2013년 12월 17일
1판 1쇄 발행__2013년 12월 26일

지은이__권정기
펴낸이__양정섭
펴낸곳__도서출판 경진
   등록__제2010-000004호
   블로그__http://kyungjinmunhwa.tistory.com
   이메일__mykorea01@naver.com

공급처__(주)글로벌콘텐츠출판그룹
   대표__홍정표
   편집__노경민 최민지 김현열 **디자인**__김미미 **기획·마케팅**__이용기 **경영지원**__안선영
   주소__서울특별시 강동구 천중로 196 정일빌딩 401호
   전화__02) 488-3280 **팩스**__02) 488-3281
   홈페이지__http://www.gcbook.co.kr

값 13,000원
ISBN 978-89-5996-235-8 03840

※ 이 책은 본사와 저자의 허락 없이 내용의 일부 또는 전체의 무단 전재나 복제, 광전자 매체 수록 등을 금합니다.
※ 잘못된 책은 구입처에서 바꾸어 드립니다.